Straight Talk on Trade

Straight Talk on Trade

IDEAS FOR A SANE WORLD ECONOMY

Dani Rodrik

PRINCETON UNIVERSITY PRESS

Princeton and Oxford

Requests for permission to reproduce material from this work should be sent to Permissions, Princeton University Press

Published by Princeton University Press,
41 William Street, Princeton, New Jersey 08540

In the United Kingdom: Princeton University Press,
6 Oxford Street, Woodstock, Oxfordshire OX20 1TR

press.princeton.edu

Cover design by Faceout Studio, Spencer Fuller

First paperback printing, 2019

Paperback ISBN 978-0-691-19608-4

Cloth ISBN 978-0-691-17784-7

Library of Congress Control Number: 2017945414

British Library Cataloging-in-Publication Data is available

This book has been composed in Bembo Std

Printed on acid-free paper. ∞

Printed in the United States of America

To my children Deniz, Odile, and Delphine, who replenish
my faith daily that the world will become a better place

CONTENTS

PREFACE

Are economists responsible for Donald Trump's shocking victory in the US presidential election? Economists might only wish they have the kind of power it takes to determine elections. But even if they may not have caused (or stopped) Trump, one thing is certain: economists would have had a greater—and much more positive—impact on the public debate had they stuck closer to their discipline's teaching, instead of siding with globalization's cheerleaders.

Nearly two decades ago, as my book *Has Globalization Gone Too Far?* went to press, I approached a well-known economist to ask him if he would provide an endorsement for the back cover. I claimed in the book that, in the absence of a more concerted government response, too much globalization would deepen societal divisions, exacerbate distributional problems, and undermine domestic social bargains— arguments that have become conventional wisdom since.

The economist demurred. He didn't really disagree with any of the analysis but worried that my book would provide "ammunition for the barbarians." Protectionists would latch on to the book's arguments about the downsides of globalization to provide cover for their narrow, selfish agenda.

It's a reaction I still get from my fellow economists. One of them will hesitantly raise his hand following a talk and ask: Don't you worry that your arguments will be abused and serve the demagogues and populists you are decrying?

There is always a risk that our arguments will be hijacked in the public debate by those with whom we disagree. But I have never understood why many economists believe this implies we should skew our argument about trade in one particular direction. The implicit premise seems to be that there are barbarians on only one side of the trade debate. Apparently, those who complain about World Trade Organization rules or trade agreements are dreadful protectionists, while those who support them are always on the side of the angels.

In truth, many trade enthusiasts are no less motivated by their own narrow, selfish agendas. Pharmaceutical firms pursuing tougher patent rules, banks pushing for unfettered access to foreign markets, or multinationals seeking special arbitration tribunals have no greater regard for the public interest than protectionists do. So when economists shade their arguments, they effectively favor one set of self-interested parties—"barbarians"—over another.

It has long been an unspoken rule of public engagement for economists that they should champion trade and not dwell too much on the fine print. This has produced a curious situation. The standard models of trade with which economists work typically yield sharp distributional effects: income losses by certain groups of producers or workers are the flip side of the "gains from trade." And economists have long known that market failures—including poorly functioning labor markets, credit market imperfections, knowledge or environmental externalities, and monopolies—can interfere with reaping those gains.

They have also known that the economic benefits of trade agreements that reach beyond borders to shape domestic regulations—as with the tightening of patent rules or the harmonization of health and safety requirements—are fundamentally ambiguous.

Nonetheless, economists can be counted on to parrot the wonders of comparative advantage and free trade whenever trade agreements come up. They have consistently minimized distributional concerns, even though it is now clear that the distributional impact of, say, the North American Free Trade Agreement or China's entry into the World Trade Organization was significant for the most directly affected communities in the United States. They have overstated the magnitude of aggregate gains from trade deals, though such gains have been relatively small since at least the 1990s. They have endorsed the propaganda portraying today's trade deals as "free trade agreements," even though Adam Smith and David Ricardo would turn over in their graves if they read the details of, say, the Trans-Pacific Partnership on intellectual property rules or investment regulations.

This reluctance to be honest about trade has cost economists their credibility with the public. Worse still, it has fed their opponents' narrative. Economists' failure to provide the full picture on trade, with all the necessary distinctions and caveats, has made it easier to tar trade, often wrongly, with all sorts of ill effects.

For example, as much as trade may have contributed to rising inequality, it is only one factor contributing to that broad trend—and in all likelihood a relatively minor one, compared to technology. Had economists been more upfront about the downside of trade, they may have had greater credibility as honest brokers in this debate.

Similarly, we might have had a more informed public discussion about social dumping if economists had been willing to recognize that imports from countries where labor rights are not protected raise serious questions about distributive justice. It may have been possible then to distinguish cases where low wages in poor countries reflect low productivity from cases of genuine rights violations. And the bulk of trade that does not raise such concerns may have been better insulated from charges of "unfair trade."

Likewise, if economists had listened to their critics who warned about currency manipulation, trade imbalances, and job losses, instead of sticking to models that assumed away unemployment and other macroeconomic problems, they might have been in a better position to counter excessive claims about the adverse impact of trade deals on employment.

In short, had economists gone public with the caveats, uncertainties, and skepticism of the seminar room, they might have become better defenders of the world economy. Unfortunately, their zeal to defend trade from its enemies has backfired. If the demagogues making nonsensical claims about trade are now getting a hearing—and actually winning power—it is trade's academic boosters who deserve at least part of the blame.

This book is an attempt to set the record straight, and not just about trade, as the title suggests, but about several areas in which economists could have offered a more balanced, principled discussion. Though trade is a central aspect of those areas, and in large part emblematic of what's happened in all of them, the same failures can be observed in policy discussions about financial globalization, the euro zone, or economic development strategies.

The book brings together much of my recent popular and nontechnical work on globalization, growth, democracy, politics, and the discipline of economics itself. The material that follows has been drawn from a variety of sources—my monthly syndicated columns for *Project Syndicate* as well as a few other short and lengthier pieces. In most cases, I have done only a light edit of the original text, updating it, providing connections with other parts of the book, and adding some references and supporting material. In places, I have rearranged the material from the original sources to provide a more seamless narrative. The full set of sources is listed at the back of the book.

The book shows how we could have constructed a more honest narrative on the world economy—one that would have prepared us for the eventual backlash and, perhaps, even rendered it less likely. It also suggests ideas for moving forward, to create better functioning national economies as well as a healthier globalization.

CHAPTER 1

A Better Balance

The global trade regime has never been very popular in the United States. Neither the World Trade Organization (WTO) nor the multitudes of regional trade deals such as the North American Free Trade Agreement (NAFTA) and the Trans-Pacific Partnership (TPP) have had strong support among the general public. But opposition, while broad, tended to be diffuse.

This has enabled policy makers to conclude a succession of trade agreements since the end of World War II. The world's major economies were in a perpetual state of trade negotiations, signing two major global multilateral deals: the General Agreement on Tariffs and Trade (GATT) and the treaty establishing the World Trade Organization. In addition, more than five hundred bilateral and regional trade agreements were signed—the vast majority of them since the WTO replaced the GATT in 1995.

The difference today is that international trade has moved to the center of the political debate. During the most recent US election, presidential candidates Bernie Sanders and Donald Trump both made opposition to trade agreements a key plank of their campaigns. And, judging from the tone of the other candidates, standing up for globalization amounted to electoral suicide in the political climate of the time. Trump's eventual win can be chalked up at least in part to his hard line on trade and his promise to renegotiate deals that he argued had benefited other nations at the expense of the United States.

Trump's and other populists' rhetoric on trade may be excessive, but few deny any longer that the underlying grievances are real. Globalization has not lifted all boats. Many working families have been devastated by the impact of low-cost imports from China, Mexico, and elsewhere.[1] And the big winners have been the financiers and skilled professionals who can take advantage of expanded markets. Although globalization has not been the sole, or even the most important, force driving inequality in the advanced economies, it has been a key contributor. Meanwhile, economists have struggled to find large gains from recent trade agreements for the economy as a whole.[2]

What gives trade particular political salience is that it often raises fairness concerns in ways that the other major contributor to inequality—technology—does not. When I lose my job because my competitor innovates and introduces a better product, I have little cause to complain. When he outcompetes me by outsourcing to firms abroad that do things that would be illegal here—for example, prevent their workers from organizing and bargaining collectively—I may have a legitimate gripe. It is not inequality per se that people tend to mind. What's problematic is *unfair* inequality, when we are forced to compete under different ground rules.[3]

During the 2016 US presidential campaign, Bernie Sanders forcefully advocated the renegotiation of trade agreements to reflect better the interests of working people. But such arguments immediately run up against the objection that any standstill or reversal on trade agreements would harm the world's poorest, by diminishing their prospect of escaping poverty through export-led growth. "If you're poor in another country, this is the scariest thing Bernie Sanders has said," ran a headline in the popular and normally sober Vox.com news site.[4]

But trade rules that are more sensitive to social and equity concerns in the advanced countries are not inherently in conflict with economic growth in poor countries. Globalization's cheerleaders do considerable damage to their cause by framing the issue as a stark choice between existing trade arrangements and the persistence of global poverty. And progressives needlessly force themselves into an undesirable trade-off.

The standard narrative about how trade has benefited developing economies omits a crucial feature of their experience. Countries that managed to leverage globalization, such as China and Vietnam, employed a mixed strategy of export promotion and a variety of policies that violate current trade rules. Subsidies, domestic-content requirements, investment regulations, and, yes, often import barriers were critical to the creation of new, higher-value industries.[5] Countries that rely on free trade alone (Mexico comes immediately to mind) have languished.[6]

That is why trade agreements that tighten the rules, such as TPP would have done, are in fact mixed blessings for developing countries. China would not have been able to pursue its phenomenally successful industrialization strategy if the country had been constrained by WTO-type rules during the 1980s and 1990s. With the TPP, Vietnam would have had some assurance of continued access to the US market (existing barriers on the US side are already quite low), but in return would have had to submit to restrictions on subsidies, patent rules, and investment regulations.

And there is nothing in the historical record to suggest that poor countries require very low or zero barriers in the advanced economies in order to benefit greatly from globalization. In fact, the most phenomenal export-oriented growth experiences to date—Japan, South

Korea, Taiwan, and China—all occurred when import tariffs in the United States and Europe were at moderate levels, and higher than where they are today.

So, for progressives who worry both about inequality in the rich countries and poverty in the rest of the world, the good news is that it is indeed possible to advance on both fronts. But to do so, we must transform our approach to trade deals in some drastic ways.

The stakes are extremely high. Poorly managed globalization is having profound effects not only in the United States but also in the rest of the developed world—especially Europe—and the low-income and middle-income countries in which a majority of the world's workers live. Getting the balance between economic openness and policy space management right is of huge importance.

Europe on the Brink

The difficulties that deep economic integration raises for governance and democracy are nowhere in clearer sight than in Europe. Europe's single market and single currency represent a unique experiment in what I have called in my previous work "hyperglobalization."[7] This experiment has opened a chasm between extensive economic integration and limited political integration that is historically unparalleled for democracies.

Once the financial crisis struck and the fragility of the European experiment came into full view, the weaker economies with large external imbalances needed a quick way out. European institutions and the International Monetary Fund (IMF) had an answer: structural reform. Sure, austerity would hurt. But a hefty dose of structural reform—liberalization of labor, product, and service markets—would make the pain bearable and help get the patient back on his feet.

As I explain later in the book, this was a false hope from the very beginning.

It is undeniable that the euro crisis has done much damage to Europe's political democracies. Confidence in the European project has eroded, centrist political parties have weakened, and extremist parties, particularly of the far right, are the primary beneficiaries. Less appreciated, but at least as important, is the damage that the crisis has done to democracy's prospects outside the narrow circle of eurozone countries. The sad fact is that Europe is no longer the shining beacon of democracy it was for other countries. A community of nations that is unable to stop the unmistakable authoritarian slide in one of its members—Hungary—can hardly be expected to foster and cement democracy in countries on its periphery. We can readily see the consequences in a country like Turkey, where the loss of the "European anchor" has played a facilitating role in enabling Erdogan's repeated power plays, and less directly in the faltering of the Arab Spring.

The costs of misguided economic policies have been the most severe for Greece. Politics in Greece has exhibited all the symptoms of a country being strangled by the trilemma of deep integration. It is impossible to have hyperglobalization, democracy, and national sovereignty all at once; we can have at most two out of three.[8] Because Greece, along with others in the euro, did not want to give up any of these, it ended up enjoying the benefits of none. The country has bought time with a succession of new programs, but has yet to emerge out of the woods. It remains to be seen whether austerity and structural reforms will eventually return the country to economic health.

History suggests some grounds for skepticism. In a democracy, when the demands of financial markets and foreign creditors clash with those of domestic workers, pensioners, and the middle class, it is usually the locals who have the last say.

As if the economic ramifications of a full-blown eventual Greek default were not terrifying enough, the political consequences could be far worse. A chaotic eurozone breakup would cause irreparable damage to the European integration project, the central pillar of Europe's political stability since World War II. It would destabilize not only the highly indebted European periphery but also core countries like France and Germany, which have been the architects of that project.

The nightmare scenario would be a 1930s-style victory for political extremism. Fascism, Nazism, and communism were children of a backlash against globalization that had been building since the end of the nineteenth century, feeding on the anxieties of groups that felt disenfranchised and threatened by expanding market forces and cosmopolitan elites.

Free trade and the gold standard had required downplaying domestic priorities such as social reform, nation-building, and cultural reassertion. Economic crisis and the failure of international cooperation undermined not only globalization but also the elites that upheld the existing order. As my Harvard colleague Jeff Frieden has written, this paved the path for two distinct forms of extremism. Faced with the choice between equity and economic integration, communists chose radical social reform and economic self-sufficiency. Faced with the choice between national assertion and globalism, fascists, Nazis, and nationalists chose nation-building.[9]

Fortunately, fascism, communism, and other forms of dictatorships are passé today. But similar tensions between economic integration and local politics have long been simmering. Europe's single market has taken shape much faster than Europe's political community has; economic integration has leaped ahead of political integration.

The result is that mounting concerns about the erosion of economic security, social stability, and cultural identity could not be handled through mainstream political channels. National political structures became too constrained to offer effective remedies, while European institutions still remain too weak to command allegiance.

It is the extreme right that has benefited most from the centrists' failure. In France, the National Front has been revitalized under Marine Le Pen and has turned into a major political force mounting a serious challenge for the presidency in 2017. In Germany, Denmark, Austria, Italy, Finland, and the Netherlands, right-wing populist parties have capitalized on the resentment around the euro to increase their vote shares and in some cases play kingmaker in their national political systems.

The backlash is not confined to eurozone members. In Scandinavia, the Sweden Democrats, a party with neo-Nazi roots, were running ahead of Social Democrats and had risen to the top of national polls in early 2017. And in Britain, of course, the antipathy toward Brussels and the yearning for national autonomy has resulted in Brexit, despite warnings of dire consequences from economists.

Political movements of the extreme right have traditionally fed on anti-immigration sentiment. But the Greek, Irish, Portuguese, and other bailouts, together with the euro's troubles, have given them fresh ammunition. Their euro skepticism certainly appears to be vindicated by events. When Marine Le Pen was asked if she would unilaterally withdraw from the euro, she replied confidently, "When I am president, in a few months' time, the eurozone probably won't exist."

As in the 1930s, the failure of international cooperation has compounded centrist politicians' inability to respond adequately to their domestic constituents' economic, social, and cultural demands. The European project and the eurozone have set the terms of debate to such an extent that, with the eurozone in tatters, these elites' legitimacy has received an even more serious blow.

Europe's centrist politicians have committed themselves to a strategy of "more Europe" that is too rapid to ease local anxieties, yet not rapid enough to create a real Europe-wide political community. They have stuck for far too long to an intermediate path that is unstable and beset by tensions. By holding on to a vision of Europe that has proven unviable, Europe's centrist elites have endangered the idea of a unified Europe itself.

The short-run and long-run remedies for the European crisis are not hard to discern in their broad outlines, and they are discussed below. Ultimately, Europe faces the same choice it always faced: it will either embark on political union or loosen the economic union. But the mismanagement of the crisis has made it very difficult to see how this eventual outcome can be produced amicably and with minimal economic and political damage to member countries.

Fads and Fashions in the Developing World

The last two decades have been good to developing countries. As the United States and Europe were reeling under financial crisis, austerity, and the populist backlash, developing economies led by China and India engineered historically unprecedented rates of economic growth and poverty alleviation. And for once, Latin America, Sub-Saharan Africa, and South Asia could join the party alongside East Asia. But even at the height of the emerging-markets hype, one could discern two dark clouds.

First, would today's crop of low-income economies be able to replicate the industrialization path that delivered rapid economic progress in Europe, America, and East Asia? And second, would they be able to develop the modern, liberal-democratic institutions that today's advanced economies acquired in the previous century? I suggest that the answers to both of these questions may be negative.

On the political side, the concern is that building and sustaining liberal democratic regimes has very special pre-requisites. The crux of the difficulty is that the beneficiaries of liberal democracy, unlike in the case of electoral democracies or dictatorships, typically have neither numbers nor resources on their side. Perhaps we should not be surprised that even advanced countries are having difficulty these days living up to liberal democratic norms. The natural tendency for countries without long and deep liberal traditions is to slide into authoritarianism. This has negative consequences not just for political development but economic development as well.

The growth challenge compounds the democracy challenge. One of the most important economic phenomena of our time is a process I have called "premature deindustrialization."[10] Partly because of automation in manufacturing and partly because of globalization, low-income countries are running out of industrialization opportunities much sooner than their earlier counterparts in East Asia did. This would not be a tragedy if manufacturing was not traditionally a powerful growth engine, for reasons I discuss below.

With hindsight, it has become clear that there was in fact no coherent growth story for most emerging markets. Unlike China, Vietnam, South Korea, Taiwan, and a few other manufacturing miracles, the recent crop of growth champions did not build many modern, export-oriented industries. Scratch the surface, and you find high growth rates driven not by productive transformation but by domestic demand, in turn fueled by temporary commodity booms and unsustainable levels of public or, more often, private borrowing. Yes, there are plenty of world-class firms in emerging markets, and the expansion of the middle class is unmistakable. But only a tiny share of these economies' labor is employed in productive enterprises, while informal, unproductive firms absorb the rest.

Is liberal democracy doomed in developing economies, or might it be saved by giving it different forms than it took in today's advanced economies? What kind of growth models are available to developing countries if industrialization has run out of steam? What are the implications of premature deindustrialization for labor markets and social inclusion? To overcome these novel future challenges, developing countries will need fresh, creative strategies that deploy the combined energies of both the private and public sectors.

No Time for Trade Fundamentalism

"One of the crucial challenges" of our era "is to maintain an open and expanding international trade system." Unfortunately, "the liberal principles" of the world trade system "are under increasing attack." "Protectionism has become increasingly prevalent." "There is great danger that the system will break down . . . or that it will collapse in a grim replay of the 1930s."

You would be excused for thinking that these lines are culled from one of the recent outpourings of concern in the business and financial media about the current backlash against globalization. In fact, they were written thirty-six years ago, in 1981.[11]

The problem then was stagflation in the advanced countries. And it was Japan, rather than China, that was the trade bogeyman, stalking—and taking over—global markets. The United States and Europe had responded by erecting trade barriers and imposing "voluntary export restrictions" on Japanese cars and steel. Talk about the creeping "new protectionism" was rife.

What took place subsequently would belie such pessimism about the trade regime. Instead of heading south, global trade exploded in the 1990s and 2000s, driven by the creation of the World Trade Organization, the proliferation of bilateral and regional trade and investment agreements, and the rise of China. A new age of globalization—in fact something more like hyperglobalization—was launched.

In hindsight, the "new protectionism" of the 1980s was not a radical break with the past. It was more a case of regime maintenance than regime disruption, as the political scientist John Ruggie has written. The import "safeguards" and "voluntary" export restrictions (VERs) of the time were ad hoc, but they were necessary responses to the distributional and adjustment challenges posed by the emergence of new trade relationships.[12]

The economists and trade specialists who cried wolf at the time were wrong. Had governments listened to their advice and not responded to their constituents, they would have possibly made things worse. What looked to contemporaries like damaging protectionism was in fact a way of letting off steam to prevent an excessive buildup of political pressure.

Are observers being similarly alarmist about today's globalization backlash? The International Monetary Fund, among others, has recently warned that slow growth and populism might lead to an outbreak of protectionism. "It is vitally important to defend the prospects for increasing trade integration," according to the IMF's chief economist, Maurice Obstfeld.[13]

So far, however, there are few signs that governments are moving decidedly away from an open economy. President Trump may yet cause trade havoc, but his bark has proved worse than his bite. The website globaltradealert.org maintains a database of protectionist measures and is a frequent source for claims of creeping protectionism. Click on its interactive map of protectionist measures, and you will see an explosion of fireworks—red circles all over the globe. It looks alarming until you click on liberalizing measures and discover a comparable number of green circles.

The difference this time is that populist political forces seem much more powerful and closer to winning elections—partly a response to the advanced stage of globalization achieved since the 1980s. Not so long ago, it would have been unimaginable to contemplate a British exit from the European Union, or a Republican president in the United States promising to renege on trade agreements, build a wall against Mexican immigrants, and punish companies that move offshore. The nation-state seems intent on reasserting itself.

But the lesson from the 1980s is that some reversal from hyperglobalization need not be a bad thing, as long as it serves to maintain a reasonably open world economy. In particular, we need to place the requirements of liberal democracy ahead of those of international trade and investment. Such a rebalancing would leave plenty of room for an open global economy; in fact, it would enable and sustain it.

What makes a populist like Donald Trump dangerous is not his specific proposals on trade. It is the nativist, illiberal platform on which he seems intent to govern. And it is as well the reality that his economic policies don't add up to a coherent vision of how the United States and an open world economy can prosper side by side.

The critical challenge facing mainstream political parties in the advanced economies today is to devise such a vision, along with a narrative that steals the populists' thunder. These center-right and center-left parties should not be asked to save hyperglobalization at all costs. Trade advocates should be understanding if they adopt unorthodox policies to buy political support.

We should look instead at whether their policies are driven by a desire for equity and social inclusion or by nativist and racist impulses, whether they want to enhance or weaken the rule of law and democratic deliberation, and whether they are trying to save the open world economy—albeit with different ground rules—rather than undermine it.

The populist revolts of 2016 will almost certainly put an end to the last few decades' hectic deal making in trade. Though developing countries may pursue smaller trade agreements, the two major regional deals on the table, the Trans-Pacific Partnership and the Transatlantic Trade and Investment Partnership, were as good as dead immediately after the election of Donald Trump as US president.

We should not mourn their passing. We should instead have an honest, principled discussion on putting globalization and development on a new footing, cognizant of our new political and technological realities and placing the requirements of liberal democracy front and center.

Getting the Balance Right

The problem with hyperglobalization is not just that it is an unachievable pipe dream susceptible to backlash—after all, the nation-state remains the only game in town when it comes to providing the regulatory and legitimizing arrangements on which markets rely. The deeper objection is that our elites' and technocrats' obsession with hyperglobalization makes it more difficult to achieve legitimate economic and social objectives at home—economic prosperity, financial stability, and social inclusion.

The questions of our day are: How much globalization should we seek in trade and finance? Is there still a case for nation-states in an age where the transportation and communications revolutions have apparently spelled the death of geographic distance? How much sovereignty do states need to cede to international institutions? What do trade agreements really do, and how can we improve them? When does globalization undermine democracy? What do we owe, as citizens and states, to others across the border? How do we best carry out those responsibilities?

All of these questions require that we restore a sane, sensible balance between national and global governance. We need a pluralist world economy where nation-states retain sufficient autonomy to fashion their own social contracts and develop their own economic strategies. I will argue that the conventional picture of the world economy as a "global commons"—one in which we would be driven to economic ruin unless we all cooperate—is highly misleading. If our economic policies fail, they do so largely for domestic rather than international reasons. The best way in which nations can serve the global good in the economic sphere is by putting their own economic houses in order.

Global governance does remain crucial in those areas such as climate change where the provision of global public goods is essential. And global rules sometimes can help improve domestic economic policy, by enhancing democratic deliberation and decision-making. But, I will argue, democracy-enhancing global agreements would look very different than the globalization-enhancing deals that have marked our age.

We begin with an entity at the very core of our political and economic existence, but which has for decades been under attack: the nation-state.

CHAPTER 2

How Nations Work

I n October 2016, British Prime Minister Theresa May shocked many when she disparaged the idea of global citizenship. "If you believe you're a citizen of the world," she said, "you're a citizen of nowhere."

Her statement was met with derision and alarm in the financial media and among liberal commentators. "The most useful form of citizenship these days," one analyst lectured her, "is one dedicated not only to the wellbeing of a Berkshire parish, say, but to the planet." *The Economist* called it an "illiberal" turn. A scholar accused her of repudiating Enlightenment values and warned of "echoes of 1933" in her speech.[1]

I know what a "global citizen" looks like: I make a perfect specimen myself. I grew up in one country, live in another, and carry the passports of both. I write on global economics, and my work takes me to far-flung places. I spend more time traveling in other countries than I do within either country that claims me as a citizen. Most of my close colleagues at work are similarly foreign-born. I devour international news, while my local paper remains unopened most weeks. In sports, I have no clue how my home teams are doing, but I am a devoted fan of a football team on the other side of the Atlantic.

And yet May's statement strikes a chord. It contains an essential truth, the disregard of which says much about how we—the world's financial, political, and technocratic elite—distanced ourselves from our compatriots and lost their trust.

Economists and mainstream politicians tend to view the backlash as a regrettable setback, fueled by populist and nativist politicians who managed to capitalize on the grievances of those who feel they have been left behind and deserted by the globalist elites. Nevertheless, today globalism is in retreat and the nation-state has shown that it is very much alive.

For years, an intellectual consensus on the declining relevance of the nation-state reigned supreme. All the craze was about global governance—the international rules and institutions needed to underpin the apparently irreversible tide of economic globalization and the rise of cosmopolitan sensibilities.

Global governance became the mantra of our era's elite. The surge in cross-border flows of goods, services, capital, and information produced by technological innovation and market liberalization has made the world's countries too interconnected, their argument went, for any country to be able to solve its economic problems on its own. We need global rules, global agreements, and global institutions. This claim is still so widely accepted today that challenging it may seem like arguing that the sun revolves around Earth.

To understand how we got to this point, let's take a close look at the intellectual case against the nation-state and the arguments in favor of globalism in governance.

The Nation-State Under Fire

The nation-state is roundly viewed as an archaic construct that is at odds with twenty-first-century realities. The assault on the nation-state transcends traditional political divisions and is one of the few things that unite economic liberals and socialists. "How may the economic unity of Europe be guaranteed, while preserving complete freedom of cultural development to the peoples living there?" asked Leon Trotsky back in 1934. The answer was to get rid of the nation-state: "The solution to this question can be reached . . . by completely liberating productive forces from the fetters imposed upon them by the national state."[2] Trotsky's answer sounds surprisingly modern in light of the eurozone's current travails. It is one to which most neoclassical economists would subscribe.

Many moral philosophers today join liberal economists in treating national borders as irrelevant, if not descriptively then certainly prescriptively. Here is Peter Singer:

> If the group to which we must justify ourselves is the tribe, or the nation, then our morality is likely to be tribal, or nationalistic. If, however, the revolution in communications has created a global audience, then we might need to justify our behavior to the whole world. This change creates the material basis for a new ethic that will serve the interests of all those who live on this planet in a way that, despite much rhetoric, no previous ethic has done.[3]

And Amartya Sen:

> There is something of a tyranny of ideas in seeing the political divisions of states (primarily, national states) as being, in some way, fundamental, and in seeing them not only as practical constraints to be addressed, but as divisions of basic significance in ethics and political philosophy.[4]

Sen and Singer think of national borders as a hindrance—a practical obstacle that can and should be overcome as the world becomes more interconnected through commerce and advances in communications.

Meanwhile, economists deride the nation-state because it is the source of the transaction costs that block fuller global economic integration. This is so not just because governments impose import tariffs, capital controls, visas, and other restrictions at their borders, impeding the global circulation of goods, money, and people. More fundamentally, it is because the multiplicity of sovereigns creates jurisdictional discontinuities and associated transaction costs. Differences in currencies, legal regimes, and regulatory practices are today the chief obstacles to a unified global economy. As overt trade barriers have come down, the relative importance of such transaction costs has grown. Import tariffs now constitute a tiny fraction of total trade costs. James Anderson and Eric van Wincoop estimated these costs to be a whopping 170 percent (in ad valorem terms) for advanced countries, an order of magnitude higher than import tariffs themselves.[5]

To an economist, this amount is equivalent to leaving $100 bills on the sidewalk. Remove the jurisdictional discontinuities, the argument goes, and the world economy would reap large gains from trade, similar to the multilateral tariff liberalization experienced over the postwar period. So, the global trade agenda has increasingly focused on efforts to harmonize regulatory regimes—everything from sanitary and phytosanitary standards to financial regulations. That is also why European nations felt it was important to move to a single currency to make their dream of a common market a reality. Economic integration requires repressing nation-states' ability to issue their own money, set different regulations, and impose different legal standards.

The Continued Vitality of the Nation-State

The death of the nation-state has long been predicted. "The critical issue for every student of world order is the fate of the nation-state," wrote political scientist Stanley Hoffman in 1966.[6] *Sovereignty at Bay* was the title of Raymond Vernon's 1971 classic.[7] Both scholars would ultimately pour cold water on the passing of the nation-state, but their tone reflects a strong current of prevailing opinion. Whether it was the European Union (on which Hoffman focused) or the multinational enterprise (Vernon's topic), the nation-state has been widely perceived as being overwhelmed by developments larger than it.

Yet the nation-state refuses to wither away. It has proved remarkably resilient and remains the main determinant of the global distribution of income, the primary locus of market-supporting institutions, and the chief repository of personal attachments and affiliations. Consider a few facts.

To test my students' intuition about the determinants of global inequality, I ask them on the first day of class whether they would rather be rich in a poor country or poor in a rich country. I tell them to consider only their own consumption level and to think of rich and poor as referring to the top and bottom 5 percent of a country's income distribution. A rich country, in turn, is one in the top 5 percent of the intercountry distribution of per-capita incomes, while a poor country is one in the bottom. Armed with this background, typically a majority of the students respond that they would rather be rich in a poor country.

They are in fact massively wrong. Defined the way I just did, the poor in a rich country are almost five times richer than the rich in a poor country.[8] The optical illusion that leads the students astray is that the superrich with the BMWs and gated mansions they have seen in poor countries are a miniscule proportion of the population—significantly fewer than the top 5 percent on which I asked them to focus. By the time we consider the average of the top ventile as a whole, we have taken a huge leap down the income scale.

The students have just discovered a telling feature of the world economy: our economic fortunes are determined primarily by where (which country) we are born and only secondarily by our location on the income-distribution scale. Or to put it in more technical but also more accurate terms, most global inequality is accounted for by inequality across rather than within nations.[9] So much for globalization having revoked the relevance of national borders.

Second, consider the role of national identity. One may imagine that attachments to the nation-state have worn thin between the push of transnational affinities, on the one hand, and the pull of local connections, on the other hand. But this does not seem to be the case. National identity remains alive and well, even in some surprising corners of the world. And this was true even before the global financial crisis and the populist backlash that has unfolded since.

To observe the continued vitality of national identification, let us turn to the World Values Survey, which covers more than eighty thousand individuals in fifty-seven countries (http://www.worldvaluessurvey .org/). The respondents to the survey were asked a range of questions about the strength of their local, national, and global attachments. I measured the strength of national attachments by computing the percentages of respondents who "agreed" or "strongly agreed" with the statement "I see myself as a citizen of [country, nation]." I measured the strength of global attachments, in turn, by the percentages of respondents who "agreed" or "strongly agreed" with the statement "I see myself as a world citizen." In each case, I subtracted these percentages from analogous percentages for "I see myself as a member of my local community" to provide for some kind of normalization. In other words, I measured national and global attachments relative to local attachments. I rely on the 2004–2008 round of the survey since it was carried out before the financial crises in Europe and the United States

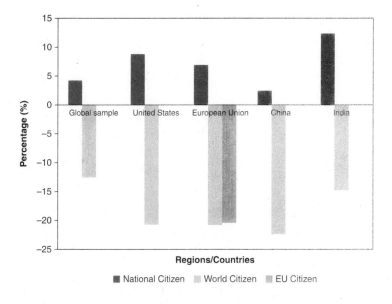

FIGURE 2.1 National, global, and EU citizenship (relative to attachment to local community). Percentages of respondents who "agree" or "strongly agree" with the statements "I see myself as a citizen of [country, nation]" and "I see myself as a world citizen," subtracted from analogous percentages for "I see myself as a member of my local community."

Source: D. Rodrik, "Who Needs the Nation State?" *Economic Geography,* 89(1), January 2013: 1–19.

and isolates the results from the confounding effects of the economic downturn.

Figure 2.1 shows the results for the entire global sample, as well as for the United States, the European Union, China, and India individually. What stands out is not so much that national identity is vastly stronger than identity as a "global citizen"—that much was predictable. The surprising finding is how it apparently exerts a stronger pull than membership in the local community, as can be observed in the positive percentages for normalized national identity. This tendency is true across the board and the strongest in the United States and India, two vast countries where we may have expected local attachments to be, if anything, stronger than attachment to the nation-state.

I find it also striking that European citizens feel so little attachment to the European Union. In fact, as Figure 2.1 shows, the idea of citizenship in the European Union seems as remote to Europeans as that of global citizenship, despite long decades of European integration and institution building.

It is not a surprise to find that global attachments have worn even thinner since 2008. Measures of world citizenship have gone down significantly in some of the European countries especially: from −18 percent to −29 percent in Germany and −12 percent to −22 percent in Spain. (These are comparisons between the 2010–2014 and 2004–2008 waves.)

One may object that such surveys obfuscate differences among subgroups within the general population. We would expect mainly the young, the skilled, and the well-educated to have been unhinged from their national mooring and to have become global in their outlook and attachments. As Figure 2.2 indicates, there are indeed differences among these groups that go in the predicted direction. But they are not as large as one may have thought and do not change the overall picture. Even among the young (less than twenty-five years old), those with a university education and professionals, national identity trumps local and—even more massively—global attachments.

Finally, any remaining doubts about the continued relevance of the nation-state must have been dispelled by the experience in the aftermath of the global financial crisis of 2008. It was domestic policy makers who had to step in to prevent an economic meltdown: it was

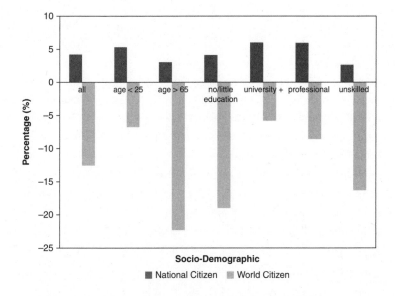

FIGURE 2.2 Effect of socio-demographics. Percentages of respondents who "agree" or "strongly agree" with the statements "I see myself as a citizen of [country, nation]" and "I see myself as a world citizen," subtracted from analogous percentages for "I see myself as a member of my local community."

Source: D. Rodrik, "Who Needs the Nation State?" *Economic Geography,* 89(1), January 2013: 1–19.

national governments that bailed out banks, pumped liquidity, provided a fiscal stimulus, and wrote unemployment checks. As Bank of England chairman Mervyn King once memorably put it, banks are global in life and national in death.

The International Monetary Fund and the newly upgraded Group of 20 were merely talking shops. In the eurozone, it was decisions taken in national capitals from Berlin to Athens that determined how the crisis would play out, not actions in Brussels (or Strasbourg). And it was national governments that ultimately took the blame for everything that went wrong—or the credit for the little that went right.

A Normative Case for the Nation-State

Historically, the nation-state has been closely associated with economic, social, and political progress. It curbed internecine violence, expanded networks of solidarity beyond local communities, spurred mass markets and industrialization, enabled the mobilization of human and financial resources, and fostered the spread of representative political institutions.[10] Civil wars and economic decline are the usual fate of today's "failed states." For residents of stable and prosperous countries, it is easy to overlook the role that the construction of the nation-state played in overcoming such challenges. The nation-state's fall from intellectual grace is in part a consequence of its achievements.

But has the nation-state, as a territorially confined political entity, truly become a hindrance to the achievement of desirable economic and social outcomes in view of the globalization revolution? Or does the nation-state remain indispensable to the achievement of those goals? In other words, is it possible to construct a more principled defense of the nation-state, one that goes beyond stating that it exists and that it has not withered away?

Let me begin by clarifying my terminology. The nation-state evokes connotations of nationalism. The emphasis in my discussion will be not on the "nation" or "nationalism" part but on the "state" part. In particular, I am interested in the state as a spatially demarcated jurisdictional entity. From this perspective, I view the nation as a consequence of a state, rather than the other way around. As Abbé Sieyès, one of the theorists of the French revolution, put it: "What is a nation? A body of associates living under one common law and represented by the same legislature."[11] I am not concerned with debates over what a nation is, whether each nation should have its own state, or how many states there ought to be.

Instead, I want to develop a substantive argument for why robust nation-states are actually beneficial, especially to the world economy. I want to show that the multiplicity of nation-states adds rather than subtracts value. My starting point is that markets require rules and that global markets would require global rules. A truly borderless global economy, one in which economic activity is fully unmoored from its national base, would necessitate transnational rule-making institutions that match the global scale and scope of markets. But this would not be desirable, even if it were feasible. Market-supporting rules are nonunique. Experimentation and competition among diverse institutional arrangements therefore remain desirable. Moreover, communities differ in their needs and preferences regarding institutional forms. And history and geography continue to limit the convergence in these needs and preferences.

So, I accept that nation-states are a source of disintegration for the global economy. My claim is that an attempt to transcend them would be counterproductive. It would get us neither a healthier world economy nor better rules.

My argument can be presented as a counterpoint to the typical globalist narrative, depicted graphically in the top half of Figure 2.3. In this narrative, economic globalization, spurred by the revolutions in transportation and communication technologies, breaks down the social and cultural barriers among people in different parts of the world and fosters a global community. It, in turn, enables the construction of a global *political* community—global governance—that underpins and further reinforces economic integration.

The globalist dynamic

The nation-state dynamic

FIGURE 2.3 Alternative reinforcing dynamics
Source: D. Rodrik, "Who Needs the Nation State?" *Economic Geography,* 89(1),
January 2013: 1–19.

My alternative narrative (shown at the bottom of Figure 2.3) emphasizes a different dynamic, one that sustains a world that is politically
divided and economically less than fully globalized. In this dynamic,
preference heterogeneity and institutional nonuniqueness, along with
geography, create a need for institutional diversity. Institutional diversity blocks full economic globalization. Incomplete economic integration, in turn, reinforces heterogeneity and the role of distance. When
the forces of this second dynamic are sufficiently strong, as I will

argue they are, operating by the rules of the first can get us only into trouble.

The Futile Pursuit of Hyperglobalization

Markets depend on nonmarket institutions because they are not self-creating, self-regulating, self-stabilizing, or self-legitimating. Anything that goes beyond a simple exchange among neighbors requires investments in transportation, communications, and logistics; enforcement of contracts, provision of information, and prevention of cheating; a stable and reliable medium of exchange; arrangements to bring distributional outcomes into conformity with social norms; and so on. Well-functioning, sustainable markets are backed by a wide range of institutions that provide the critical functions of regulation, redistribution, monetary and fiscal stability, and conflict management.

These institutional functions have so far been provided largely by the nation-state. Throughout the postwar period, this not only did not impede the development of global markets but it facilitated it in many ways. The guiding philosophy behind the Bretton Woods regime, which governed the world economy until the 1970s, was that nations—not only the advanced nations but also the newly independent ones—needed the policy space within which they could manage their economies and protect their social contracts. Capital controls, restricting the free flow of finance between countries, were viewed as an inherent element of the global financial system. Trade liberalization remained limited to manufactured goods and to industrialized nations; when imports of textiles and clothing from low-cost countries threatened domestic social bargains by causing job losses in affected industries and regions, these, too, were carved out as special regimes.

Yet trade and investment flows grew by leaps and bounds, in no small part because the Bretton Woods recipe made for healthy domestic policy environments. In fact, economic globalization relied critically on the rules maintained by the major trading and financial centers. As John Agnew has emphasized, national monetary systems, central banks, and financial regulatory practices were the cornerstones of financial globalization.[12] In trade, it was more the domestic political bargains than GATT rules that sustained the openness that came to prevail.

The nation-state was the enabler of globalization, but also the ultimate obstacle to its deepening. Combining globalization with healthy domestic polities relied on managing this tension well. Veer too much in the direction of globalization, as in the 1920s, and we would erode the institutions' underpinning markets. Veer too much in the direction of the state, as in the 1930s, and we would forfeit the benefits of international commerce.

From the 1980s on, the ideological balance took a decisive shift in favor of markets and against governments. The result internationally was an all-out push for what I have called "hyperglobalization"[13]—the attempt to eliminate all transaction costs that hinder trade and capital flows. The World Trade Organization was the crowning achievement of this effort in the trade arena. Trade rules were now extended to services, agriculture, subsidies, intellectual property rights, sanitary and phytosanitary standards, and other types of what were previously considered to be domestic policies. In finance, freedom of capital mobility became the norm, rather than the exception, with regulators focusing on the global harmonization of financial regulations and standards. A majority of European Union members went the furthest by first reducing exchange-rate movements among themselves and ultimately adopting a single currency.

The upshot was that domestic governance mechanisms were weakened while their global counterparts remain incomplete. The flaws of the new approach became evident soon enough. One type of failure arose from pushing rule making onto supranational domains too far beyond the reach of political debate and control. This failure was exhibited in persistent complaints about the democratic deficit, lack of legitimacy, and loss of voice and accountability. These complaints became permanent fixtures attached to the World Trade Organization and Brussels institutions.

Where rule making remained domestic, another type of failure arose. Growing volumes of trade with countries at different levels of development and with highly dissimilar institutional arrangements exacerbated inequality and economic insecurity at home. What was even more destructive, the absence of institutions at the global level that have tamed domestic finance (a lender of last resort, deposit insurance, bankruptcy laws, and fiscal stabilizers) rendered global finance a source of instability and periodic crises of massive proportions. Domestic policies alone were inadequate to address the problems that extreme economic and financial openness created.

Suitably enough, the countries that did the best in the new regime were those that did not let their enthusiasm for free trade and free flows of capital get the better of them. China, which engineered history's most impressive poverty reduction and growth outcomes, was, of course, a major beneficiary of others' economic openness. But for its part, it followed a highly cautious strategy that combined extensive industrial policies with selective, delayed import liberalization and capital controls. Effectively, China played the globalization game by Bretton Woods rules rather than by hyperglobalization rules.

Is Global Governance Feasible or Desirable?

By now it is widely understood that globalization's ills derive from the imbalance between the global nature of markets and the domestic nature of the rules that govern them. As a matter of logic, the imbalance can be corrected in only one of two ways: expand governance beyond the nation-state or restrict the reach of markets. In polite company, only the first option receives much attention.

Global governance means different things to different people. For policy officialdom, it refers to new intergovernmental forums, such as the Group of 20 and the Financial Stability Forum. For some analysts, it means the emergence of transnational networks of regulators setting common rules from sanitary to capital adequacy standards.[14] For other analysts, it is "private governance" regimes, such as fair trade and corporate social responsibility.[15] Yet others imagine the development of accountable global administrative processes that depend "on local debate, is informed by global comparisons, and works in a space of public reasons."[16] For many activists, it signifies greater power for international nongovernmental organizations.

It remains without saying that such emergent forms of global governance remain weak. But the real question is whether they can develop and become strong enough to sustain hyperglobalization and spur the emergence of truly global identities. I do not believe they can. I develop my argument in four steps: (1) market-supporting institutions are not unique, (2) communities differ in their needs and preferences regarding institutional forms, (3) geographic distance limits the convergence in those needs and preferences, and (4) experimentation and competition among diverse institutional forms is desirable.

Market-supporting Institutions Are Not Unique

It is relatively straightforward to specify the *functions* that market-supporting institutions serve, as I did previously. They create, regulate, stabilize, and legitimate markets. But specifying the *form* that institutions should take is another matter altogether. There is no reason to believe that these functions can be provided only in specific ways or to think that there is only a limited range of plausible variation. In other words, institutional function does not map uniquely into form.

All advanced societies are some variant of a market economy with dominantly private ownership. But the United States, Japan, and the European nations have evolved historically under institutional setups that differ significantly. These differences are revealed in divergent practices in labor markets, corporate governance, social welfare systems, and approaches to regulation. That these nations have managed to generate comparable amounts of wealth under different rules is an important reminder that there is not a single blueprint for economic success. Yes, markets, incentives, property rights, stability, and predictability are important. But they do not require cookie-cutter solutions.

Economic performance fluctuates, even among advanced countries, so institutional fads are common. In recent decades, European social democracy, Japanese-style industrial policy, the US model of corporate governance and finance, and Chinese state capitalism have periodically come into fashion, only to recede from attention once their stars faded. Despite efforts by international organizations, such as the World Bank and the Organisation for Economic Co-operation and Development (OECD), to develop "best practices," institutional emulation rarely succeeds.

One reason is that elements of the institutional landscape tend to have a complementary relationship to each other, dooming partial reform to failure. For example, in the absence of labor market training programs and adequate safety nets, deregulating labor markets by making it easier for firms to fire their workers can easily backfire. Without a tradition of strong stakeholders that restrain risk taking, allowing financial firms to self-regulate can be a disaster. In their well-known book *Varieties of Capitalism*, Peter Hall and David Soskice identified two distinct institutional clusters among advanced industrial economies, which they called "liberal market economies" and "coordinated market economies."[17] We can certainly identify additional models as well if we turn to Asia.

The more fundamental point has to do with the inherent malleability of institutional designs. As Roberto Unger has emphasized, there is no reason to think that the range of institutional divergence we observe in the world today exhausts all feasible variation.[18] Desired institutional functions—aligning private incentives with social optimality, establishing macrostability, achieving social justice—can be generated in innumerable ways, limited only by our imagination. The idea that there is a best-practice set of institutions is an illusion.

This is not to say that differences in institutional arrangements do not have real consequences. Institutional malleability does not mean that institutions always perform adequately: there are plenty of societies whose institutions patently fail to provide for adequate incentives for production, investment, and innovation, not to mention social justice. But even among relatively successful societies, different institutional configurations often have varying implications for distinct groups. Compared to coordinated market economies, liberal market economies, for example, present better opportunities for the most creative and successful members of society, but also tend to produce greater inequality and economic insecurity for their working classes. Richard Freeman has shown that more highly regulated labor market environments produce less dispersion in earnings but not necessarily higher rates of unemployment.[19]

There is an interesting analogy here to the second fundamental theorem of welfare economics. The theorem states that any Pareto-efficient equilibrium can be obtained as the outcome of a competitive equilibrium with an appropriate distribution of endowments. Institutional arrangements are, in effect, the rules that determine the allocation of rights to a society's resources; they shape the distribution of endowments in the broadest term. Each Pareto-efficient outcome can be sustained by a different set of rules. And conversely, each set of rules has the potential to generate a different Pareto-efficient outcome. (I say potential because "bad" rules will clearly result in Pareto-inferior outcomes.)

It is not clear how we can choose ex ante among Pareto-efficient equilibria. It is precisely this indeterminacy that makes the choice among alternative institutions a difficult one, best left to political communities themselves.

Heterogeneity and Diversity

Immanuel Kant wrote that religion and language divide people and prevent a universal monarchy.[20] But there are many other things that divide us. As I discussed in the previous section, institutional arrangements have distinct implications for the distribution of well-being and many other features of economic, social, and political life. We do not agree on how to trade equality against opportunity, economic security against innovation, stability against dynamism, economic outcomes against social and cultural values, and many other consequences of institutional choice. Differences in preferences are ultimately the chief argument against institutional harmonization globally.

Consider how financial markets should be regulated. There are many choices to be made. Should commercial banking be separated from investment banking? Should there be a limit on the size of banks? Should there be deposit insurance, and, if so, what should it cover? Should banks be allowed to trade on their own account? How much information should they reveal about their trades? Should executives' compensation be set by directors, with no regulatory controls? What should the capital and liquidity requirements be? Should all derivative contracts be traded on exchanges? What should be the role of credit-rating agencies? And so on.

A central trade-off here is between financial innovation and financial stability. A light approach to regulation will maximize the scope for financial innovation (the development of new financial products), but at the cost of increasing the likelihood of financial crises and crashes. Strong regulation will reduce the incidence and costs of crises, but potentially at the cost of raising the cost of finance and excluding many from its benefits. There is no single ideal point along this trade-off. Requiring that communities whose preferences over the innovation-stability continuum vary all settle on the same solution may have the virtue that it reduces transaction costs in finance. But it would come at the cost of imposing arrangements that are out of sync with local preferences. This is the conundrum that financial regulation faces at the moment, with banks pushing for common global rules and domestic legislatures and policy makers resisting.

Here is another example from food regulation. In a controversial 1998 case, the World Trade Organization sided with the United States in ruling that the European Union's ban on beef reared on certain growth hormones violated the Agreement on Sanitary and Phytosanitary Standards (SPS). It is interesting that the ban did not discriminate against imports and applied to imported and domestic beef alike. There did not seem to be a protectionist motive behind the ban, which had been pushed by consumer lobbies in Europe that were alarmed by the potential health threats. Nonetheless, the World Trade Organization judged that the ban violated the requirement in the SPS agreement that policies be based on "scientific evidence." (In a similar case in 2006, the World Trade Organization also ruled against the European Union's restrictions on genetically modified food and seeds [GMOs], finding fault once again with the adequacy of the European Union's scientific risk assessment.)

There is indeed scant evidence to date that growth hormones pose any health threats. The European Union argued that it had applied a broader principle not explicitly covered by the World Trade Organization, the "precautionary principle," which permits greater caution in the presence of scientific uncertainty. The precautionary principle reverses the burden of proof. Instead of asking, "Is there reasonable evidence that growth hormones, or GMOs, have adverse effects?" it requires policy makers to ask, "Are we reasonably sure that they do *not*?" In many unsettled areas of scientific knowledge, the answer to both questions can be no. Whether the precautionary principle makes sense depends both on the degree of risk aversion and on the extent to which potential adverse effects are large and irreversible.

As the European Commission argued (unsuccessfully), regulatory decisions here cannot be made purely on the basis of science. Politics, which aggregates a society's risk preferences, must play the determining role. It is reasonable to expect that the outcome will vary across societies. Some (like the United States) may go for low prices; others (like the European Union) will go for greater safety.

The suitability of institutional arrangements also depends on levels of development and historical trajectory. Alexander Gerschenkron famously argued that lagging countries would need institutions—such as large banks and state-directed investments—that differed from those present in the original industrializers.[21] To a large extent, his arguments have been validated. But even among rapidly growing developing nations, there is considerable institutional variation. What works in one place rarely does in another.

Consider how some of the most successful developing nations joined the world economy. South Korea and Taiwan relied heavily on export subsidies to push their firms outward during the 1960s and 1970s and liberalized their import regime only gradually. China established special economic zones in which export-oriented firms were allowed to operate under different rules than those applied to state enterprises and to others focused on the internal market. Chile, by contrast, followed the textbook model and sharply reduced import barriers to force domestic firms to compete with foreign firms directly in the home market. The Chilean strategy would have been a disaster if applied in China, because it would have led to millions of job losses in state enterprises and incalculable social consequences. And the Chinese model would not have worked as well in Chile, a small nation that is not an obvious destination for multinational enterprises.

Alberto Alesina and Enrico Spolaore have explored how heterogeneity in preferences interacts with the benefits of scale to determine endogenously the number and size of nations. In their basic model, individuals differ in their preferences over the type of public goods— or, in my terms, the specific institutional arrangements—provided by the state.[22] The larger the population over which the public good is provided, the lower the unit cost of provision. On the other hand, the larger the population, the greater the number of people who find their preferences ill served by the specific public good that is provided. Smaller countries are better able to respond to their citizens' needs. The optimum number of jurisdictions, or nation-states, trades off the scale benefits of size against the heterogeneity costs of the provision of public good.

The important analytical insight of the Alesina-Spolaore model is that it makes little sense to optimize along the market-size dimension (and eliminate jurisdictional discontinuities) when there is heterogeneity in preferences along the institutional dimension. The framework does not tell us whether we have too many nations at present or too few. But it does suggest that a divided world polity is the price we pay for institutional arrangements that are, in principle at least, better tailored to local preferences and needs.

Distance Lives: The Limits to Convergence

We need to consider an important caveat to the discussion on heterogeneity—namely, the *endogenous* nature of many of the differences that set communities apart. That culture, religion, and language are in part a side product of nation-states is an old theme that runs through the long trail of the literature on nationalism. From Ernest Renan down, theorists of nationalism have stressed that cultural differences are not innate and can be shaped by state policies. Education, in particular, is a chief vehicle through which national identity is molded. Ethnicity has a certain degree of exogeneity, but its salience in defining identity is also a function of the strength of the nation-state. A resident of Turkey who defines himself as Muslim is potentially a member of a global community, whereas a "Turk" owes primary loyalty to the Turkish state.

Much the same can be said about other characteristics along which communities differ. If poor countries have distinctive institutional needs arising from their low levels of income, we may perhaps expect these distinctions to disappear as income levels convergence. If societies have different preferences over risk, stability, equity, and so on, we may similarly expect these differences to narrow as a result of greater communication and economic exchange across jurisdictional boundaries. Today's differences may exaggerate tomorrow's differences. In a world where people are freed from their local moorings, they are also freed from their local idiosyncrasies and biases. Individual heterogeneity may continue to exist, but it need not be correlated across geographic space.

There is some truth to these arguments, but they are also counterweighed by a considerable body of evidence that suggests that geographic distance continues to produce significant localization effects despite the evident decline in transportation and communication costs and other man-made barriers. One of the most striking studies in this vein was by Anne-Celia Disdier and Keith Head, which looked at the effect of distance on international trade over the span of history.[23] It is a stylized fact of the empirical trade literature that the volume of bilateral trade declines with the geographic distance between trade partners. The typical distance elasticity is around −1.0, meaning that trade falls by 10 percent for every 10 percent increase in distance. This is a fairly large effect. Presumably, what lies behind it is not just transportation and communication costs but the lack of familiarity and cultural differences. (Linguistic differences are often controlled for separately.)

Disdier and Head undertook a meta-analysis, collecting 1,467 distance effects from 103 papers covering trade flows at different points in time, and stumbled on a surprising result: distance matters more now than it did in the late nineteenth century. The distance effect seems to have increased from the 1960s, remaining persistently high since then (see Figure 2.4). If anything, globalization seems to have raised the penalty that geographic distance imposes on economic exchange. This apparent paradox was also confirmed by Matias Berthelon and Caroline Freund, who found an increase in the (absolute value) of the distance elasticity from −1.7 to −1.9 between 1985 and 1989 and between 2001 and 2005 using a consistent trade data set. Berthelon and Freund showed that the result was not due to a compositional switch from low- to high-elasticity goods but to "a significant and increasing impact of distance on trade in almost 40 percent of industries."[24]

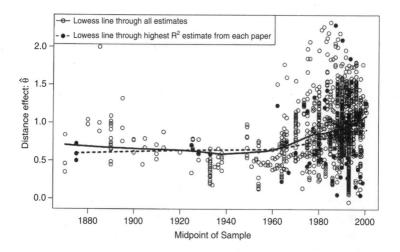

FIGURE 2.4 Estimated distance effect ($\hat{\theta}$) over time

Source: Disdier, A.-C., and Head, K. 2008. "The Puzzling Persistence of the Distance Effect on Bilateral Trade," *The Review of Economics and Statistics* 90(1): 37–48. With permission from MIT Press Journals.

Leaving this puzzle aside for the moment, let us turn to an altogether different type of evidence. [25] In the mid-1990s a new housing development in one of the suburbs of Toronto engaged in an interesting experiment. The houses were built from the ground up with the latest broadband telecommunications infrastructure and came with a host of new Internet technologies. Residents of Netville (a pseudonym) had access to high-speed Internet, a videophone, an online jukebox, online health services, discussion forums, and a suite of entertainment and educational applications. These new technologies made the town an ideal setting for nurturing global citizens. The people of Netville were freed from the tyranny of distance. They could communicate with anyone in the world as easily as they could with a neighbor, forge their own global links, and join virtual communities in cyberspace. One might expect they would begin to define their identities and interests increasingly in global, rather than in local, terms.

What actually transpired was quite different. Glitches experienced by the telecom provider left some homes without a link to the broadband network. This situation allowed researchers to compare wired and nonwired households and reach some conclusions about the consequences of being wired. Far from letting local links erode, wired people actually strengthened their existing local social ties. Compared to nonwired residents, they recognized more of their neighbors, talked to them more often, visited them more frequently, and made many more local phone calls. They were more likely to organize local events and mobilize the community around common problems. They used their computer network to facilitate a range of social activities, from organizing barbecues to helping local children with their homework. Netville exhibited, as one resident put it, "a closeness that you don't see in many communities." What was supposed to have unleashed global engagement and networks had instead strengthened local social ties.

There are plenty of other examples that belie the death of distance. One study identified strong "gravity" effects on the Internet: "Americans are more likely to visit websites from nearby countries, even controlling for language, income, immigrant stock, etc."[26] For digital products related to music, games, and pornography, a 10 percent increase in physical distance reduces the probability that an American will visit the website by 33 percent—a distance elasticity even higher (in absolute value) than for trade in goods.

Despite the evident reduction in transportation and communication costs, the production location of globally traded products is often determined by regional agglomeration effects. When the *New York Times* recently examined why Apple's iPhone is manufactured in China, rather than in the United States, the answer turned out to have little to do with comparative advantage. China had already developed a massive network of suppliers, engineers, and dedicated workers in a complex known informally as Foxconn City that provided Apple with benefits that the United States could not match.[27]

More broadly, incomes and productivity do not always exhibit a tendency to converge as markets for goods, capital, and technology become more integrated. The world economy's first era of globalization produced a large divergence in incomes between the industrializing countries at the center and lagging regions in the periphery that specialized in primary commodities. Similarly, economic convergence has been the exception rather than the rule in the postwar period. Economic development depends perhaps more than ever on what happens at home. If the world economy exerts a homogenizing influence, it is at best a partial one, competing with many other influences that go the other way.

Relationships based on proximity are one such offsetting influence. Many, if not most, exchanges are based on relationships, rather than textbook-style anonymous markets. Geographic distance protects relationships. As Ed Leamer put it, "geography, whether physical or cultural or informational, limits competition since it creates cost-advantaged relationships between sellers and buyers who are located 'close' to one another."[28] But relationships also create a role for geography. Once relationship-specific investments are made, geography becomes more important. The iPhone could have been produced anywhere, but once relationships with local suppliers were established, there are lock-in effects that make it difficult for Apple to move anywhere else.

Technological progress has an ambiguous effect on the importance of relationships. On the one hand, the decline in transportation and communication costs reduces the protective effect of distance in market relationships. It may facilitate the creation of long-distance relationships that cross national boundaries. On the other hand, the increase in complexity and product differentiation, along with the shift from Fordist mass production to new, distributed modes of learning, increases the relative importance of spatially circumscribed relationships. The new economy runs on tacit knowledge, trust, and cooperation—which still depend on personal contact. As Kevin Morgan put it, spatial reach does not equal "social depth."[29]

Hence, market segmentation is a natural feature of economic life, even in the absence of jurisdictional discontinuities. Neither economic convergence nor preference homogenization is the inevitable consequence of globalization.

Experimentation and Competition

Finally, since there is no fixed, ideal shape for institutions and diversity is the rule rather than exception, a divided global polity presents an additional advantage. It enables experimentation, competition among institutional forms, and learning from others. To be sure, trial and error can be costly when it comes to society's rules. Still, institutional diversity among nations is as close as we can expect to a laboratory in real life. Josiah Ober has discussed how competition among Greek city-states during 800–300 BCE fostered institutional innovation in areas of citizenship, law, and democracy, sustaining the relative prosperity of ancient Greece.[30]

There can be nasty sides to institutional competition. One of them is the nineteenth-century idea of a Darwinian competition among states, whereby wars are the struggle through which we get progress and self-realization of humanity.[31] The equally silly, if less bloody, modern counterpart of this idea is the notion of economic competition among nations, whereby global commerce is seen as a zero-sum game. Both ideas are based on the belief that the point of competition is to lead us to the one perfect model. But competition works in diverse ways. In economic models of "monopolistic competition," producers compete not just on price but on variety—by differentiating their products from others'.[32] Similarly, national jurisdictions can compete by offering institutional "services" that are differentiated along the dimensions I discussed earlier.

One persistent worry is that institutional competition sets off a race to the bottom. To attract mobile resources—capital, multinational enterprises, and skilled professionals—jurisdictions may lower their standards and relax their regulations in a futile dynamic to outdo other jurisdictions. Once again, this argument overlooks the multidimensional nature of institutional arrangements. Tougher regulations or standards are presumably put in place to achieve certain objectives: they offer compensating benefits elsewhere. We may all wish to be free to drive at any speed we want, but few of us would move to a country with no speed limit at all where, as a result, deadly traffic accidents would be much more common. Similarly, higher labor standards may lead to happier and more productive workers; tougher financial regulation to greater financial stability; and higher taxes to better public services, such as schools, infrastructure, parks, and other amenities. Institutional competition can foster a race to the top.

The only area in which some kind of race to the bottom has been documented is corporate taxation. Tax competition has played an important role in the remarkable reduction in corporate taxes around the world since the early 1980s. In a study on OECD countries, researchers found that when other countries reduce their average statutory corporate tax rate by 1 percentage point, the home country follows by reducing its tax rate by 0.7 percentage points.[33] The study indicated that international tax competition takes place only among countries that have removed their capital controls. When such controls are in place, capital and profits cannot move as easily across national borders and there is no downward pressure on capital taxes. So, the removal of capital controls appears to be a factor in driving the reduction in corporate tax rates.

On the other hand, there is scant evidence of similar races to the bottom in labor and environmental standards or in financial regulation. The geographically confined nature of the services (or public goods) offered by national jurisdictions often presents a natural restraint on the drive toward the bottom. If you want to partake of those services, you need to be in that jurisdiction. But corporate tax competition is also a reminder that the costs and benefits need not always neatly cancel each other. Although it is not a perfect substitute for local sourcing, international trade does allow a company to serve a high-tax market from a low-tax jurisdiction. The problem becomes particularly acute when the arrangement in question has a "solidarity" motive and is explicitly redistributive (as in many tax examples). In such cases, it becomes desirable to prevent "regulatory arbitrage" even if it means tightening controls at the border.

What Do Global Citizens Do?

Let's circle back to Teresa May's comments at the beginning of this chapter. What does it even mean to be a "global citizen"? The Oxford English Dictionary defines "citizen" as "a legally recognized subject or national of a state or commonwealth." Hence, citizenship presumes an established polity—"a state or commonwealth"—of which one is a member. Countries have such polities; the world does not.

Proponents of global citizenship quickly concede that they do not have a literal meaning in mind. They are thinking figuratively.

Technological revolutions in communications and economic globalization have brought citizens of different countries together, they argue. The world has shrunk, and we must act bearing the global implications in mind. And besides, we all carry multiple, overlapping identities. Global citizenship does not—and need not—crowd out parochial or national responsibilities.

All well and good. But what do global citizens really do?

Real citizenship entails interacting and deliberating with other citizens in a shared political community. It means holding decision makers to account and participating in politics to shape the policy outcomes. In the process, my ideas about desirable ends and means are confronted with and tested against those of my fellow citizens.

Global citizens do not have similar rights or responsibilities. No one is accountable to them, and there is no one to whom they must justify themselves. At best, they form communities with like-minded individuals from other countries. Their counterparts are not citizens everywhere but self-designated "global citizens" in other countries.

Of course, global citizens have access to their *domestic* political systems to push their ideas through. But political representatives are elected to advance the interests of the people who put them in office. National governments are meant to look out for national interests, and rightly so. This does not exclude the possibility that constituents might act with enlightened self-interest, by taking into account the consequences of domestic action for others.

But what happens when the welfare of local residents comes into conflict with the well-being of foreigners—as it often does?[34] Isn't disregard of their compatriots in such situations precisely what gives so-called cosmopolitan elites their bad name?

Global citizens worry that the interests of the global commons may be harmed when each government pursues its own narrow interest.

This is certainly a concern with issues that truly concern the global commons, such as climate change or pandemics. But in most economic areas—taxes, trade policy, financial stability, fiscal and monetary management—what makes sense from a global perspective also makes sense from a domestic perspective. Economics teaches that countries should maintain open economic borders, sound prudential regulation, and full-employment policies, not because these are good for other countries but because they serve to enlarge the domestic economic pie.

Of course, policy failures—for example, protectionism—do occur in all of these areas. But these reflect poor domestic governance, not a lack of cosmopolitanism. They result either from policy elites' inability to convince domestic constituencies of the benefits of the alternative, or from their unwillingness to make adjustments to ensure that everyone does indeed benefit.

Hiding behind cosmopolitanism in such instances—when pushing for trade agreements, for example—is a poor substitute for winning policy battles on their merits. And it devalues the currency of cosmopolitanism when we truly need it, as we do in the fight against global warming.

Few have expounded on the tension between our various identities—local, national, global—as insightfully as the philosopher Kwame Anthony Appiah. In this age of "planetary challenges and interconnection between countries," he wrote in response to May's statement, "the need has never been greater for a sense of a shared human fate."[35] It is hard to disagree.

Yet cosmopolitans often come across like the character from Fyodor Dostoyevsky's *The Brothers Karamazov* who discovers that the more he loves humanity in general, the less he loves people in particular. Global citizens should be wary that their lofty goals do not turn into an excuse for shirking their duties toward their compatriots.

We have to live in the world we have, with all its political divisions, and not the world we wish we had. The best way to serve global interests is to live up to our responsibilities within the political institutions that matter: those that exist, within national borders.

Who Needs the Nation-State?

The design of institutions is shaped by a fundamental trade-off. On the one hand, relationships and preference heterogeneity push governance down. On the other hand, the scale and scope of the benefits of market integration push governance up. A corner solution is rarely optimal. An intermediate outcome, a world divided into diverse polities, is the best that we can do.

Our failure to internalize the lessons of this simple point leads us to pursue dead ends. We push markets beyond what their governance can support. We set global rules that defy the underlying diversity in needs and preferences. We downgrade the nation-state without compensating improvements in governance elsewhere. The failure lies at the heart of globalization's unaddressed ills as well as the decline in our democracies' health.

Who needs the nation-state? We all do.

CHAPTER 3

Europe's Struggles

The eurozone was an unprecedented experiment. Its members tried to construct a single, unified market—in goods, services, and money—while political authority remained vested in the constituting national units. There would be one market, but many polities.

The closest historical parallel was that of the Gold Standard. Under the Gold Standard, countries effectively subordinated their economic policies to a fixed parity against gold and the requirements of free capital mobility. Monetary policy consisted of ensuring the parity was not endangered. Since there was no conception of countercyclical fiscal policy or the welfare state, the loss of policy autonomy that these arrangements entailed had little political cost. Or so it seemed at the time. Starting with Britain in 1931, the Gold Standard would eventually unravel precisely because the high interest rates required to maintain the gold parity became politically unsustainable in view of domestic unemployment.

The postwar arrangements that were erected on the ashes of the gold standard were consciously designed to facilitate economic management by national political authorities. John Maynard Keynes's signal contribution to saving capitalism was recognizing that it required national economic management. Capitalism worked only one country at a time, and economic interactions among countries had to be regulated to ensure they did not impinge too much on domestic social and political bargains.

The European single market initiative and, even more so, the single currency flew in the face of this understanding. It is worth considering the possible narratives under which such a leap into the danger zone could have made sense.

What Were We Thinking?

One theory, perhaps held most strongly by conservative economists, rejected the Keynesian perspective and re-enshrined the "self-equilibrating market" at the center stage of policy. In this worldview, the apparent malfunctions of markets—the boom and bust cycles in finance and macroeconomics, inequality, and low growth—were the product not of market failures but of too much government intervention to begin with. Do away with moral hazard in financial markets, institutionalized labor markets, countercyclical fiscal policy, high taxes, and the welfare state, and all these problems would disappear.

This free-market nirvana had little use for economic governance at any level—national or European. The single market and currency would force governments into their proper role—which was to do very little. Transnational political institutions were a distraction at best, and harmful at worst.

A second theory was that Europe would eventually develop the quasi-federal political institutions that would transnationalize its democracies. Yes, the single market and currency had created an imbalance between the reach of markets and the reach of political institutions. But this was temporary. In time, the institutional gaps would be filled in, and Europe would develop its own Europe-wide political space. Not only banking and finance but fiscal and social policy as well would become EU-wide.

This image envisaged a significant amount of convergence in the social models that exist around the EU. Differences in tax regimes, labor-market arrangements, and social insurance schemes would have to be narrowed. Otherwise, it would be difficult to fit them under a common political umbrella and finance them out of a largely common fiscal pot. The British, with their own sense of uniqueness, understood this well, which is why they always pushed for a narrow economic union and resisted anything that smacked of political union as well.

Neither of the two theories—the minimalist nor the federalist—could be articulated too openly. Doing so would have raised a torrent of criticism and objections. The minimalist economic model had little attraction beyond a narrow group of economists. And the federalist model would run up against widely divergent views even among the pro-European elites about the political future of the union. That these opposing, but at least internally coherent, visions could not even be widely discussed in polite company should have told us something: neither, in fact, offered a practical solution to the eurozone's institutional imbalance. But the absence of public discussion and debate meant that they would not be explicitly repudiated. So, both justifications lingered on in the background, providing their adherents some comfort about the sustainability of the union's arrangements.

The eurozone's problems—deflation; unemployment; and economic stagnation on the economic side, and voter dissatisfaction and the rise of extremist parties on the political—no longer allow such equivocation.

The Elusive Promise of Structural Reform

The immediate problem in Europe is how to revive growth. Here, Germans and other creditor nations have clung far too long to the notion that the answer lies in what's known as structural reform.

Structural reform—or more accurately talk of structural reform—is everywhere nowadays. Every country struggling for economic growth, it seems, is getting the same message from the chattering classes as well as the deep-pocketed multilateral finance agencies like the IMF and the European Central Bank: half measures are not enough.

In practice, structural reform has come to represent a grab bag of policies meant to enhance productivity and improve the functioning of the supply side of the economy. These measures aim to sweep away impediments to the functioning of labor, goods, and services markets—to make it easier for firms to fire unwanted employees, to break business and union monopoly power, to privatize state assets, to reduce regulation and red tape, to remove licensing fees and other costs that deter market entry, to improve the efficiency of the courts, to enforce property rights, to enhance contract enforcement, and so on. Indeed, the grab bag is even bigger. Often, for example, structural reform includes changes in taxes and social security programs with an eye toward fiscal sustainability.

The overarching goal of structural reform is to increase the efficiency with which labor and capital are allocated in the economy, ensuring that these resources go where their contribution to national income is largest. Success comes in the form of increased productivity, more private investment, and, of course, more rapid economic growth.

Perhaps nowhere in recent years has the gospel of structural reform been promoted with greater vehemence than in Greece. Indeed, Greece's creditors have made it crystal clear that structural reform, boldly conceived and implemented without slippage, is critical to economic recovery and growth—and most persuasively to Greeks, that bailout funds will not be forthcoming without it.

The International Monetary Fund and European public lenders understood that the fiscal austerity they prescribed would be costly to incomes and employment (though a retrospective IMF study later showed they significantly underestimated by how much[1]). But there would be a compensatory boost to the economy, they argued, that would come from the long-delayed and much-needed opening of the Greek economy to competitive market forces.

The specifics demanded from Greece ranged from mundane to gut-wrenching. They included (in no particular order) lower barriers to entry in service businesses such as notaries, pharmacies, and taxis; reduced scope of collective bargaining; privatization of state assets; a rollback of pensions; and the cleanup of Greece's notoriously inefficient and arguably corrupt tax administration. The IMF's then-chief economist, Olivier Blanchard, (among others) argued that such reforms were critical in light of the "dismal productivity growth record of Greece before the program."[2] Less ambitious reforms wouldn't do because they would have less impact on growth potential and necessitate greater debt relief.

Partial Amnesia

But the policy prescribers, it seems, suffered from selective memory. Structural reform as a remedy for slow (or no) growth has been around at least since the early 1980s. At that time, in return for "structural adjustment" loans, the World Bank insisted on economy-wide liberalizing reforms for developing countries in Asia, Africa, and the Middle East. These policies were then extended and codified in Latin America during the 1990s under the umbrella of the Washington Consensus. Many of the former socialist economies adopted similar policies (in some cases, voluntarily) when they opened up their economies during the 1990s.

A serious look at the vast experience with privatization, deregulation, and liberalization since the 1980s—in Latin America, postsocialist economies, and Asia in particular—would have produced much less optimism about the reforms Athens was asked to swallow.

That experience suggests that structural reform yields growth only over the longer term, at best. More often than not, the short-run effects are negative. One meta-study of forty-six different research papers on postsocialist economies found that the impact of structural reform varied across the board. The modal estimate of the impact was statistically insignificant, meaning that it was impossible to conclude with any confidence whether the effects were positive or negative.[3]

In Latin America, for example, some economies have flourished in the wake of reform (think Chile) and some have lagged (as in Mexico).

These results may seem surprising at first glance but are, in fact, consistent with what economic theory teaches. The standard convergence framework that economists use to analyze growth across countries gives us little reason to expect strong short-term growth-promoting effects. Reform works by raising the potential income of the economy in the long run.

In Greece, opening the regulated professions will eventually lead more productive firms to drive out inefficient suppliers. The privatization of state enterprises will lead to the rationalization of production (and dismissal of all the excess workers employed through political patronage). These changes will require years to work themselves through the economy. In the short run, they may yield perverse effects. For example, the loss of the (however disappointing) output of workers laid off by privatized enterprises will subtract from, rather than add to, national income.

Economists have spent significant effort at estimating the speed with which economies tend to converge to their long-run levels of income. The near-consensus of academic studies is that convergence is pretty slow, at a rate of about 2 percent per year.[4] That is, an economy tends to close 2 percent of the gap each year between its actual and potential income levels.

This estimate helps us gauge the magnitude of growth we can expect from structural reform. Let's be wildly optimistic and suppose that structural reforms enable Greece to double its potential income over three years, which would push Greece's potential per-capita gross domestic product (GDP) significantly beyond the European Union average. Applying convergence math, this would produce an annual growth boost of only about 1.3 percent per year on average over the next three years. To place this number in perspective, remember that since 2009 Greek GDP has shrunk by 25 percent.

So, if structural reforms have so far not paid off in Greece, it is not necessarily because the country's governments have slacked off. Indeed, it is easy—but also largely erroneous—to blame successive Greek governments for unenthusiastic implementation of structural reform and significant slippages. Certainly, Greece has not delivered on every measure it agreed to adopt. Given the magnitude of effort needed, which government could? Yet, remarkably, Greece moved up by nearly 40 positions between 2010 and 2015 in the World Bank's Ease of Doing Business rankings.[5] The country's labor markets are more "flexible"—or liberalized—today than those of most other euro-zone countries. Greece's "failure" arises instead from the very logic of structural reform: the bulk of the benefits comes much later, not when their creditors (and unemployed Greeks) need them most.

Takeoffs?

This leaves us with an apparent puzzle. There are numerous instances of abrupt takeoffs in East Asia and elsewhere. If structural reforms deliver their growth payoffs so slowly, how are we to explain these? If such takeoffs are not the product of conventional structural reform, what does drive them?

A decade ago, Ricardo Hausmann, Lant Pritchett, and I published an article that documented the basic stylized facts about what we called "growth accelerations."[6] We defined a growth acceleration as an increase in per-capita growth of two percentage points or more (with most of the episodes we identified exceeding this threshold by a wide margin). To qualify as acceleration, the increase in the growth rate had to be sustained for at least eight years, and the postacceleration rate had to be at least 3.5 percent annually (per capita). In addition, to rule out cases of acceleration purely attributable to recovery from recession, we required that postacceleration output exceed the pre-episode peak level of income.

We were surprised to discover how frequent these episodes of growth acceleration are. We identified more than eighty cases over the thirty-five-year period from 1957 to 1992. This meant the probability that any given country would experience a growth acceleration sometime during a decade was as high as 25 percent. Of the 110 countries included in the sample, sixty had at least one acceleration in the 1957–1992 period.

More important, we found that standard factors economists think play a role in growth do not do a good job of predicting acceleration. In particular, structural reforms were only loosely correlated with turning points in economic performance. Fewer than 15 percent of significant economic liberalizations produced growth accelerations, and only 16 percent of growth accelerations were preceded by economic liberalization.

Some growth accelerations were obviously the result of fortuitous external conditions (such as a rise in the world prices of a country's major exports) or other changes not directly attributable to economic policy (such as changes in political regime). But in most cases, there was no smoking gun. That got us thinking about what might lie behind these instances when economic prospects suddenly brightened.

India's growth acceleration in the early 1980s is perhaps a paradigmatic case. The country's growth rate more than doubled, from 1.7 percent in 1950–1980 to 3.8 percent in 1980–2000, with a clear turning point in 1981–1982. Yet serious liberalizing reforms in India did not arrive until 1991, when Manmohan Singh slashed trade barriers, welcomed foreign investment, and began both privatization and the dismantling of what is derisively called the license raj. In other words, the pickup in India's growth preceded the 1991 liberalization by a full decade.

Arvind Subramanian and I concluded that the trigger to India's economic growth was a shift in attitude toward the private sector on the part of the national government in 1980.[7] Until that time, the rhetoric of the reigning Congress Party had been all about socialism and pro-poor policies. When Indira Gandhi returned to power in 1980, she realigned herself politically with the organized private sector and dropped her previous rhetoric. The national government's attitude toward business went from being outright hostile to supportive.

Note that this was a pro-business shift rather than a pro-market shift. It was not supported by strong liberalizing reforms, which would only come a decade down the road. Indira Gandhi's switch was further reinforced, in a more explicit manner, by Rajiv Gandhi after his rise to power in 1984. This seems to have been the key change that unleashed what Keynes called the "animal spirits" of the Indian private sector.

The moral of the Indian story is that in economies that suffer from multiple distortions, small changes can make a big difference. The Chinese growth acceleration after 1978 very much bears this out. The Chinese economic takeoff wasn't the product of economy-wide reforms or a major liberalization. It was the consequence of specific reforms that loosened collective farming rules and allowed farmers to sell excess production—after state quotas were fulfilled—at uncontrolled market prices. The same type of selective, targeted reforms in urban industrial development, trade, foreign investment, and finance would unfold over the next three decades, keeping the Chinese miracle going and going.

Or consider Mauritius, one of Africa's few growth successes in the twentieth century, which experienced its growth acceleration in 1971. The trigger there seems to have been the establishment of a largely unregulated export processing zone that led to a boom in garment exports, even as the rest of the economy remained heavily controlled and protected.

What is common to these cases is that the takeoffs were associated with a targeted removal of key obstacles to growth, rather than broad liberalization and economy-wide reforms. India, China, and Mauritius all benefited from growth strategies that specifically focused on removing binding constraints on growth. Targeting reforms on areas where the growth returns are the greatest maximizes early benefits. It also ensures that scarce political capital and administrative resources are spent on the battles that really matter.

Maximum Gain for Minimum Pain

In a 2005 article, Ricardo Hausmann, Andres Velasco, and I sought to identify these binding constraints to growth in specific settings.[8] For example, an economy in which the main constraint on growth was poor access to finance should exhibit different symptoms (high interest rates, strong responsiveness of domestic investment to foreign capital inflows, and so on) than an economy whose main problem was low profitability of private investment (low interest rates, ample liquidity in the banking system, and so on). When entrepreneurship is hampered primarily by market failures rather than government failures, the country may rank high on standard creditworthiness measures like transparency or institutional quality, but private investment will remain low.

A focus on binding constraints helps us see why remedies that are not well targeted—broad structural reforms—are ineffective, at best, and sometimes counterproductive. Cutting red tape and reducing regulation does little to spur private economic activity when the constraint lies on the finance side. Improving financial intermediation does not raise private investment when entrepreneurs expect low profits. Successful policy design must rely more on domestic experimentation and local institutional innovations—and much less on "best practices" and blueprints adopted from international experience.

Going back to Greece, where was the binding constraint on that economy while structural reforms and fiscal austerity were being applied? With a quarter of the labor force out of work, the quickest way to get the economy back on its feet would have been to increase the private sector's demand for workers. Supply-side measures, such as conventional structural reforms, would not be particularly effective because the binding constraint was on aggregate demand rather than the supply side of the economy. Deregulating professions could not boost entry by new firms when existing firms cannot find customers. Making it easier to fire workers would not induce firms to invest and produce more; it just facilitated laying off workers. As helpful as these measures may be in promoting long-term growth, they don't do much for the economy in the short run and may even make things worse.

Conventional demand-side remedies like government spending, tax cuts, or devaluation were ruled out both by the burden of public debt and by Greece's membership in the eurozone. In principle, wage deflation could have been a substitute for currency depreciation, making Greek goods and services cheaper in foreign markets. And Greek wages did come down substantially. But here, too, the absence of a single-minded focus on the binding constraints proved costly.

In particular, different elements in the structural reforms had conflicting effects on export competitiveness. In manufacturing, for example, the competitiveness benefits of wage cuts were offset by the cost of increases in energy prices resulting from fiscal austerity measures and state enterprise price adjustments.[9] A better prioritized reform strategy could have protected export activities from this adverse effect.

The absence of the ability to devalue or depreciate the currency remains a serious impediment to Greek recovery. But the experience of other countries provides a rich menu of alternative tools for export promotion ranging from tax incentives to special zones to targeted infrastructure projects. Greece and its creditors should have recognized the importance (and priority) of improving the profitability of sectors that produce tradable goods and services, and to reorganize reforms around that primary task.

As an illustration, the government could have set up an institution close to the prime minister tasked with fostering a dialogue with potential investors—both domestic and foreign—in export-oriented projects. This institution would have had the authority and ability to remove obstacles identified in the process, to avoid having its proposals languish in ministries with other priorities. Typically, these obstacles are highly specific to the investment—a zoning regulation here, the lack of a labor-training program there—and are unlikely to be targeted by broad structural reforms. They need a government agency dedicated to identifying them and endowed with the capability to remove them.

Some observers of the Greek economy have derided the value of export promotion, arguing that the country was hindered by a lack of diversity in tradable goods and services, and thus was unlikely to respond to incentives. But the experience of other countries makes clear that low export and diversification levels are not destiny. Sizable—and credible—changes in export incentives can produce robust responses, even where exports are confined to a few traditional crops. Taiwan exported sugar, rice, and little else before its trade took off in the early 1960s.

Closer by, export pessimism had been the dominant mood among Turkey's elites before the reforms in the early 1980s. These reforms mainly consisted of export subsidies, and they produced a rapid rise in the export-GDP ratio. In Taiwan, Turkey, and elsewhere, new exports rather than traditional products have led the way. There's no straightforward way to predict what these new exports will be before the incentives are put in place. But this opacity should not be grounds for pessimism about their likelihood of emerging.

Pay Now, Pay Later

Ultimately, the choice of reform boils down to one of two approaches. The conventional structural reform agenda relies on a "big bang"—as many changes as possible, as quickly as feasible. Politically, this approach typically exploits a window of opportunity created by economic crisis that reformers fear will close when normal times return. The costs of big-bang reform—higher unemployment, slower recovery—are tolerated in order to reap what is hoped will be sizable benefits down the line. This kind of reform perhaps works best when there are external anchors that prevent backsliding as short-term costs mount.

Poland in the early 1990s is arguably the model. After a half century of isolation from the West, the prospect of European Union membership and the promise of becoming a "normal European country"—held the reforms there together despite high unemployment and serious economic dislocation early on.

In the absence of external anchors, however, there is a real threat that the backlash to harsh reforms will dominate. Bolivia and Venezuela in Latin America during the 1980s and 1990s fit this latter mold.

The second approach, sequential targeting of binding constraints, is less ambitious. The political strategy underpinning this style of reform is the expectation that early wins will create political support for reforms (and the reformers) over time. If reforms identify and target the binding constraints, the early growth payoffs can be quite spectacular.

China is the quintessential model, but versions have been at play at different times in South Korea, Taiwan, and India. Because the reforms are partial, they never quite do away with the insiders (and their ability to extract gains through market power and political connections). These insiders are typically less than enthusiastic about continuing reforms. So, there is always the risk that such reforms get stuck midway and the early growth benefits will dissipate.

Greece has taken the first route—likely less because this was the country's choice than because its creditors left it with little alternative. If the results have been disappointing to date, it is for reasons that should have been expected at the outset. We will see whether Greeks' evident desire to remain in the eurozone (or their fears of the alternative) will prove sufficient counterweight to the pain that the country has yet to endure.

As desirable as broad structural reforms may be in the medium to long run, they do very little to solve the short-run problem of inadequate demand. Dealing with this problem through supply-side reforms aimed at increasing productivity is like pushing on a string. What is needed instead is some good old-fashioned Keynesianism: policies to boost eurozone–wide demand and stimulate greater spending in creditor countries, especially Germany.

Back to Politics and Democracy

At the heart of this economic misdiagnosis is also the absence of EU-wide democratic accountability. As long as the costs of harsh policies are borne primarily by the debtor countries with high unemployment, there is little prospect that the German electorate will change its mind and give up on austerity. So, the lack of transnational politics aggravates the economic crisis, which in turn poisons domestic politics in the high-unemployment countries further. There is no mechanism that forces German policy makers to internalize the costs of their decisions on the rest of the eurozone. To be sure, austerity policies are short-sighted even from the perspective of Germany's own economic interest. But the fact remains that it is not Germany that bears the bulk of these costs.

The German argument for structural reform does make a lot more sense for the longer run, for political as well as economic reasons. Ultimately, a workable European economic union does require greater structural homogeneity and institutional convergence (especially in labor markets) among its members. If they want to inhabit the same house for the long haul, EU countries need to look more like one another.

We should understand well the reason behind this need for structural convergence. It does not derive, as many economists presume, from the inherent superiority of any particular economic-social model. It is based, instead, on the idea that legitimacy is essential to the functioning of a common, unified market. It becomes increasingly difficult to maintain legitimacy when market outcomes appear to reflect structural differences—or what is called, in common parlance, a lack of a level playing field. I may grudgingly accept my fate when my losses are the result of my competitors' thrift, hard work, or ingenuity. But I am likely to think the fault lies with the system itself when these losses are the product of weaker labor standards, larger government subsidies, or poorer enforcement of regulations under another sovereign. I may be willing to bail out others when they fall into hard times, but not when it looks like I would be thereby underwriting their "irresponsibility" or "inappropriate" economic policies—their economic and social arrangements that differ from mine.

To some extent, cross-national solidarity may ameliorate this sense of unfairness, especially when the beneficiaries in other countries are poorer (and to that extent more "deserving"). But it is unlikely that solidarity—such as there may be—can bear the full weight of the burden that large institutional differences place on markets.

This argument for institutional convergence in an economic union goes significantly beyond integration in the fiscal and financial domains. But it leaves open the question of what shape those common institutions should ultimately take. It certainly does not suggest that other countries in the European Union should converge to Germany's social arrangements. What common set of institutions should look like is a question that requires democratic deliberation and decision-making.

Here again, we confront the need for EU-wide democracy. The more such questions are settled by fiat or under duress, in moments of relative weakness of indebted countries, the greater the future risk. One danger is that some of the countries will commit to institutional arrangements that have poor fit and will be eventually repudiated. Another is the likelihood of backlash when reasonably normal times return. Yet another is that the union will lack mechanisms of review and revision, and lock itself into arrangements that outlive their usefulness.

The absence of transnational democratic mechanisms creates vicious cycles in the short term and the long term—how do we get out of the present economic crisis, and how do we create durable EU-wide institutional arrangements? The inability to transcend national sovereignty has aggravated the crisis not just in Greece but for Europe as a whole.

Sovereignty, Economic Union, and Democracy

In a true economic union, underpinned by union-wide political institutions, the financial problems of Greece, Spain, and the others would not have blown up to their current proportions, threatening the existence of the union itself. In the United States, no one even keeps track of Florida's current-account deficit with the rest of the country, but since the state is home to many retirees living off benefits that come from elsewhere, we can safely guess that it is huge. When Florida's state government goes bankrupt, Florida's banks continue to operate normally, because they are under federal rather than state jurisdiction. When Florida's banks go belly-up, state finances are insulated, because the banks are ultimately the responsibility of federal institutions. When Florida's workers become unemployed, they get unemployment checks from Washington, DC. And when Florida's voters are disenchanted about the economy, they do not riot outside the state capital; they put pressure on their representatives in Congress to push for changes in federal policies. US states do not have any abundance of sovereignty.

Restricting the exercise of sovereign power is not necessarily undemocratic. Political scientists talk about "democratic delegation"—the idea that a sovereign might want to tie its hands (through international commitments or delegation to autonomous agencies) in order to achieve better outcomes. The delegation of monetary policy to an independent central bank is the archetypal example: in the service of price stability, daily management of monetary policy is insulated from politics.

However, even if selective limitations on sovereignty may enhance democratic performance, there is no guarantee that all limitations implied by market integration would do so. In domestic politics, delegation is carefully calibrated and restricted to a few areas where the issues tend to be highly technical and partisan differences are not large. Similarly, a truly democracy-enhancing globalization respects these boundaries. It imposes only those limits that are consistent with democratic delegation, possibly along with a limited number of procedural norms (such as transparency, accountability, representativeness, use of scientific evidence, etc.) that enhance democratic deliberation domestically. I will come back to this when I consider the reform of globalization at the end of the book.

But what about Europe's principle of subsidiarity? Doesn't this principle simultaneously allow local self-rule and a single market, by restricting the competencies of the union only to those that need to be transnationalized? There is nothing wrong with the idea of subsidiarity per se. But the crisis has clarified how narrow the room for national sovereignty really is when we talk about European economic integration. It is no longer a matter of open borders to goods, services, capital, and people. A single currency and unified financial markets also require harmonization of labor-market rules, banking and financial regulations, bankruptcy procedures, and a good deal of fiscal policy as well. The nation-states of the eurozone may not disappear as a result. But they would become largely empty shells from a political/policy standpoint, requiring compensation through an expansion of a transnational political space.

, The EU's institutional reforms to date following the crisis (banking union, stricter fiscal oversight) fall far short of what is needed. It is understandable that these efforts have gone into the areas most immediately implicated by the crisis. But in many ways, the reforms have deepened the democratic deficit of the union. They have made union-wide arrangements more technocratic, less accountable, and more distant from the European electorates. In the one uniquely European space of politics, the European Parliament, the voice of anti-EU groups has in fact become louder, in part as a result of the growing democratic deficit.

A European Dilemma

As the American example illustrates, it is possible to give up on sovereignty—as Florida, Texas, California, and the other states have done—without giving up on democracy. But combining market integration with democracy requires the creation of supranational political institutions that are representative and accountable. Otherwise, the conflict between democracy and globalization becomes acute, as economic integration restricts the domestic articulation of policy preferences without a compensating expansion of democratic space at the regional/global level. Europe is already on the wrong side of this boundary.

This is what I have called the political trilemma of the world economy: we cannot have globalization, democracy, and national sovereignty simultaneously. We must choose two among the three. Nowhere is this trilemma clearer than in Europe. If European leaders want to maintain democracy, they must make a choice between political union and economic disintegration. They must either explicitly renounce economic sovereignty or actively put it to use for the benefit of their citizens. The first would entail coming clean with their own electorates and building democratic space above the level of the nation-state. The second would mean giving up on monetary union in order to be able to deploy national monetary and fiscal policies in the service of longer-term recovery.

Those who propose to save democracy in the eurozone with intermediate solutions—a little democracy at the national level, a little more democracy at the EU-level—ignore the extremity of economic union. Such intermediate solutions might work with limited or managed economic interdependence; they are inadequate when individual countries essentially give up economic management wholesale—as they must with economic, financial, and monetary union.

The longer this choice is postponed, the greater the economic and political cost that will ultimately have to be paid.

History and Denial

European politicians' instinct has been to deny the trade-offs. As the French parliament debated Europe's new fiscal treaty in 2012, the country's socialist government vehemently rejected the idea that ratification of the treaty would undermine French sovereignty. It places "not one constraint on the level of public spending," Jean-Marc Ayrault, the prime minister, asserted. "Budget sovereignty remains in the parliament of the French Republic."

As Ayrault was trying to reassure his skeptical colleagues, including many members of his own party, European Commissioner for Competition Joaquin Almunia was delivering a similar message to his fellow social democrats in Brussels. To succeed, he argued, Europe must prove wrong those who believe there is a conflict between globalization and sovereignty.

A precondition for the creation of a true European political space is the transfer of sovereignty to supranational entities. Nobody likes to give up national sovereignty, neither politicians of the right nor politicians on the left. Yet, by denying the obvious fact that the eurozone's viability depends on substantial restraints on sovereignty, Europe's leaders have been misleading their voters, delaying the Europeanization of democratic politics, and raising the political and economic costs of the ultimate reckoning.

Or consider the July 2015 referendum in Greece, in which the Greek electorate resoundingly rejected demands for further austerity by the country's foreign creditors: the European Central Bank, the International Monetary Fund, and the other eurozone governments, led by Germany. Whatever the economic merits of the decision, the Greek people's voice rang loud and clear: we are not going to take it anymore.

Many viewed this as a straightforward victory for democracy, as the country's prime minister, Alexis Tsipras, and his supporters claimed at the time. But what the Greeks called democracy came across in many other—equally democratic—countries as irresponsible unilateralism. There was, in fact, little sympathy for the Greek position in other eurozone countries, where similar referendums would have undoubtedly shown overwhelming public support for the continuation of the austerity policies imposed on Greece.

And it wasn't just citizens of the large creditor countries, such as Germany, who had little patience for Greece. Exasperation was especially widespread among the eurozone's poorer members. Ask the average person on the street in Slovakia, Estonia, or Lithuania and you are likely to get a response not too different from this one from a Latvian pensioner: "We learned our lesson—why can't the Greeks learn the same lesson?"

Perhaps Europeans were not well-informed about the plight of the Greeks and the damage that austerity has done to the country. And, indeed, it is possible that with better information, many among them would change their position. But the forces of public opinion on which democracies rest rarely take shape in ideal conditions. Indeed, one need look no further than the Greek vote itself to find an example of raw emotions and outrage winning out over a rational calculation of economic costs and benefits.

It is important to remember that the creditors in this instance were not a bunch of oligarchs or wealthy private bankers but the governments of the other eurozone countries, democratically accountable to their own electorates. (Whether they did the right thing by lending to Greece so that their own bankers could be repaid is a legitimate, but separate question.) This was not a conflict between the Greek *demos*— its people—and the bankers, as much as it was a conflict between European democracies.

When the Greeks voted "no," they reaffirmed their democracy. But more than that, they asserted the priority of their democracy over those in other eurozone countries. In other words, they asserted their national sovereignty—their right as a nation to determine their own economic, social, and political path. If the Greek referendum was a victory for anything, it was a victory for national sovereignty.

That is what made it so ominous for Europe. The European Union, and even more so the eurozone, was constructed on the expectation that the exercise of national sovereignty would fade away over time. This was rarely made explicit; sovereignty is popular after all. But as economic unification narrowed each country's room for maneuver, it was hoped that national action would be exercised less frequently.

The Greek referendum put perhaps the final nail in the coffin of that idea.

Students of economic history are familiar with a classic, much earlier example of this tension: Britain's exit from the Gold Standard in 1931. Having made the mistake in 1925 of restoring parity with gold at a level that left the economy desperately uncompetitive, Britain struggled for several years with deflation and rising unemployment. Industries such as coal, steel, and shipbuilding were hit hard, and labor strife became rampant. Even as unemployment reached 20 percent, the Bank of England was obliged to maintain high interest rates in order to prevent a massive outflow of gold. Eventually, increasing financial-market pressure pushed the country off gold in September 1931.

This wasn't the first time that financial probity had required the real economy to suffer under the Gold Standard. What was different was that Britain had become a more democratic society: the working class had become unionized, the political franchise had expanded fourfold since the end of World War I, mass media publicized ordinary people's economic plight, and a socialist movement was waiting in the wings. Despite their own instincts, central bankers and their political masters understood that they could no longer remain aloof from the consequences of economic recession and high unemployment.

Even more importantly, investors understood this too. As soon as financial markets begin to question the credibility of a government's commitment to a fixed exchange rate, they become a force for instability. At the slightest hint of things going awry, investors and depositors pull up stakes and move capital out of the country, thereby precipitating the collapse of the currency.

A similar scenario played out in Argentina in the late 1990s. The linchpin of Argentina's economic strategy after 1991 was the convertibility law, which legally anchored the peso to the US dollar at a one-to-one exchange rate and prohibited restrictions on capital flows. Argentine economy minister Domingo Cavallo had envisioned the convertibility law as both a harness and an engine for the economy. The strategy worked well initially by bringing much-needed price stability. But, by the end of the decade, the Argentine nightmare had returned with a vengeance.

The Asian financial crisis and the Brazilian devaluation in early 1999 left the Argentinean peso looking decidedly overvalued. Doubts about Argentina's ability to service its external debt multiplied, confidence collapsed, and before too long, Argentina's creditworthiness slid below that of some African countries.

Ultimately, what sealed Argentina's fate was not its leaders' lack of political will but rather their inability to impose ever-more costly policies on their domestic constituents. In fact, the Argentine government was willing to abrogate contracts with virtually all domestic constituencies—public employees, pensioners, provincial governments, and bank depositors—in order to meet its obligations to foreign creditors. But investors grew increasingly skeptical that the Argentine congress, provinces, and ordinary people would tolerate the austerity policies needed to continue servicing foreign debt. As mass protests spread, they were proved right. In early 2002, the convertibility law was repealed and the peso was devalued.

Sometimes, there is another path. Consider Latvia, which found itself experiencing economic difficulties similar to those of Argentina fifteen years ago. Latvia had grown rapidly since joining the European Union in 2004, on the back of large-scale external borrowing and a domestic property bubble. It had run up a current-account deficit and a foreign-debt burden that were literally of Greek proportions. Predictably, the global financial crisis and abrupt reversal in capital flows in 2008 left the Latvian economy in dire straits. As lending and property prices collapsed, unemployment rose to 20 percent and GDP declined by 18 percent in 2009. In January 2009, the country had its worst riots since the collapse of the Soviet Union.

Just like Argentina, Latvia had a fixed exchange rate and free capital flows. Its currency has been pegged to the euro since 2005. Unlike Argentina, however, the country's politicians managed to tough it out without devaluing the currency and introducing capital controls.

What seems to have changed the balance of political costs and benefits was similar to what happened in Poland: the prospect of reaching the promised land of eventual membership in the eurozone compelled Latvian policy makers to foreclose any options that would endanger that objective. That, in turn, increased the credibility of their actions—despite the very high economic and political costs.

The Latvian example notwithstanding, democracies find it difficult to swallow the bitter pill of austerity when economic and monetary integration leaves no other option. And when globalization collides with domestic politics, the smart money bets on the home team. National sovereignty can be repressed only for so long.

Can Macron Pull It Off?

Emmanuel Macron's victory over Marine Le Pen in France's presidential elections in May 2017 was much-needed good news for all who favor open, liberal democratic societies over their nativist, xenophobic counterparts. But the battle against right-wing populism is far from won and Europe's prospects remain uncertain.

Le Pen received more than a third of the second-round vote, even though only one party other than her own National Front—Nicolas Dupont-Aignan's small *Debout la France*—gave her any backing. And turnout was down from previous presidential elections, indicating a large number of disaffected voters. If Macron fails during the next five years, Le Pen will be back with a vengeance, and nativist populists will gain strength in Europe and elsewhere.

As a candidate, Macron was helped in this age of antiestablishment politics by the fact that he stood outside traditional political parties. As president, however, that same fact is a singular disadvantage. His political movement, *En Marche!*, was brand new. He will have to build from scratch a legislative majority following the National Assembly elections in June 2017.

Macron's economic ideas resist easy characterization. During the presidential campaign, he was frequently accused of lacking specifics. To many on the left and the extreme right, he is a neoliberal, with little to distinguish himself from the mainstream policies of austerity that failed Europe and brought it to its current political impasse. The French economist Thomas Piketty, who supported the socialist candidate Benoit Hamon, described Macron as representing "yesterday's Europe."[10]

Many of Macron's economic plans did indeed have a neoliberal flavor. He has vowed to lower the corporate tax rate from 33.5 percent to 25 percent, cut 120,000 civil service jobs, keep the government deficit below the EU limit of 3 percent of GDP, and increase labor-market flexibility (a euphemism for making it easier for firms to fire workers). But he has promised to maintain pension benefits, and his preferred social model appears to be Nordic-style flexicurity—a combination of high levels of economic security with market-based incentives.[11]

None of these steps will do much—certainly not in the short run—to address the key challenge that will define Macron's presidency: creating jobs. Employment was the French electorate's top concern and will be the new administration's top priority. Since the eurozone crisis, French unemployment has remained high, at 10 percent—and close to

25 percent for people under twenty-five years old. As we have seen, conventional structural reforms have weak and ambiguous effects on employment, especially during times of depressed demand. There is virtually no reliable evidence that liberalizing labor markets will increase employment, unless the French economy receives a significant boost in aggregate demand as well.

This is where the other component of Macron's economic program comes into play. He has also proposed a five-year, €50 billion ($54.6 billion) stimulus plan, which would include investments in infrastructure and green technologies, along with expanded training for the unemployed. This plan on its own lacks ambition. The stimulus amounts to barely more than 2 percent of France's annual GDP, and may not do too much to lift overall employment.

Macron's more ambitious idea is to take a big leap toward a eurozone fiscal union, with a common treasury and a single finance minister. This would enable, in his view, permanent fiscal transfers from the stronger countries to countries that are disadvantaged by the eurozone's common monetary policy. The eurozone budget would be financed by contributions from member states' tax receipts. A separate eurozone parliament would provide political oversight and accountability. Such fiscal unification would make it possible for countries like France to increase infrastructure spending and boost job creation without busting fiscal ceilings.

A fiscal union backed by deeper political integration makes eminent sense. It represents a coherent path out of the eurozone's present no-man's land. But Macron's unabashedly Europeanist policies are not just a matter of politics or principle. They are also critical to the success of his economic program. Without either greater fiscal flexibility or transfers from the rest of the eurozone, France is unlikely to get out of its employment funk soon. The success of Macron's presidency thus depends to a large extent on European cooperation.

And that brings us to Germany. Angela Merkel's initial reaction to the election's outcome was not encouraging. She congratulated Macron, who "carries the hopes of millions of French people," but she also stated that she would not consider changes in eurozone fiscal rules.[12] Even if Merkel (or a future government under her Social Democratic challenger Martin Schulz) were more willing, there is the problem of the German electorate. Having portrayed the eurozone crisis not as a problem of interdependence but as a morality tale—thrifty, hard-working Germans pitted against profligate, duplicitous debtors—German politicians will not have an easy time bringing their voters along on any common fiscal project.

Macron is well aware of the difficulties he faces with Germany. Anticipating the German reaction, he countered it thus: "You cannot say, 'I am for a strong Europe and globalization, but over my dead body for a transfer union.'" That, he believes, is a recipe for disintegration and reactionary politics: "Without transfers, you will not allow the periphery to converge and will create political divergence toward extremists."[13]

France may not be in the European periphery—at least not yet— but Macron's message to Germany has been clear: Either you help me out and we build a true union—economic, fiscal, and eventually political—or we will be run over by the extremist onslaught.

Macron is almost certainly right. (A third alternative, along the lines of my argument here, would be the deliberate scaling back of economic integration.) Those who wish Europe to retain both a single market and a healthy democracy must hope that his victory will be followed by a German change of heart.

What Future for the European Union?

In March 2017, the European Union celebrated the sixtieth anniversary of its founding treaty, the Treaty of Rome, which established the

European Economic Community. There was much to celebrate for sure. After centuries of war, upheaval, and mass killings, Europe is peaceful and democratic. In an age of inequality, European nations exhibit the lowest income gaps anywhere in the world. And the EU has successfully guided the transition of eleven formerly socialist countries, by bringing them into its fold.

These are past achievements. Today the union remains mired in deep existential crisis, and its future is very much in doubt. The symptoms are everywhere: Brexit, crushing levels of youth unemployment in Greece and Spain, debt and stagnation in Italy, the rise of populist movements, and the backlash against immigrants and the euro. They all point in the same direction: Europe's institutions are in need of major overhaul.

If European democracies are to regain their health, economic integration and political integration cannot remain out of sync. Either political integration catches up with economic integration or economic integration needs to be scaled back. The EU will remain dysfunctional as long as this decision is avoided.

When confronted with this stark choice, member states are likely to make different choices along the continuum of economic-political integration. That, in turn, implies Europe must develop the flexibility and institutional arrangements to accommodate them.

From the very beginning, Europe was built on a "functionalist" argument, which posited that political integration would follow economic integration. The founder of the European Economic Community (and French prime minister) Robert Schuman said in 1950, "Europe will not be made all at once, or according to a single plan. It will be built through concrete achievements which first create a de facto solidarity." Build the mechanisms of economic cooperation first, and this will prepare the ground for broader, political institutions.

The approach worked fine at first. It enabled economic integration to remain one step ahead of political integration—but not too far ahead. After the 1980s, the EU made a big leap into the darkness. It adopted an ambitious single market agenda that aimed to unify Europe's economies, whittling away at national policies that hampered the free movement not just of goods but also of services, people, and capital. The euro, which established a single currency among a subset of member states, was the logical extension of this agenda. This was hyperglobalization on a European scale.

As we saw at the beginning of this chapter, there were two lines of thought on how this would work out. Many economists and technocrats thought Europe's governments had become too interventionist and that deep economic integration and a single currency would discipline the overactive state. From this perspective, the imbalance between the economic and political legs of the integration process was a feature, not a bug. On the other side, many practical politicians did recognize that the imbalance was potentially problematic, but assumed functionalism would eventually come to the rescue. Quasi-federal political institutions needed to underpin that the single market would develop, given sufficient time.

The leading European powers played their part. The French thought shifting economic authority to bureaucrats in Brussels would enhance French national power and prestige on the global stage. The Germans went along with the French as the price of German unification.

There was an alternative. Europe could have developed a social model and allowed it to develop alongside economic integration. This would require integrating not only markets but also social policies, labor market institutions, and fiscal arrangements. The diversity of social models across Europe, and the difficulties in reaching agreement on common rules, would naturally have put a brake on the pace and scope of integration. Far from being a disadvantage, this would have injected a useful corrective on the desirable speed and extent of integration. We may have ended up with a smaller EU, more deeply integrated across the board. Or we could have had an EU with as many members as today, but much less ambitious in economic scope.

Macron notwithstanding, today it may be too late to entertain fiscal and political integration within the EU. As I write these words, less than one in five Europeans favor moving power away from nation-states.[14]

An optimist might say this is due less to aversion to Brussels or Strasbourg per se than to "more Europe" being associated in the public's mind with a technocratic focus on the single-market and the absence of an appealing alternative model. Perhaps new leaders and political formations will manage to sketch out such a model and generate excitement about a reformed European project.

A pessimist, on the other hand, will hope there are some deep, dark corners in the corridors of power in Berlin and Paris where economists and lawyers are readying a secret plan B to deploy for the day when loosening of the economic union can no longer be postponed.

CHAPTER 4

Work, Industrialization, and Democracy

Not so long ago, economic analysts were giddy with optimism about the prospects for economic growth in the developing world. In contrast to the United States and Europe, where the growth outlook looked weak at best, emerging markets were expected to sustain their strong performance from the decade preceding the global financial crisis, and thus become the engine of the global economy.

Economists at Citigroup, for example, boldly concluded that circumstances had never been this conducive to broad, sustained growth around the world, and they projected rapidly rising global output until 2050, led by developing countries in Asia and Africa. The accounting and consulting firm Price Waterhouse Coopers predicted that per-capita GDP growth in China, India, and Nigeria would exceed 4.5 percent well into the middle of the century. McKinsey & Company christened Africa, long synonymous with economic failure, the land of "lions on the move."

Today, such talk has been displaced by concern about what *The Economist* calls "the great slowdown." China and India have slowed down, while Brazil and Turkey are mired in political crises. Latin American nations are experiencing the weakest growth performance in years. Optimism has given way to doubt.

Of course, just as it was inappropriate to extrapolate from a decade of strong growth, one should not read too much into short-term fluctuations. Nevertheless, there are strong reasons to believe that rapid growth will prove the exception rather than the rule in the decades ahead.

To see why, we need to understand how "growth miracles" are made. These are countries that grew rapidly in a sustained fashion beyond the bursts of growth I examined in the previous chapter. Except for a handful of small countries that benefited from natural-resource bonanzas, all of these successful economies owe their growth to rapid industrialization. If there is one thing that everyone agrees on about the East Asian recipe, it is that Japan, South Korea, Singapore, Taiwan, and of course China all were exceptionally good at moving their labor from the countryside (or informal activities) to organized manufacturing. Earlier cases of successful economic catch-up, such as the United States or Germany, were no different.

Manufacturing enables rapid catch-up because it is relatively easy to copy and implement foreign production technologies, even in poor countries that suffer from multiple disadvantages. My research shows that manufacturing industries tend to close the gap with the technology frontier at the rate of about 3 percent per year regardless of policies, institutions, or geography.[1] Consequently, countries that are able to transform farmers into factory workers reap a huge growth bonus.

To be sure, some modern service activities are capable of productivity convergence as well. But most high-productivity services require a wide array of skills and institutional capabilities that developing economies accumulate only gradually. A poor country can easily compete with Sweden in a wide range of manufactures, but it takes many decades, if not centuries, to catch up with Sweden's institutions.

India demonstrates the limitations of relying on services rather than industry in the early stages of development. The country has developed remarkable strengths in IT services, such as software and call centers. But the bulk of the Indian labor force lacks the skills and education to be absorbed into such sectors. In East Asia, unskilled workers were put to work in urban factories, making several times what they earned in the countryside. In India, they remain on the land or move to construction and petty services (where their productivity is not much higher). Structural change is limited by the growth of domestic demand for nontraditional products.

Two Mexicos: Productive Dualism

When researchers at the McKinsey Global Institute (MGI) recently dug into the details of Mexico's lagging economic performance, they made a remarkable discovery: an unexpectedly large gap in productivity growth between large and small firms. From 1999 to 2009, labor productivity had risen by a respectable 5.8 percent per year in large firms with five hundred or more employees. In small firms with ten or fewer employees, by contrast, labor productivity growth had declined, at an annual rate of 6.5 percent.[2]

Moreover, the share of employment in these small firms, already at a high level, had increased from 39 percent to 42 percent over this period. In view of the huge gulf separating what the authors called the "two Mexicos," it is no wonder that the economy performed so poorly overall. As rapidly as the large, modern firms improved, through investments in technology and skills, the economy was dragged down by its unproductive small firms.

This may seem like an anomaly, but it is increasingly common. Look around the developing world, and you will see a bewildering fissure opening between economies' leading and lagging sectors.

Productive heterogeneity—or what development economists used to call economic dualism—has always been a central feature of low-income societies. What *is* new—and distressing—is that developing economies' low-productivity segments are not shrinking. On the contrary, in many cases, they are expanding.

Typically, economic development occurs as workers and farmers move from traditional, low-productivity sectors (such as agriculture and petty services) to modern factory work and services. As this takes place, two things happen. First, the economy's overall productivity increases, because more of its labor force becomes employed in modern sectors. Second, the productivity gap between the traditional and modern parts of the economy shrinks, and dualism gradually diminishes. Agricultural productivity increases during the process, owing to better farming techniques and a decline in the number of farmers working the land.

This was the classic pattern of postwar development in the European periphery—countries like Spain and Portugal. It was also the mechanism that generated the Asian growth "miracles" in South Korea, Taiwan, and eventually China (the most phenomenal example of all).

One thing that all of these high-growth episodes had in common was rapid industrialization. Expansion of modern manufacturing drove growth even in countries that relied mostly on the domestic market, as Brazil, Mexico, and Turkey did until the 1980s. It was structural change that mattered, not international trade per se. Today, the picture is very different. Though young people are still flocking to the cities from the countryside, they end up not in factories but mostly in informal, low-productivity services.

Indeed, structural change has become increasingly perverse: from manufacturing to services, tradable to nontradable activities, organized sectors to informality, modern to traditional firms, and medium-size and large firms to small firms. Such patterns of structural change are exerting a substantial drag on economic growth in Latin America, Africa, and in many Asian countries.

This could be a sign of troubling effects to come. To understand what these new trends in structural change portend, let's take a look at how societies have generally industrialized, and then deindustrialized, in the past.

A Brief History of Work

In the beginning, there were farmers and animal husbanders. Life was hard, brutal, and short. Taxes and other requirements imposed by chiefs, landlords, or the state were onerous. Many people were serfs or slaves, devoid of autonomy and dignity. Poverty and injustice were the norm, save for the lucky few.

Then came the Industrial Revolution, first in Britain, then in Western Europe and North America. Men and women flocked from the countryside to towns to satisfy factories' growing demand for labor. New technologies in cotton textiles, iron and steel, and transport delivered steadily rising levels of labor productivity. But for decades, few of these benefits trickled to the workers themselves. They worked long hours in stifling conditions, lived in jam-packed housing, and experienced few gains in earnings. Some indicators, such as average height levels of workers, suggest that standards of living may have even declined for a while.

Eventually, capitalism transformed itself, and its gains began to be shared more widely. This was in part because wages naturally started to rise as the surplus of workers from the countryside dried up. But equally importantly, workers organized themselves to claim their rights. It was not just their grievances that gave their demands urgency. It was also that the conditions of modern industrial production made it more difficult for the elites to pursue their usual tactics of divide and rule. Factory work, concentrated in major cities, facilitated coordination among laborers, mass mobilization, and militant activism.

Fearing revolution, the industrialists compromised. Political rights and the franchise were extended to the working class. And democracy in turn tamed capitalism. Conditions in the workplace improved as state-mandated or negotiated arrangements led to reduced working hours; greater safety; and vacation, family, health, and other benefits. Public investment in education and training made workers both more productive and freer to exercise choice. Labor's share of the enterprise surplus rose. Factory jobs never became pleasant. But at least blue-collar work now enabled a middle-class existence, with all its consumption possibilities and lifestyle opportunities.

Technological progress fostered industrial capitalism, but would eventually undermine it. Labor productivity in manufacturing industries rose much faster than in the rest of the economy. That meant that the same or higher quantity of steel, cars, and electronics could be produced with many fewer workers. Manufacturing's share of total employment began to decline steadily in all the advanced industrial countries sometime after the Second World War. Workers moved to service industries—education, health, entertainment, and public administration. Thus was born the postindustrial economy.

For some, work became more pleasant. For those with the skills, capital, and savvy to prosper in the postindustrial age, services offered inordinate opportunities. Bankers, consultants, and engineers earned much higher wages. Equally important, office work allowed a degree of freedom and personal autonomy that factory work had never provided. Hours may have been long—longer perhaps than in factory work—but service professionals enjoyed much greater control over their daily lives and workplace decisions. Teachers, nurses, and waiters were not paid nearly as well, but they too were released from the humdrum mechanical drudgery of the shop floor.

On the other hand, for less skilled workers, service sector jobs meant giving up the negotiated benefits of industrial capitalism. The transition to a service economy often went hand in hand with the decline of unions, job protections, and norms of pay equity, greatly weakening workers' bargaining power and job security.

So, the postindustrial economy opened a new chasm between those with good jobs in services, which were stable, high paying, and rewarding, and those with bad jobs, which were fleeting, low paying, and unsatisfying. Two things determined the mix between these two types of jobs and the extent of inequality the postindustrial transition produced. First, the greater the education and skill level of the workforce, the higher the level of wages in general. Second, the greater the institutionalization of labor markets in services (in addition to manufacturing), the higher the quality of service sector jobs in general. So, inequality, exclusion, and duality became more marked in countries where skills were poorly distributed, and many services approximated the textbook ideal of impersonal, unfettered markets. The United States, where many workers are forced to hold multiple jobs in order to make an adequate living, remains the canonical example of this model.

This is the story mainly for advanced, Western countries. A few places in the non-Western world have gone through a similar evolution. The most notable cases are Japan, South Korea, and Taiwan. Each has experienced significant industrialization, and then deindustrialization. They now share with other advanced countries the feature that they are postindustrial economies where the nature of jobs is determined by the interplay between productivity and labor market practices in service sectors. High productivity combined with labor market protections make for good jobs. Low productivity combined with atomistic labor markets are a recipe for poor jobs.

It is tempting to extrapolate this story straightforwardly to countries that have lagged economically. These are the low-income and middle-income countries in which a majority of the world's workers live. The recipe for them would seem clear. Foster rapid industrialization so you can grow. Invest in good institutions and human capital so you have a productive workforce, making sure no one is left behind. When deindustrialization naturally sets in, do not resist it. Instead, ensure the legal and regulatory setting within which services operate provides adequate protections for employees.

This message is not wrong in its broad outlines. But we have two ask two questions: How desirable is it to emulate the historical experience of today's advanced countries? And how feasible is it to do so? Let me take up each in turn.

Should Developing Nations Emulate the Historical Pattern?

Historically, the early stages of industrialization rarely produced an improvement in the living conditions of most workers. There was a significant delay between the onset of industrialization and its benefits being shared widely. A similar lag is visible in many low-income countries that have made successful inroads into world markets in manufactures in recent decades. This has kindled a debate on sweatshops in exporting countries. According to labor-rights activists, export gains are being built on the back of exploited workers, often female, earning very little and working long hours in hazardous conditions. The employment of child workers is a particularly sensitive bone of contention.

Others, typically economists, respond by arguing that so-called sweatshops are simply a stepping stone on the path of economic and eventual human development. As shabby as they may look, sweatshops represent an improvement compared to the alternatives most workers have—a precarious existence in subsistence farming perhaps or worse urban jobs. And low pay and poor work conditions reflect the low productivity of workers. Besides, isn't this exactly how today's advanced countries got rich?

The question that this debate raises is whether the benefits of labor protection cannot be made available at earlier stages of development than has occurred historically. Is there an iron rule that good labor standards must lag behind development? This is similar to the question of whether political democracy requires economic development as a precondition.

The answer to the latter question informs the answer to the first. Historically, democracy has followed the Industrial Revolution and the rise in incomes. But there is no reason to think countries cannot become democratic at much earlier levels of development. Political participation and contestation are intrinsic values. They also serve an instrumental purpose: empirical research has established that democratic governments possibly perform better than authoritarian regimes and produce greater stability on top.

Two shining models of democracy in low-income settings exemplify the point: India and Mauritius. These two countries differ greatly in size. But they are both highly heterogeneous countries that were born amid ethnic strife and violence. In both cases, democracy early on has tempered social conflict and enabled political stability. Mauritius grew rapidly several years after independence. India's growth performance lagged until the 1980s, but has been more than decent since (even overtaking China in recent years).

Similarly, there is no reason why workers in low income countries should be deprived of fundamental labor rights for the sake of industrial development and export performance. These include freedom of association and collective bargaining, reasonably safe working conditions, nondiscrimination, maximum hours, and restrictions on arbitrary dismissal. As with democracy, these are basic requirements of a decent society. Their first-order effect is to level the bargaining relationship between employers and employees, rather than to raise overall costs of production. And even when costs are affected, any adverse effects could be easily offset by improved morale, better incentives, and reduced turnover of the workforce.

Minimum wages are somewhat different in that they directly raise the cost of labor. Minimum wages that are not too far from the market-clearing competitive level may not do much damage to overall employment while improving labor conditions somewhat. The same cannot be said of minimum wages that are far above this level. The danger then is that many job-seekers will be denied opportunities of employment by being priced out of the market. Labor-market dualism, whereby a comparably small minority of "insiders" protect their state-mandated privileges at the expense of a large majority of "outsiders," is unfortunately a common feature of economies around the world. This stunts both human development and growth prospects.

The bottom line, however, is that basic labor rights, as encapsulated in the International Labor Organization's core conventions, for example, are not an impediment to economic development. They need not be postponed until economic takeoff takes place and is firmly entrenched. History need not be a guide here.

Can Developing Nations Emulate the Historical Pattern?

As I mentioned previously, manufacturing is an escalator for poor countries for several important reasons. First, there tends to be a positive productivity dynamic in many manufacturing industries. Establish a beach head in one of the "easy" manufacturing sectors—such as garments—and the chances are that you will experience steady increases in productivity and will be able to jump on to other, more sophisticated industries in time. Second, manufacturing is a tradable sector. This means that your successful manufacturing industries can expand almost indefinitely, by gaining market share in world markets, without running into demand constraints. Third, manufacturing is a great absorber of unskilled labor, a low-income country's most plentiful resource. Activities such as garments, footwear, toys, and electronics assembly require few skills, so farmers can easily be transformed into assembly line workers.

These are the reasons why historically industrialization has been the main engine of rapid economic growth. Productivity convergence, export expansion, and labor absorption create a virtuous cycle that propel the economy forward until the gap with the global frontier closes and the demands of technological progress become substantially greater.

Again, that is how things worked in the past. The conventional view is that today's low-income countries in Africa, Asia, and Latin America will have to do something similar if they want to experience rapid and sustained economic growth.

But this expectation may not be fulfilled. Ours is a very different world. The forces of globalization and technological progress have combined to alter the nature of manufacturing work in a way that makes it very difficult, if not impossible, for latecomers to emulate the industrialization experience of East Asian tigers, or the European and North American economies before them.

Consider some of the facts. Since the 1960s, every decade has brought lower levels of industrial employment and output (as a share of the economy) in developing countries, controlling for standard income and demographic determinants. Peak levels of industrialization are lower than ever and are being reached at a fraction of the incomes experienced by previous industrializers. This means that many (if not most) developing nations are becoming service economies without having had a proper experience of industrialization—a process I have called "premature deindustrialization." While early industrializers managed to place 30 percent or more of their workforce in manufacturing, the most recent rounds of latecomers have rarely managed that feat. Brazil's manufacturing employment peaked at 16 percent and Mexico's at 20 percent. In India, manufacturing employment began to lose ground (in relative terms) after it reached 13 percent.[3]

Latin America appears to be the worst-hit region. But worryingly similar trends are very much evidenced in Sub-Saharan Africa too, where few countries had much industrialization to begin with. The only countries that seem to have escaped the curse of premature industrialization are a relatively small group of Asian countries and manufactures exporters. The advanced countries themselves have experienced significant employment deindustrialization. But manufactures output at constant prices has held its own comparatively well in the advanced world, something that is typically overlooked since so much of the discussion on deindustrialization focuses on nominal rather than real values.

The reasons behind these trends have to do both with technology and trade. Rapid global technological progress in manufacturing has reduced the prices of manufactured goods relative to services, discouraging newcomers in developing countries from entry. At the same time, manufacturing has become much more capital and skill intensive, substantially reducing the labor-absorbing potential of the sector for workers from agriculture or informality. On the trade front, competition from China and other successful exporters combined with the reduction in protection levels means that few poor countries now have the opportunity to develop simple manufactures for home consumption. The room for import-substitution was squeezed out.

It is not implausible that the East Asian tiger economies will be the last countries to ever experience industrialization in the manner to which economic history has accustomed us. If true, this is bad news for economic growth for all the reasons described earlier. It is also bad news for equity. The chasm in earnings and working conditions between bankers and managers, on the one hand, and participants in informal activities such as petty trade or household help is incomparably larger in developing countries. Earlier transition to services, prior to substantial accumulation of human capital and institutional capabilities, greatly exacerbates the problems of inequality and exclusion in the labor market with which advanced economies are struggling.

Future Paths for Work

Can this process of premature deindustrialization nonetheless prove to be a blessing in disguise? I noted previously some of the advantages of services in terms of personal autonomy and freedom. James C. Scott notes that a very high percentage of industrial workers in the United States would rather open a shop, restaurant, or work on a farm. "The unifying theme of these dreams is the freedom from close supervision and autonomy of the working day that, in their mind, more than compensates for the long hours and risks of such small businesses." Scott contrasts this with the work in a factory setting "where the assembly line is fine-tuned to reduce autonomy to the vanishing point. . . ."[4] Perhaps workers in the developing world can somehow take a shortcut and bypass the drudgery of manufacturing?

Perhaps, but how such a future can be constructed is not at all clear. A society in which most workers are self-proprietors—shopkeepers, independent professionals, artists—and set their own terms of employment while making an adequate living is feasible only when productivity is very high. High productivity enables the generation of plentiful demand for these services and, correspondingly, high incomes for independent proprietors. The trouble is that services, in aggregate, have not experienced nearly as much productivity growth as manufacturing over the course of history; it takes as many waiters to run a restaurant today as it did a century ago. So, it has fallen on industrialization to provide the high incomes and demand for the rest of the economy.

What is clear therefore is that policy makers will face an altogether new challenge when they turn to the future of work and human development. More economic growth will have to come from productivity advances in services. This means in turn that the partial, sectoral approaches that worked so well to stimulate export-oriented industrialization during the early stages of rapid growth in Asia and beyond will have to be replaced (or at least complemented) by massive economy-wide investments in human capital and institutions. When manufacturing is the engine of the economy, selective reforms such as export incentives, special economic zones, or incentives to foreign investors can be highly effective. After all, it is enough to have a few export successes, facing nearly infinite demand on world markets, to pull the economy along. But when growth must rely on (mostly) non-tradable services, selective efforts will not work. Reform efforts will have to be more comprehensive, targeting productivity growth in all services simultaneously.

Marx famously envisioned a society in which it would be possible for people "to do one thing today and another tomorrow, to hunt in the morning, fish in the afternoon, rear cattle in the evening, criticize after dinner . . . without ever becoming hunter, fisherman, herdsman or critic." A precondition for this, however, was that the productive forces of the economy develop sufficiently. To date, industrial capitalism has been pretty much the only path to a productive society. Factory work was not pleasant and it generated significant social tensions (as Marx highlighted), but it got the productivity job done.

Today this path looks both less desirable and less feasible. A new path will have to be invented. The broad contours of this alternative are easy to state. It will be a model based on services. It will focus more on soft infrastructure—learning and institutional capabilities—and less on physical capital accumulation—plant and equipment in manufacturing industries. Beyond that, however, much remains up for grabs.

Economic and Political Institutions

For some time now it has been conventional wisdom that institutions—beyond policy reforms here and there—were central in the process of economic development. Economists focused on two types of institutions in particular: those that protected property rights and those that enforced contracts. Though this was not always explicit, economists also tended to have a universalist conception of institutions, presuming that what worked well in one setting could be transplanted in others. Over time, this best-practice mind-set would come to dominate the practical and policy work of international organizations such as the World Bank, the International Monetary Fund, and the Organization for Economic Co-operation and Development. The detailed but fairly specific prescriptions of the Washington Consensus would be augmented by open-ended recommendations on reducing corruption, improving regulatory and judicial institutions, and enhancing governance more broadly.

In an article published in 2000, I argued that the prevailing technocratic views on institutional reform were missing an important part of the picture.[5] They ignored both the malleability and the context specificity of institutional designs.

You can step off a plane in a country you have never been to and spout these commandments—"Keep inflation low and stable," "Ensure that entrepreneurs feel safe and can retain the return to their investments"—without going wrong. Who would possibly invest in the economy otherwise? We can agree that growth-supporting institutions must perform certain universal tasks, such as safeguarding macroeconomic stability or ensuring that investors do not fear expropriation. These are universal functions in the sense that it is difficult to envisage how any market-based economy can develop in their absence.

But these tasks do not tell us much about the form that the requisite institutions should take. As East Asia has amply shown, market incentives can be generated with institutions that take, from the best-practice perspective, highly unusual forms. Even private property rights can be dispensed with, it seems, if there are arrangements (as in the case of China's TVEs, township and village enterprises) that provide effective and substantial control rights to investors. Function does not map into unique forms.[6]

I also argued that democracy was a sort of metainstitution, allowing each society to choose and shape its institutions in contextually appropriate ways. China is not a democracy, of course. But, its experimental approach to institutional design, ensuring that reforms are locally effective and do not generate large redistributions, mimics in some essential ways how democratic deliberation and decision-making operate. I also provided some cross-national evidence suggesting that democracies do indeed generate high-quality growth, providing greater predictability, stability, and resilience and better distributional outcomes.[7]

When the piece was published, the number of democracies in the world was swiftly rising. Today, by one count, there are more democracies in the world than autocracies—something never experienced before in world history.[8] This is something to be celebrated. But for the world's new democracies, the picture is hardly rosy.

Democratic Failures

In a prescient article in 1997, Fareed Zakaria wrote about "democratically elected regimes . . . routinely ignoring constitutional limits on their power and depriving their citizens of basic rights and freedoms." Observers began to notice most countries with more or less free elections hardly operated along Western lines. Today experts are more likely to talk of "democratic recession" than to applaud democracy's advance.[9] Zakaria called these regimes "illiberal democracies."[10]

As he and others have noted, electoral democracy is different from liberal democracy. Sharun Mukand and I have formalized the difference by distinguishing among three sets of rights.[11] *Property* rights are rights that protect asset holders and investors against expropriation by the state or other groups. *Political* rights guarantee free and fair electoral contests and allow the winners of such contests to determine policy subject to the constraints set by other rights (when provided). *Civil* rights ensure equality before the law—that is, nondiscrimination in the provision of public goods such as justice, security, education, and health. Political and civil rights can bleed into each other and be difficult to distinguish. But they are not the same. Tabulations based on Freedom House raw scores, for example, show that it is far more common for countries to provide political rights, in the sense defined here, than it is for them to provide civil rights.

The distinction between political and civil rights allows us to operationalize the difference between electoral and liberal democracies. An electoral democracy provides property and political rights. A liberal democracy provides civil rights in addition. We can classify countries accordingly, using the 2×2 matrix in Figure 4.1. (Our classification is based on unpublished Freedom House raw scores; details are in the original paper.)

Countries that provide civil rights but no political rights—what we call "liberal autocracies"—are extremely rare. Britain in the early nineteenth century before the extension of the franchise is the prime historical example. Perhaps the only contemporary example is the principality of Monaco.

The literature on economic development recognizes, to some extent, the importance of liberal practices by stressing the importance of the "rule of law." But, when economists and others talk of the rule of law, they often confound two things that are best kept distinct. On the one hand, the weakness of legal administration and enforcement in poor

		Political Rights	
		no	yes
Civil Rights	no	illiberal autocracies	electoral democracies (Argentina, Croatia, Ukraine, . . .)
	yes	liberal autocracies (Monaco)	liberal democracies (Canada, Chile, S. Korea, Uruguay, . . .)

FIGURE 4.1 A taxonomy of political regimes

countries can render judicial remedies against rights violations and the abuse of power ineffective. On the other, the governing coalition—the "majority"—can deliberately discriminate against ethnic, religious, or ideological minorities in order to solidify their hold on power or disproportionately divert public goods to their supporters. India ranks low on rule-of-law indicators, in part, because it takes a very long time for courts to reach a verdict, not because the legal regime exhibits explicit bias against members of a certain caste or religion. In Turkey, the rule of law fails whenever government opponents—whether they are secularists, liberals, or Kurdish activists— are on the wrong side of a dispute. Inefficiency and deliberate bias are quite different things. The first can be ameliorated by improved capabilities and enhanced bureaucratic capacity. The second is part and parcel of the deliberate operations of the judicial machinery. Violations of the second type are more insidious and perhaps also more damaging. Rights violations targeting minorities or government opponents become the modus operandi of governments hoping to hold on to power. They also deepen identity and ideological cleavages in society, making the establishment of liberal democracy that much harder.

Historically, liberal democracy has never come easy. The United States is perhaps the oldest democracy today, though for all its pretensions, it would have been hard to call the country fully liberal until after the civil rights struggles of the 1960s bore fruit. With the notable exception of Britain, most western European countries reverted to various forms of autocratic government periodically before the Second World War. The reestablishment of liberal democracy in Western Europe after 1945 was by no means a foregone conclusion and presumably owes much to the discrediting of the fascist regimes of the prewar period. Japan too was an unlikely success in Asia. We do not have to idealize the political regimes in these advanced postindustrial societies to acknowledge that it has been very difficult to follow their examples in the developing world. The temptations of illiberalism have been evidenced in the postsocialist countries of eastern and south-eastern Europe as well. Despite membership in the European Union, Hungary is well on its way to becoming a model illiberal democracy. Today, the vast majority of countries that became democratic in the third wave of democratization and thereafter are electoral rather than liberal democracies.

Why Is Liberal Democracy So Rare?

To understand why liberal democracy is such a rare beast, it is useful to consider the circumstances under which countries make a transition from autocracy to democracy. The voluminous literature in political science and political economy on democratic transitions tends to focus on two kinds of processes.[12] The first has to do with splits and bargaining within the elite. When the elite are divided and have a hard time coordinating, democracy can emerge as a system of power sharing. The second has to do with struggles between nonelites and the elite. When the elites can no longer keep nonelites in check, they may prefer to give the nonelites the vote instead of facing the prospect of political instability and mass revolt.

The democratic settlements that such transitions produce are unlikely to be liberal. This is because the primary beneficiaries of liberal democracy—as opposed to electoral democracy—are disenfranchised minority groups who hold little power in either kind of settlement. Elites want to protect their property rights first and foremost. And the dominant groups within the nonelite—let us call them the "majority"—want electoral rights so they can choose policies to their liking. The ethnic, religious, or ideological minorities that would most benefit from nondiscrimination will rarely sit at the negotiating table. The political logic of democratization produces electoral rather than liberal democracy. The real puzzle is not that liberal democracy is so rare but that it exists at all.

There are several circumstances that can bend this dismal logic in a direction that is more favorable to liberal democracy. First, there may be reasons why the elite want civil rights in addition to property rights. The landlords and wealthy merchants who prevailed over the king in Britain's Glorious Revolution sought to protect themselves from the king in both the religious sphere and the economic sphere. They feared James II would impose his Catholicism on them as much as they worried about the crown's ability to expropriate them through exorbitant taxes. So, in Britain, property and civil rights were entrenched together. British liberals would in time make little distinction between these two sets of rights, presuming that they were part and parcel of the same process. T. H. Marshall's famous essay "Citizenship and Social Class," for example, would fold property rights under civil rights.[13]

South Africa is a very different case, but the continued and somewhat improbable presence of liberal norms appears to be due to an analogous set of circumstances. At the time of the democratic transition in 1994, the minority government was intent on protecting not only the property rights of the whites but also their civil rights.[14] As in the Glorious Revolution, the elites shared "identity markers" with the minority, rendering them easy targets for discrimination and making them particularly interested in safeguarding civil rights. (Sadly, liberal norms have been in retreat for a number of years in South Africa. Our index of liberal democracy no longer classifies South Africa as one since 2009.)

A second path arises when society is relatively homogeneous and there are no marked identity cleavages. In this case, the majority have no clear minority against whom they can discriminate. Liberal democracy and electoral democracy become effectively indistinguishable. Japan and South Korea are perhaps apt illustrations of this model.

Finally, it is possible to maintain liberal democracy if there is no clear majority and if no identifiable group can hope to hold on to power indefinitely. Repeated-game incentives may then sustain a regime of moderation and tolerance: each group respects the rights of others for fear that it too may become a minority one day.

Such modi vivendi are fragile for a number of reasons. Successful political leaders can forge and sustain majority governing coalitions even when society is divided by multiple, cross-cutting cleavages. Such leaders will be less concerned about the rights of groups outside the coalition, even when the nature of the coalition changes over time. Turkey's Recep Tayyip Erdogan provides a good example of this tactic. Alternatively, leaders may simply overestimate how long they will remain in power. In this case, they will overlook that sooner rather than later they may need the goodwill of today's opposition groups.

These problems plague developed and developing countries alike. Liberal democracy in continental Europe—at least until the postwar period—was fragile partly because identity cleavages (based on religion, ethnicity, or language) competed with affiliations based on income and class. Fascists and Nazis were successful because they could forge large enough governing alliances based on constructed identity narratives that blamed and excluded "others" (foreigners, Jews, Gypsies, and "cosmopolitans"). But, in many respects, the challenges that developing nations face today are much greater.

Political Disadvantages of Backwardness

In the West, liberalism developed and spread before the franchise was expanded. Restraints on the executive, the rule of law, religious tolerance, and free speech were well established in Britain by the early part of the nineteenth century. Democracy was a latecomer, and liberals themselves were quite dubious about its benefits. The best-known theorist of classical liberalism, John Stuart Mill, thought democracy required a certain level of societal maturity, one that Britain had reached only recently (and that other societies like Russia or India lacked). Along with de Tocqueville, he fretted about the "tyranny of the masses" that elections might bring. As Edmund Fawcett explains, liberals grudgingly made their peace with democracy in the decades before First World War. They gave their support to the expansion of the franchise, hoping in return that popular forces would accept "liberal limits on the authority of the people's will."[15]

The difference with the developing world could not be bigger. Liberals rarely held the upper hand in developing nations, and there was no liberal tradition to speak of in decolonizing countries before democracy arrived. (India is perhaps the exception, thanks to British influence among the elite.)

Second, the forces of industrialization, which promoted liberal democracy in the West, are much weaker today in the developing world, as we saw earlier in this chapter. Industrialization was important to democracy because it unleashed the social forces that destabilized the old aristocratic order. But it also meant that the main axis of conflict between the elite and nonelite would consist of bread-and-butter issues having to do with pay, labor rights, and taxes and benefits. These were conflicts liberal democracy could handle. Labor market regulation and the welfare state were the upshot. Over time these institutional innovations would alter the nature of capitalism, but they did not pose a serious threat to liberal practices.

In developing countries, mass political mobilization typically took place in very different circumstances. It was the product of decolonization or wars of national liberation, where the main cleavage was not class, based on economic interests, but identity. Politics revolved around nation building, with an implicit or explicit "other" against which mobilized masses were aligned—a colonial adversary, a neighboring nation, or an ethnic group supposedly standing in the way of independence.

From the standpoint of politics, identity cleavages are not primordial or independent; they can be deepened or manipulated, spurring political mobilization based on ethnicity, language, or religion. Historical tensions and cultural diversity provide the raw material for clever politicians to fashion electoral majorities. Populism of this kind—populism of the right—differs in one important respect from populism of the left, centered on income and class cleavages. "Left-populists" promise (income-boosting or redistributive) policies that aim to overcome the income and class cleavages that animate them. "Right-populists," on the other hand, depend on the continued prevalence—and deepening—of identity cleavages to maintain their hold on power. So, unlike populism of the left, populism of the right directly blocks the emergence of liberal democracy.

The politics of identity can sometimes produce stable arrangements, typically temporary, where, in the absence of a clear majority group, each ethnic or linguistic group can hold on to its rights. Before 1975, Lebanon's consociational democracy was a classic case of this.[16] But, once the main political cleavages are identity based, the political balance is fragile and can be easily destabilized by demographic changes or opportunistic politicians (as indeed happened subsequently in Lebanon with the influx of Jordanian Palestinians and the subsequent civil war).

It is true, of course, that by definition developing countries are still poor and that the structural changes that today's rich countries underwent during the nineteenth and early twentieth centuries are perhaps still ahead of them. It is also the case that successful industrializers among them have ended up becoming liberal democracies. Consider South Korea or Taiwan. In both cases, industrialization produced a significant working class, which in turn played an important role in democratization. Even more impressive is the case of Mauritius, which is an ethnically divided society but remains a liberal democracy. As in the case of Switzerland, it appears that major identity cleavages are not necessarily an insurmountable obstacle to liberal democracy. But industrialization—and especially the creation of a significant labor movement—seems to be important in opening up space for liberal politics and repressing identity politics.

The Costs of Dictatorship

The degradation of democracy has clear costs for human rights and civil liberties. But it also has less obvious costs for economic performance as well.

The relationship between a nation's politics and its economic prospects is one of the most fundamental—and most studied—subjects in all of social science. Which is better for economic growth—a strong guiding hand that is free from the pressure of political competition, or a plurality of competing interests that fosters openness to new ideas and new political players? East Asian examples (South Korea, Taiwan, and China) seem to suggest the former. But how, then, can one explain the fact that almost all wealthy countries—except those that owe their riches to natural resources alone—are democratic? Should political openness precede, rather than follow, economic growth?

When we look at systematic historical evidence, instead of individual cases, we find that authoritarianism buys little in terms of economic growth. For every authoritarian country that has managed to grow rapidly, there are several that have floundered. For every Lee Kuan Yew of Singapore, there are many like Mobutu Sese Seko of the Congo. Democracies outperform dictatorships in long-term economic growth, and in several other important respects as well. They provide much greater economic stability, measured by the ups and downs of the business cycle. They are better at adjusting to external economic shocks (such as terms-of-trade declines or sudden stops in capital inflows). They generate more investment in health and education, or human capital. And they produce more equitable societies.

Authoritarian regimes, by contrast, ultimately produce economies that are as fragile as their political systems. Their economic potency, when it exists, rests on the strength of individual leaders, or on favorable but temporary circumstances. They cannot aspire to continued economic innovation or to global economic leadership.

At first sight, China seems to be an exception. Since the late 1970s, following the end of Mao's disastrous experiments, China has done extremely well, experiencing unparalleled rates of economic growth. Even though it has democratized some of its local decision-making, the Chinese Communist Party maintains a tight grip on national politics, and the human-rights picture is marred by frequent abuses. But China also remains a comparatively poor country. Its future economic progress depends in no small part on whether it manages to open its political system to competition, in much the same way that it has opened up its economy. Without this transformation, the lack of institutionalized mechanisms for voicing and organizing dissent will eventually produce conflicts that will overwhelm the capacity of the regime to suppress. Political stability and economic growth will both suffer.

Still, Russia and China are both large and powerful economies. Their example can sway leaders elsewhere to think that they can aspire to economic ascendancy while tightening the screws on domestic political opposition.

Consider Turkey, a rising economic power in the Middle East that seemed destined until recently to become the region's sole Muslim democracy. During his first term in office, Prime Minister Recep Tayyip Erdogan relaxed some restrictions on Kurdish minorities and passed reforms that aligned the country's legal regime with European norms.

But since the late 2000s Erdogan and his allies have launched a thinly disguised campaign to intimidate their opponents and cement government control over the media and public institutions. Early on, they incarcerated hundreds of military officers, academics, and journalists on fabricated charges of fomenting terror and plotting coups. Once Erdogan broke from his former allies, followers of Fethullah Gulen, the witch hunt turned on the latter, especially after the failed coup of July 2016. More than a hundred thousand public sector workers were dismissed and the country became the world's largest jailer of journalists. This rapid slide toward authoritarianism has greatly damaged prospects for the Turkish economy. It will have corrosive effects on the quality of policy making, as well as undermine Turkey's claim to global economic standing.

External observers and financial markets are not always good at reading such political developments. Turkey was still receiving plaudits from Western experts and emerging-market analysts long after it became clear that its politics had taken a nasty turn.

Brazil's experience provides a sharply contrasting case. Brazil's currency has been hammered since mid-2014—much worse than most other emerging markets—in large part because of the unfolding of a major corruption scandal. Prosecutors there have laid bare a wide-ranging kickback scheme centered on the state-oil company

Petrobras and involving executives, parliamentarians, and state officials. So, it may seem natural that financial markets have been spooked.

Yet what we have learned since the corruption story first broke is the remarkable strength of Brazil's legal and democratic institutions rather than their weakness. The prosecutor and judge on the case have been allowed to do their jobs, despite the Dilma Rousseff government's natural instinct to quash the investigation. And from all appearances the probe follows proper judicial procedures and is not used to advance the political agenda of the government's opponents. Beyond the judiciary, a slew of institutions, including the federal police and the finance ministry, have taken part and worked in sync. Leading businessmen and politicians have been jailed, among them the former treasurer of the ruling Workers' Party.

Financial markets are supposed to be forward- rather than backward looking. A proper comparison of Brazil's experience with that of other emerging market economies, where corruption is no less a problem, would, if anything, lead to an upgrade of Brazil's standing.

Going back to Turkey, corruption there reaches higher and is more widespread than in Brazil. Leaked phone conversations have directly implicated Erdogan and his family along with several government ministers in a hugely lucrative corruption ring revolving around trade with Iran and construction deals. It is an open secret that government procurement has long been used to enrich politicians and their business cronies. Yet today it is the police officers who led the corruption probe against Erdogan who are in jail. The media outlets that supported the probe have been closed down and taken over by the government. Erdogan has argued that the police officers are followers of Gulen and that the investigation was politically motivated, aiming to unseat Erdogan. Both claims are most likely true. But neither justifies the blatant unlawfulness with which the government has clamped down on the corruption allegations.

Turkey's institutions are sinking into a morass that will make recovery very difficult. Brazil's political institutions, on the other hand, will emerge stronger, even though the country has incurred a bigger economic cost in the short term.

Does Economic Development Buy Good Politics?

What about the connection in the other direction, from economics to politics?

In 2010, just prior to the Arab Spring, the United Nations published its twentieth-anniversary *Human Development Report* (HDI). Perhaps the biggest surprise in it was the outstanding performance of the Muslim countries of the Middle East and North Africa. Here was Tunisia, ranked sixth among 135 countries in terms of improvement in its Human Development Index over the previous four decades, ahead of Malaysia, Hong Kong, Mexico, and India. Not far behind was Egypt, ranked fourteenth.

The HDI is a measure of development that captures achievements in health and education alongside economic growth. Egypt and (especially) Tunisia did well enough on the growth front, but where they really shone was on these broader indicators. At seventy-four, Tunisia's life expectancy edged out Hungary's and Estonia's, countries that are more than twice as wealthy. Some 69 percent of Egypt's children were in school, a ratio that matched much richer Malaysia's. Clearly, these were states that did not fail in providing social services or distributing the benefits of economic growth widely.

Yet in the end it didn't matter. The Tunisian and Egyptian people were, to paraphrase Howard Beale, mad as hell at their governments, and they were not going to take it anymore. If Tunisia's Zine El Abidine Ben Ali or Egypt's Hosni Mubarak were hoping for political popularity as a reward for economic gains, they must have been sorely disappointed.

One lesson of the Arab *annus mirabilis*, then, is that good economics doesn't always mean good politics; the two can part ways for quite some time. It is true that the world's wealthy countries are almost all democracies. But democratic politics is neither a necessary nor a sufficient condition for economic development over a period of several decades.

Despite the economic advances they registered, Tunisia, Egypt, and many other Middle Eastern countries remained authoritarian countries ruled by a narrow group of cronies, with corruption, clientelism, and nepotism running rife. These countries' rankings on political freedoms and corruption stand in glaring contrast to their rankings on development indicators. In Tunisia, Freedom House reported prior to the Jasmine revolution, "the authorities continued to harass, arrest, and imprison journalists and bloggers, human rights activists, and political opponents of the government."[17] The Egyptian government was ranked 111th out of 180 countries in Transparency International's 2009 survey of corruption. And of course, the converse is also true: India has been democratic since independence in 1947, yet the country didn't begin to escape its low "Hindu rate of growth" until the early 1980s.

A second lesson is that rapid economic growth on its own does not buy political stability, unless political institutions are allowed to develop and mature rapidly as well. In fact, economic growth itself generates social and economic mobilization, a fundamental source of political instability.

As the late political scientist Samuel Huntington put it more than forty years ago, "social and economic change—urbanization, increases in literacy and education, industrialization, mass media expansion—extend political consciousness, multiply political demands, broaden political participation."[18] Now add social media such as Twitter and Facebook to the equation, and the destabilizing forces that rapid economic change sets into motion can become overwhelming. These forces become most potent when the gap between social mobilization and the quality of political institutions widens. When a country's political institutions are mature, they respond to demands from below through a combination of accommodation, response, and representation. When they are underdeveloped, they shut those demands out in the hope that they will go away—or be bought off by economic improvements.

The events in the Middle East amply demonstrate the fragility of the second model. Protesters in Tunis and Cairo were not demonstrating about lack of economic opportunity or poor social services. They were rallying against a political regime that they felt was insular, arbitrary, and corrupt, and that did not allow them adequate voice.

A political regime that can handle these pressures need not be democratic in the Western sense of the term. One can imagine responsive political systems that do not operate through free elections and competition among political parties. Some would point to Oman or Singapore as examples of authoritarian regimes that are durable in the face of rapid economic change. Perhaps so. But the only kind of political system that has proved itself over the long haul is that associated with Western democracies.

Which brings us to back to China. At the height of the Egyptian protests, Chinese Web surfers who searched the term *Egypt* or *Cairo* were returned messages saying that no results could be found.

Evidently, the Chinese government did not want its citizens to read up on the Egyptian protests and get the wrong idea. With the memory of the 1989 Tiananmen Square movement ever present, China's leaders are intent on preventing a repeat.

China is not Tunisia or Egypt, of course. The Chinese government has experimented with local democracy and has tried hard to crack down on corruption. Even so, protest has spread over the last decade. There were eighty-seven thousand instances of what the government calls "sudden mass incidents" in 2005, the last year that the government released such statistics, which suggests that the rate has since increased. Dissidents challenge the supremacy of the Communist Party at their peril. The Chinese leadership's gamble is that a rapid increase in living standards and employment opportunities will keep the lid on simmering social and political tensions. That is why it is so intent on maintaining high rates of economic growth and props up public and private investment through credit.

But the Arab Spring sent a sobering message to China and other authoritarian regimes around the world: don't count on economic progress to keep you in power forever.

Substitutes for Classical Liberal Politics?

The developments I have discussed in this chapter, and the reality of premature deindustrialization in particular, makes for rather poor prospects for liberal democracy in developing countries. Could there be alternative paths to liberal democracy that do not rely on mass industrialization or prior experience with liberalism? Perhaps today's developing countries can still get there, even though they will necessarily take a different road.

Let me draw an analogy with economic reform. It was Alexander Gerschenkron's enduring insight that latecomers in the economic development game would have to rely on institutions quite a bit different from those that had worked well in early industrializers. This insight has been vindicated time and again in the developing world. Economic growth miracles happened not where policy makers slavishly copied policies and institutional arrangements from the West but where they crafted new arrangements more appropriate to their conditions. China has been a master of that game, but the point applies equally well to South Korea, Taiwan, or Mauritius—where heterodox development strategies prevailed early on. As we've already repeatedly seen so far, the market economy admits a wide variety of institutional possibilities.

Could there be a similar possibility with political reform? Can something that looks like liberal democracy—equal treatment before the law—be achieved without Western-style institutions—an independent judiciary, for example, or separation of church and state?

Consider the system in Lebanon as it operated prior to the country's civil war in 1975. The regime that had been created in 1943 by a national pact between the Muslim and Christian communities looked in some respects as the antithesis of a liberal regime. Instead of disregarding religious differences, the regime explicitly apportioned public offices among religious denominations. At the apex of the political system the presidency was allocated to a Christian Maronite, the premiership to a Muslim Sunni, and the speakership to a Muslim Shiite. This principle extended downward to other government positions. As long as the system was stable, the country was regarded as a model democracy in a region sorely lacking in liberal politics. Political scientists counted it, alongside Austria and Switzerland, among the world's liberal democracies.[19] It was a nonliberal arrangement that nevertheless produced a liberal outcome.

An important reason that developing countries have difficulty sustaining liberal regimes is that they lack agencies of restraint. Elected governments can do whatever they want, and if courts or the media stand in their way, they can easily manipulate those too. Paul Collier has suggested that there is one important, and powerful, institution that can often fill the gap: the military. As Collier argues, the military is often the only well-trained, meritocratic institution with an esprit de corps that favors interests of the country as a whole rather than a particular ethnic or religious group. Perhaps it can act as the institution of restraint for elected governments in countries where the judiciary is not up to the task.[20]

Such an arrangement, of course, is at best a mixed blessing. The pros and cons have been easy to observe in Turkey. On the one hand, the military did prevent, while it was powerful, religious sectarian political groups from becoming dominant. It did promote a kind of procedural legalism and rule of law—to the point that it buckled rather than be perceived to act unlawfully when those same legal instruments were used against it in a series of sham trials. At the same time, the military had its own ideology of intolerance: for observant Muslims or Kurdish nationalists, the Turkish republic was hardly liberal. And the frequent interruptions of civilian politics prevented the long-term institutionalization of political parties and the development of a culture of political compromise and moderation.

As a third example consider the future direction that China's political regime may take. Might the country possibly develop a more liberal regime while retaining the monopoly of the Communist Party? One can envisage a sort of Singapore writ large—where political competition takes place within the dominant political party and judicial institutions are effective in enforcing the rule of law. One can think of many reasons why such a regime might fall far short of the standards of liberal democracy we are accustomed to in the West. But as in China's imperfect market economy, the outcome may be better than the most likely alternative.

Fourth, there is the media. We are accustomed to think of a free press as the sine qua non of a liberal democracy. But what if the bulk of mainstream media, as in many developing and some advanced economies, is bankrolled and controlled by business interests who have little interest in presenting fair and balanced views? What if a sensationalist media plays up and aggravates identity cleavages to maximize its readership? The usual answer to such dilemmas is to call for more competition in media markets. But in the real world there is no guarantee that this solves the problem. We cannot rule out the possibility that more aggressive regulation of the media than would be acceptable in the West might sometimes provide a better outcome.

As I have argued throughout, market-supporting institutions can take diverse institutional forms. We should not be institutional purists. These considerations lead me to think that the same may be true perhaps of liberal-democracy-supporting institutions too. Perhaps liberalism admits diverse institutional forms. I hasten to add that I am considerably less sure of this point than I was of my original argument, in the domain of economics. I would certainly like to see more examples of heterodox liberal democracy before I would push this idea strongly. But to remain optimistic about the prospects for liberal democracy, we need to at least entertain the idea that there may be a gist of truth to it.

CHAPTER 5

Economists and Their Models

conomists have played a big part in constructing the world in
which we live. They have provided the intellectual constructs,
narratives, and justifications for the arrangements that have
underpinned the liberal—or neoliberal, if you prefer—international
economic order of the last few decades. Will they also play a part in
its destruction? Or will they help redesign it, thereby saving it from its
own extremes and contradictions?

Economics is a science that can be tremendously powerful and useful. But at the hands of its practitioners, it often goes wrong—as it did
in preparing the ground for the global financial crisis and pushing for
an unsustainable, unhealthy model of globalization. Where did we go
wrong? Why, to take one prominent problem discussed here, were
economists so dismissive of the distributional consequences of trade
agreements—consequences that their own models had predicted so
well?

Hubris, overconfidence, and naïve politics are all to blame. But perhaps the most surprising answer offered here is that economists are
often not true to their own discipline and training. Economists often
forget, especially when they engage in public debates, that economics

is not a set of predetermined conclusions or policy prescriptions but a highly context-specific discipline that provides only contingent answers.[1] There is virtually no question in economics to which "it depends" is not an appropriate answer. (Of course, the strength of economics is that we can usually also tell precisely what it depends on.) Many of the difficulties economists run into, as this chapter illustrates, derive not from taking economics too seriously but from not taking it seriously enough.

Economists are often dragged into public debates by the policy relevance of their work, but they are rarely very self-conscious about their public responsibility. Should they shade their answers if they worry that what they say will be hijacked by special interest groups? If an unsavory dictator's son asks them for help developing his country's economy, should they accept? Should they just say "I don't know" when their science has not developed strong evidence and let others with even worse understanding take over the public conversation? If economists want to enhance their public engagement, they will need to pay greater attention to these and other questions discussed in the next few chapters.

Nobel Confusion?

When the 2013 Nobel Prize in economics (technically the Sveriges Riksbank Prize in Economic Sciences in Memory of Alfred Nobel) was awarded to Eugene Fama and Robert Shiller, along with Lars Peter Hansen, many were puzzled by the selection. Fama and Shiller are both distinguished and highly regarded scholars, so it was not their qualifications that raised eyebrows. What seemed odd was that the committee had picked them together.

The two economists seem to hold diametrically opposed views on how financial markets work. Fama, the University of Chicago economist, is the father of the "efficient market hypothesis," the theory that asset prices reflect all publicly available information, with the implication that it is impossible to consistently beat the market. Shiller, the Yale economist, meanwhile, has spent much of his career demonstrating that financial markets work poorly: they overshoot, are subject to "bubbles" (sustained rises in asset prices that cannot be explained by fundamentals), and are often driven by "behavioral" rather than rational forces. Could both be right? Was the Nobel committee simply hedging its bets?

We can't read the jury's mind, but its selection highlighted a central feature of economics—and a key difference between it and the natural sciences. Economics deals with human behavior, which depends on social and institutional context. That context in turn is the creation of human behavior, purposeful or not. This implies that propositions in economic science are typically context specific, rather than universal. The best, and most useful, economic theories are those that draw clear causal links from a specific set of contextual assumptions to predicted outcomes.

So, financial markets behave sometimes like Fama's theory and sometimes like Shiller's. The value of their respective theories is that they discipline our understanding of what type of financial market behavior to expect under specific conditions. Ideally, they also help us choose which model/theory we should apply in a particular conjuncture, although this happens too rarely as we will see below. (Aptly, the third laureate, Lars Peter Hansen, was given his prize for devising statistical techniques to test whether markets behave in a fully rational fashion.)

What is true of finance is true also of other fields within economics. Labor economists focus not only on how trade unions can distort markets but also how, under certain conditions, they can enhance productivity. Trade economists study how globalization can reduce or increase, as the case may be, inequality within and across countries. Open-economy macroeconomists examine conditions under which global finance stabilizes or destabilizes national economies. Development economists study conditions under which foreign aid does and does not reduce poverty. Training in economics requires learning not only about how markets work but also about market failures and the myriad ways in which governments can help markets work better.

When Economists Misbehave

The flexible, contextual nature of economics is both its strength and its weakness. The downside was in ample display during the buildup to the global financial crisis and its aftermath. As the world economy tumbled off the edge of a precipice, critics of the economics profession rightly raised questions about its complicity in the crisis. It was economists who had legitimized and popularized the view that unfettered finance was a boon to society. They had spoken with near unanimity when it came to the "dangers of government over-regulation." Their technical expertise—or what seemed like it at the time—had given them a privileged position as opinion makers, as well as access to the corridors of power. Very few among them had raised alarm bells about the crisis to come (Robert Shiller was one such Cassandra). Perhaps worse, the profession failed to provide helpful guidance in steering the world economy out of its mess. Economists' opinion on monetary, fiscal, and regulatory remedies for longer term recovery and growth never converged.

Many outsiders concluded that economics was in need of a major shake-up. Burn the textbooks and rewrite them from scratch, they said.

The paradox is that macroeconomics and finance did not lack the tools needed to understand how the crisis arose and unfolded. In fact, without recourse to the economist's toolkit, we cannot even begin to make sense of the crisis. What, for example, is the link between China's decision to accumulate large amounts of foreign reserves and a mortgage lender in California taking excessive risks? It is impossible to decipher such interrelationships without relying on elements from behavioral economics, agency theory, information economics, and international economics. The academic literature is chock-full of models of financial bubbles, asymmetric information, incentive distortions, self-fulfilling crises, and systemic risk. Pretty much everything needed to explain the crisis and its aftermath was in the research journals! But in the years leading up to the crisis, many economists downplayed these models' lessons in favor of models of efficient and self-correcting markets, which resulted in inadequate government oversight over financial markets. There was too much Fama, not enough Shiller.

"Economics is a science of thinking in terms of models," Keynes once said, "joined to the art of choosing models which are relevant." It was the art that fell short in this instance. Economists (and those who listen to them) became overconfident in their preferred models of the moment: markets are efficient, financial innovation transfers risk to those best able to bear it, self-regulation works best, and government intervention is ineffective and harmful. They forgot that there were many other models that led in radically different directions. Hubris creates blind spots. The science of the profession was fine—its craft and sociology, not so much.

Economists and the Public

Noneconomists tend to think of economics as a discipline that idolizes markets and a narrow concept of (allocative) efficiency at the expense of ethics or social concerns. If the only economics course you take is the typical introductory survey, or if you are a journalist asking an economist for a quick opinion on a policy issue, that is indeed what you will encounter. But take a few more economics courses, or spend some time in advanced seminar rooms, and you will get a different picture.

Economists get stuck with the charge of being narrowly ideological because they are their own worst enemy when it comes to applying their theories to the real world. Instead of communicating the full panoply of perspectives that their discipline offers, they display excessive confidence in particular remedies—often those that best accord with their own personal ideologies.

In my book *The Globalization Paradox*, I contemplate the following thought experiment. Let a journalist call an economics professor for his view on whether free trade with country X or Y is a good idea. We can be fairly certain that the economist, like the vast majority of the profession, will be enthusiastic in his support of free trade.[2]

Now let the reporter go undercover as a student in the professor's advanced graduate seminar on international trade theory. Let him pose the same question: Is free trade good? I doubt that the answer will come as quickly and be as succinct this time around. In fact, the professor is likely to be stymied by the question. "What do you mean by 'good'?" he will ask. "And good for whom?"

The professor would then launch into a long and tortured exegesis that will ultimately culminate in a heavily hedged statement: "So if the long list of conditions I have just described are satisfied, and assuming we can tax the beneficiaries to compensate the losers, freer trade has the potential to increase everyone's well-being." If he were in an expansive mood, the professor might add that the effect of free trade on an economy's growth rate is not clear, either, and depends on an altogether different set of requirements.

A direct, unqualified assertion about the benefits of free trade has now been transformed into a statement adorned by all kinds of ifs and buts. Oddly, the knowledge that the professor willingly imparts with great pride to his advanced students is deemed to be inappropriate (or dangerous) for the general public. This is particularly true of the effects of trade on income distribution, which economists elaborate at great length in their academic studies, but tend to stay away from in public.

Economists ignore the impact of the manner in which they frame their theories in introductory courses. I was invited once by two Harvard colleagues to make a guest appearance in their course on globalization. "I have to tell you," one of them warned me beforehand, "this is a pretty pro-globalization crowd." In the very first meeting, he had asked the students how many of them preferred free trade to import restrictions. Even though this was before the students had been instructed in the wonders of comparative advantage, the response was more than 90 percent.

We know that when the same question is asked in real surveys with representative samples—not just Harvard students—the outcome is quite different. In the United States, respondents favor trade restrictions by a two-to-one margin. But the Harvard students' response was not entirely surprising. Highly skilled and better-educated respondents tend to be considerably more pro–free trade than blue-collar workers are. Perhaps the Harvard students were simply voting with their own (future) wallets in mind.

Or maybe they did not understand how trade really works. When I met with them, I posed the same question in a different way, emphasizing the distributional effects of trade. This time, the free-trade consensus evaporated—even more rapidly than I had anticipated.

I began the class by asking students whether they would approve of my carrying out a particular magic experiment. I picked two volunteers, Nicholas and John, and told them that I was capable of making $200 disappear from Nicholas's bank account—*poof!*—while adding $300 to John's. This feat of social engineering would leave the class as a whole better off by $100. Would they allow me to carry out this magic trick?

Only a tiny minority voted affirmatively. Many were uncertain. Even more opposed the change.

Clearly the students were uncomfortable about condoning a significant redistribution of income, even if the economic pie grew as a result. How is it possible, I asked, that almost all of them had instinctively favored free trade, which entails a similar—in fact, most likely greater—redistribution from losers to winners? They appeared taken aback.

Let's assume, I said next, that Nicholas and John own two small firms that compete with each other. Suppose that John got richer by $300 because he worked harder, saved and invested more, and created better products, driving Nicholas out of business and causing him a loss of $200. How many of the students now approved of the change? This time a vast majority did—in fact, everyone except Nicholas approved.

I posed other hypotheticals, now directly related to international trade. Suppose John had driven Nicholas out of business by importing higher-quality inputs from Germany? By outsourcing to China, where labor rights are not well protected? By hiring child workers in Indonesia? Support for the proposed change dropped with each one of these alternatives.

But what about technological innovation, which, like trade, often leaves some people worse off. Here, few students would condone blocking technological progress. Banning the light bulb because candle makers would lose their jobs strikes almost everyone as a silly idea.

So, the students were not necessarily against redistribution. They were against certain kinds of redistribution. Like most of us, they care about procedural fairness.

To pass judgment on redistributive outcomes, we need to know about the circumstances that cause them. We do not begrudge Bill Gates or Warren Buffett their billions, even if some of their rivals have suffered along the way, presumably because they and their competitors operate according to the same ground rules and face pretty much the same opportunities and obstacles. We would think differently if Gates and Buffett had enriched themselves not through perspiration and inspiration but by cheating, breaking labor laws, ravaging the environment, or taking advantage of government subsidies abroad. If we do not condone redistribution that violates widely shared moral codes at home, why should we accept it just because it involves transactions across political borders?

Similarly, when we expect redistributive effects to even out in the long run, so that everyone eventually comes out ahead, we are more likely to overlook reshufflings of income. That is a key reason why we believe that technological progress should run its course, despite its short-run destructive effects on some. When, on the other hand, the forces of trade repeatedly hit the same people—less educated, blue-collar workers—we may feel less sanguine about globalization.

Too many economists are tone-deaf to such distinctions. They are prone to attribute concerns about globalization to crass protectionist motives or ignorance, even when there are genuine ethical issues at stake. By ignoring the fact that international trade sometimes—certainly not always—involves redistributive outcomes that we would consider problematic at home, they fail to engage the public debate properly. They also miss the opportunity to mount a more robust defense of trade when ethical concerns are less warranted.

Economics instruction suffers from the same problem. In their zeal to display the profession's crown jewels in untarnished form—market efficiency, the invisible hand, comparative advantage—economists skip over the real-world complications and nuances. It is as if introductory physics courses assumed a world without gravity, because everything becomes so much simpler that way. Downplaying the diversity of intellectual frameworks within their own discipline does not make economists better analysts of the real world. Nor does it make them more popular.

Consider how economists have used their models in recent trade policy debates.

Economists and the Trade Numbers Game

The Trans-Pacific Partnership—a mega trade deal covering twelve countries that together produce more than a third of global GDP and a quarter of the world's exports—has been the latest battleground in the decades-long confrontation between proponents and opponents of trade agreements.

True to form, the pact's advocates have marshalled quantitative models that make the agreement look like a no-brainer. Their favorite model (developed by Peter Petri and Michael Plummer, from Brandeis and Johns Hopkins Universities, respectively, building on a long line of similar frameworks by them and others) predicts increases in real incomes down the line that range from 0.5 percent for the United States to 8 percent in Vietnam, at relatively insignificant cost to employment in affected industries.[3] TPP opponents latched on to a competing model that generates very different projections. This model, produced by Jeronim Capaldo of Tufts University and Alex Izurieta of the U.N. Conference on Trade and Development (along with Jomo Kwame Sundaram, a former U.N. Assistant Secretary-General), predicts wage cuts and increased unemployment all around as well as income declines in two key countries, the United States and Japan.[4]

There is no disagreement between the models on the trade effects: in fact, Capaldo and his collaborators take as their starting point the trade predictions from an earlier version of the Petri-Plummer study. The differences arise largely from contrasting assumptions about how economies respond to changes in trade volumes sparked by liberalization.

Petri and Plummer assume sufficiently flexible labor markets so that job losses in adversely affected parts of the economy are compensated by job gains elsewhere. Unemployment is ruled out at the get-go. Proponents of TPP often fudged that this is an outcome that is built into the model. The Peterson Institute, which published the underlying study, inexplicably stated in its brief: "The agreement will raise US wages but is not projected to change US employment levels . . ."[5] The result on wages is a conclusion of the study, whereas the employment "projection" might as well have been made before the computer crunched a single number.

Capaldo and his collaborators meanwhile projected a competitive race to the bottom in labor markets, with a decline in wages and government spending keeping the lid down on aggregate demand and employment. Unfortunately, their paper does a poor job of explaining how their model works, and the particulars of their simulation are somewhat murky.

The Petri-Plummer model is squarely rooted in decades of academic trade modeling, which makes a sharp distinction between effects that are microeconomic (that shape resource allocation across sectors) and those that are macroeconomic (that relate to overall levels of demand

and employment). In this tradition, trade liberalization is a microeconomic "shock" that affects the composition of employment, but not its overall level. Trade economists tend to analyze trade agreements in such terms, which renders the Petri-Plummer model more congenial to them. By comparison, the Capaldo framework lacks sectoral and country detail; its behavioral assumptions remain opaque; and its extreme Keynesian assumptions sit ill at ease with its medium-term perspective.

The trouble is that the real world has not lined up so neatly with trade economists' presumptions. Trade critics have marshalled countless anecdotes about the adverse effects of imports on wages and employment in affected communities. The empirical work of three academic economists—David Autor, David Dorn, and Gordon Hanson—shows that critics have more than a point.[6] They document that the expansion of Chinese exports has produced "substantial adjustment costs and distributional consequences" in the United States. In regions hard hit by imports from China, wages have remained depressed and unemployment levels elevated for more than a decade. In industries that came under Chinese competition, employment has fallen, which was expected. But there have been no offsetting employment gains in other industries, which is a surprise.

Trade advocates have long maintained that deindustrialization and loss of low-skill jobs in advanced economies have little to do with trade and are the product of new technologies rather than growing international trade. In the debate on TPP, many prominent proponents still clung to this line. In light of the new empirical findings, such nonchalance toward trade has become untenable.[7] Incidentally, the Petri-Plummer model does indicate that TPP will accelerate the movement of jobs from manufacturing to services, a result that the pact's advocates do not trumpet.

Economists do not fully understand why expanded trade has interacted with the macroeconomy to produce the negative consequences for wages and employment that it has. We do not yet have a good alternative framework to replace the kind that trade advocates use. But we should not act as if our cherished standard model has not been severely tarnished by reality. It would be far better to consider the full range of possibilities highlighted by all models on offer, instead of putting all the weight on a single one.

The uncertainties do not end with macroeconomic interactions. The Petri-Plummer study predicts that the bulk of the economic benefits of TPP will come from reductions in nontariff barriers (such as regulatory barriers on imported services) and lower obstacles to foreign investment. But the modeling of these effects is an order of magnitude more difficult than in the case of tariff reductions. The assumptions needed to do so are not standard and require many arbitrary shortcuts.

The bottom line is that neither side's models generate numbers reliable enough on which a case for or against TPP could be made. Just about the only thing we can say with some certainty is that there would have been gainers and losers. Perhaps the agreement would have galvanized investment and knowledge flows across the Pacific, giving the world economy a much-needed boost. Perhaps not. But those who believe that the trade agreement, like previous ones, would have provided lopsided benefits had ample reason to be concerned.

Economists and Democracy

By the time my book *The Globalization Paradox* was published in 2011, I was used to all types of comments from audiences to whom I'd present the book. But at one book-launch event an economist assigned to discuss the book surprised me with an unexpected criticism. "Rodrik wants to make the world safe for politicians," he huffed. Lest the message be lost, he then illustrated his point by reminding the audience of "the former Japanese minister of agriculture who argued that Japan could not import beef because human intestines are longer in Japan than in other countries."

The comment drew a few chuckles. Who doesn't enjoy a joke at the expense of politicians?

But the remark had a more serious purpose and was evidently intended to expose a fundamental flaw in my argument. My discussant found it self-evident that allowing politicians greater room for maneuver was a cockamamie idea—and he assumed that the audience would concur. Remove constraints on what politicians can do, he implied, and all you will get are silly interventions that throttle markets and stall the engine of economic growth.

This criticism reflects a serious misunderstanding of how markets really function. Raised on textbooks that obscure the role of institutions, economists often imagine that markets arise on their own, with no help from purposeful, collective action. Adam Smith may have been right that "the propensity to truck, barter, and exchange" is innate to humans, but a wide array of nonmarket institutions is needed to capitalize on this propensity.

Consider all that is required. Modern markets need an infrastructure of transport, logistics, and communication, much of it the result of public investments. They need systems of contract enforcement and property-rights protection. They need regulations to ensure that consumers make informed decisions, externalities are internalized, and market power is not abused. They need central banks and fiscal institutions to avert financial panics and moderate business cycles. They need social protections and safety nets to legitimize distributional outcomes.

Well-functioning markets are always embedded within broader mechanisms of collective governance. That is why the world's wealthier economies, those with the most productive market systems, also have large public sectors.

Once we recognize that markets require rules, we must next ask who writes those rules. Economists who denigrate the value of democracy sometimes talk as if the alternative to democratic governance is decision-making by high-minded Platonic philosopher-kings—ideally economists!

This scenario is neither relevant nor desirable. For one thing, the lower the political system's transparency, representativeness, and accountability, the more likely it is that special interests will hijack the rules. Of course, democracies can be captured too. But they are still our best safeguard against arbitrary rule. Moreover, rule making is rarely about efficiency alone; it may entail trading off competing social objectives—such as stability versus innovation—or making distributional choices. These are not tasks that we would want to entrust to economists, who might be authorities on the price of a lot of things, but not necessarily their value.

True, the quality of democratic governance can sometimes be augmented by reducing the discretion of elected representatives. As we saw in the previous chapter, well-functioning democracies often delegate rule-making power to quasi-independent bodies when the issues at hand are technical and do not raise distributional concerns; when logrolling would otherwise result in suboptimal outcomes for all; or when policies are subject to myopia, with heavy discounting of future costs.

Independent central banks provide an important illustration of this. It may be up to elected politicians to determine the inflation target, but the means deployed to achieve that target are left to the technocrats at the central bank. Even then, central banks typically remain accountable to politicians and must provide an accounting when they miss the targets.

Similarly, there can be useful instances of democratic delegation to international organizations. Global agreements to cap tariff rates or reduce toxic emissions are indeed valuable. But economists have a tendency to idolize such constraints without sufficiently scrutinizing the politics that produce them.

It is one thing to advocate external restraints that enhance the quality of democratic deliberation—by preventing short-termism or demanding transparency, for example. It is another matter altogether to subvert democracy by privileging particular interests over others.

For instance, we know that the global capital-adequacy requirements produced by the Basel Committee reflect overwhelmingly the influence of large banks. If the regulations were to be written by economists and finance experts, they would be far more stringent. Alternatively, if the rules were left to domestic political processes, there could be more countervailing pressure from opposing stakeholders (even though financial interests are powerful at home too).

Similarly, despite the rhetoric, many World Trade Organization agreements are the result not of the pursuit of global economic well-being but the lobbying power of multinationals seeking profit-making opportunities. International rules on patents and copyright reflect the ability of pharmaceutical companies and Hollywood—to take just two examples—to get their way. These rules are widely derided by economists for having imposed inappropriate constraints on developing economies' ability to access cheap pharmaceuticals or technological opportunities.

So, the choice between democratic discretion at home and external restraint is not always a choice between good and bad policies. Even when the domestic political process works poorly, there is no guarantee that global institutions will work any better. Often, the choice is between yielding to domestic rent-seekers or to foreign ones. In the former case, at least the rents stay at home!

Ultimately, the question concerns whom we empower to make the rules that markets require. The unavoidable reality of our global economy is that the principal locus of legitimate democratic accountability still resides within the nation-state. So, I readily plead guilty to my economist critic's charge. I *do* want to make the world safe for democratic politicians. And, frankly, I wonder about those who do not.

Milton Friedman's Magical Thinking

Probably no other economist since Keynes has had as much impact on policy makers' understanding of how economies work as Milton Friedman. Friedman was one of the twentieth century's leading economists, a Nobel Prize winner who made notable contributions to monetary policy and consumption theory. But he will be remembered primarily as the visionary who provided the intellectual firepower for free-market enthusiasts during the second half of the century, and as the *éminence grise* behind the dramatic shift in the economic policies that took place after 1980.

At a time when skepticism about markets ran rampant, Friedman explained in clear, accessible language that private enterprise is the foundation of economic prosperity. All successful economies are built on thrift, hard work, and individual initiative. He railed against government regulations that encumber entrepreneurship and restrict markets. What Adam Smith was to the eighteenth century, Milton Friedman was to the twentieth.

As Friedman's landmark television series *Free to Choose* was being broadcast in 1980, the world economy stood in the throes of a singular transformation. Inspired by Friedman's ideas, Ronald Reagan, Margaret Thatcher, and many other government leaders began to dismantle the government restrictions and regulations that had been built up over the preceding decades.

China moved away from central planning and allowed markets to flourish—first in agricultural products and, eventually, in industrial goods. Latin America sharply reduced its trade barriers and privatized its state-owned firms. When the Berlin Wall fell in 1989, there was no doubt as to which direction the former command economies would take: toward free markets.

But Friedman also produced a less felicitous legacy. In his zeal to promote the power of markets, he drew too sharp a distinction between the market and the state. In effect, he presented government as the enemy of the market. He therefore blinded us to the evident reality that all successful economies are, in fact, mixed. Unfortunately, the world economy is still contending with that blindness in the aftermath of a financial crisis that resulted, in no small part, from letting financial markets run too free.

The Friedmanite perspective greatly underestimates the institutional prerequisites of markets. Let the government simply enforce property rights and contracts, and—presto!—markets can work their magic. In fact, the kind of markets that modern economies need are not self-creating, self-regulating, self-stabilizing, or self-legitimizing. Governments must invest in transport and communication networks; counteract asymmetric information, externalities, and unequal bargaining power; moderate financial panics and recessions; and respond to popular demands for safety nets and social insurance.

Markets are the essence of a market economy in the same sense that lemons are the essence of lemonade. Pure lemon juice is barely drinkable. To make good lemonade, you need to mix it with water and sugar. Of course, if you put too much water in the mix, you ruin the lemonade, just as too much government meddling can make markets dysfunctional. The trick is not to discard the water and the sugar but to get the proportions right. Hong Kong, which Friedman held up as the exemplar of a free-market society, remains the exception to the mixed-economy rule—and even there the government has played a large role in providing land for housing.

The image most people will retain of Friedman is the smiling, diminutive, unassuming professor holding up a pencil in front of the cameras in *Free to Choose* to illustrate the power of markets. It took thousands of people all over the world to make this pencil, Friedman said—to mine the graphite, cut the wood, assemble the components, and market the final product. No single central authority coordinated their actions; that feat was accomplished by the magic of free markets and the price system.

Nearly forty years later, there is an interesting coda to the pencil story (which in fact was based on an article by the economist Leonard E. Read). Today, most of the world's pencils are produced in China—an economy that is a peculiar mix of private entrepreneurship and state direction.

A modern-day Friedman might want to ask how China has come to dominate the pencil industry, as it has so many others. There are better sources of graphite in Mexico and South Korea. Forest reserves are more plentiful in Indonesia and Brazil. Germany and the United States have better technology. China has lots of low-cost labor, but so does Bangladesh, Ethiopia, and many other populous low-income countries.

Undoubtedly, most of the credit belongs to the initiative and hard work of Chinese entrepreneurs and laborers. But the present-day pencil story would be incomplete without citing China's state-owned firms, which made the initial investments in technology and labor training; forest management policies, which kept wood artificially cheap; generous export subsidies; and government intervention in currency markets, which gives Chinese producers a significant cost advantage. China's government has subsidized, protected, and goaded its firms to ensure rapid industrialization, thereby altering the global division of labor in its favor.

Friedman himself would have rued these government policies. Yet the tens of thousands of workers that pencil factories in China employ would most likely have remained poor farmers if the government had not given market forces a nudge to get the industry off the ground. Given China's economic success, it is hard to deny the contribution made by the government's industrialization policies.

Free-market enthusiasts' place in the history of economic thought will remain secure. But thinkers like Friedman leave an ambiguous and puzzling legacy, because it is the interventionists who have succeeded in economic history, where it really matters.

The Mercantilist Challenge

The history of economics is largely a struggle between two opposing schools of thought, liberalism and mercantilism. Economic liberalism, with its emphasis on private entrepreneurship and free markets, remains today's dominant doctrine. But its intellectual victory has blinded us to the great appeal—and frequent success—of mercantilist practices. In fact, mercantilism remains alive and well, and its continuing conflict with liberalism is likely to be a major force shaping the future of the global economy.

Today, mercantilism is typically dismissed as an archaic and blatantly erroneous set of ideas about economic policy. And, in their heyday, mercantilists certainly did defend some very odd notions, chief among which was the view that national policy ought to be guided by the accumulation of precious metals—gold and silver. Adam Smith's 1776 treatise *The Wealth of Nations* masterfully demolished many of these ideas. Smith showed, in particular, that money should not be confused for wealth. As he put it, "the wealth of a country consists, not in its gold and silver only, but in its lands, houses, and consumable goods of all different kinds."

But it is more accurate to think of mercantilism as a different way to organize the relationship between the state and the economy—a vision that holds no less relevance today than it did in the eighteenth century. Mercantilist theorists such as Thomas Mun were in fact strong proponents of capitalism; they just propounded a different model than liberalism. The liberal model views the state as necessarily predatory and the private sector as inherently rent-seeking. So, it advocates a strict separation between the state and private business. Mercantilism, by contrast, offers a corporatist vision in which the state and private business are allies and cooperate in pursuit of common objectives, such as domestic economic growth or national power.

The mercantilist model can be derided as state capitalism or cronyism. But when it works, as it has so often in Asia, the model's "government-business collaboration" or "pro-business state" quickly garners heavy praise. Lagging economies have not failed to notice that mercantilism can be their friend. Even in Britain, classical liberalism arrived only in the mid-nineteenth century—that is, *after* the country had become the world's dominant industrial power.

A second difference between the two models lies in whether consumer or producer interests are privileged. For liberals, consumers are king. The ultimate objective of economic policy is to increase house-holds' consumption potential, which requires giving them unhindered access to the cheapest-possible goods and services. Mercantilists, by contrast, emphasize the productive side of the economy. For them, a sound economy requires a sound production structure. And consumption needs to be underpinned by high employment at adequate wages.

These different models have predictable implications for international economic policies. The logic of the liberal approach is that the economic benefits of trade arise from imports: the cheaper the imports, the better, even if the result is a trade deficit. Mercantilists, however, view trade as a means of supporting domestic production and employment, and prefer to spur exports rather than imports.

Today's China is the leading bearer of the mercantilist torch, though Chinese leaders would never admit it—too much opprobrium still attaches to the term. Much of China's economic miracle is the product of an activist government that has supported, stimulated, and openly subsidized industrial producers—both domestic and foreign.

Although China phased out many of its explicit export subsidies as a condition of membership in the World Trade Organization, which it joined in 2001, mercantilism's support system remains largely in place. In particular, the government has managed the exchange rate to maintain manufacturers' profitability, resulting in a sizable trade surplus (which has come down recently). Moreover, export-oriented firms continue to benefit from a range of tax incentives.

From the liberal perspective, these export subsidies impoverish Chinese consumers while benefiting consumers in the rest of the world. A study by the economists Fabrice Defever and Alejandro Riaño of the University of Nottingham puts the "losses" to China at around 3 percent of Chinese income, and gains to the rest of the world at around 1 percent of global income.[8] From the mercantilist perspective, however, these are simply the costs of building a modern economy and setting the stage for long-term prosperity.

As the example of export subsidies shows, the two models can coexist happily in the world economy. Liberals should be happy to have their consumption subsidized by mercantilists. Indeed, that, in a nutshell, is the story of the last six decades: a succession of Asian countries managed to grow by leaps and bounds by applying different variants of mercantilism. Governments in rich countries for the most part looked the other way while Japan, South Korea, Taiwan, and China protected their home markets, appropriated "intellectual property," subsidized their producers, and managed their currencies.

We have now reached the end of this happy coexistence. The liberal model has become severely tarnished, owing to the rise in inequality and the plight of the middle class in the West, together with the financial crisis that deregulation spawned. Medium-term growth prospects for the American and European economies range from moderate to bleak. Unemployment will remain a major headache and preoccupation for policy makers. So, mercantilist pressures will likely intensify in the advanced countries too.

As a result, the new economic environment will produce more tension than accommodation between countries pursuing liberal and mercantilist paths. It may also reignite long-dormant debates about the type of capitalism that produces the greatest prosperity.

Economics Hijacked

When the stakes are high, it is no surprise that battling political opponents use whatever support they can garner from economists and other researchers. That is what happened when conservative American politicians and European Union officials latched on to the work of two Harvard professors—Carmen Reinhart and Kenneth Rogoff—to justify their support of fiscal austerity.[9]

Reinhart and Rogoff had published a paper that appeared to show that public-debt levels above 90 percent of GDP do significant damage to economic growth. The paper was criticized by three economists from the University of Massachusetts at Amherst, who argued their findings were brittle.[10] They had found a relatively minor spreadsheet error. But more importantly, they charged that Reinhart and Rogoff had made some questionable methodological assumptions that cast doubt on their results. Even though debt levels and growth seemed to be negatively correlated, the evidence for a stark 90 percent threshold was weak. And many others have argued that the correlation itself could be the result of reverse causation—from low growth to high indebtedness, rather than the other way around.

Reinhart and Rogoff strongly contested accusations by many commentators that they were willing, if not willful, participants in a game of political deception. They defended their empirical methods and insisted that they are not the deficit hawks that their critics portrayed them to be.

The Reinhart-Rogoff affair was not just an academic quibble. Because the 90 percent threshold had become political fodder, its subsequent demolition also became politicized. Despite their protests, Reinhart and Rogoff were accused of providing scholarly cover for a set of policies for which there was, in fact, limited supporting evidence. A similar criticism was leveled at a paper by two other economists, Alberto Alesina and Silvia Ardagna, which apparently showed that fiscal austerity could stimulate the economy—the opposite of the standard Keynesian presumption.[11] This paper too had been influential in policy circles, until the austerity camp had to concede defeat under the weight of accumulating evidence to the contrary.[12]

Clearly, we can use better rules of engagement between economic researchers and policy makers. I discuss how economists should relate to the public in my book *Economics Rules.* But one approach that does not work is for economists to second-guess how their ideas will be used or misused in public debate and to shade their public statements accordingly. For example, Reinhart and Rogoff might have downplayed their results—such as they were—in order to prevent them from being misused by deficit hawks. But few economists are sufficiently well attuned to have a clear idea of how the politics will play out. Moreover, when economists adjust their message to fit their audience, the result is the opposite of what is intended: they rapidly lose credibility.

This is clearly what happened in the globalization debate, where such shading of research is established practice. For fear of empowering the "protectionist barbarians," trade economists have been prone to exaggerate the benefits of trade and downplay its distributional and other costs. In practice, this often leads to their arguments being captured by interest groups on the other side—for example, global corporations that seek to manipulate trade rules to their own advantage. As a result, economists are rarely viewed as honest brokers in the public debate about globalization.

A far better strategy for economists is to be open about the ambiguity and context-specificity of most results in economics—to flaunt the diversity rather than hide it. Instead, as we'll see in the next chapter, economists' tendency is to celebrate consensus and rue discord, even when they should know better.

CHAPTER 6

The Perils of Economic Consensus

The Initiative on Global Markets, based at the University of Chicago, periodically surveys a group of leading academic economists, of varying political persuasions, on the issues of the day. Despite the difference in the political orientation, there is often overwhelming consensus. For example, when the group was asked whether President Barack Obama's stimulus plan helped to reduce unemployment in the United States, the responses were virtually unanimous. Officially known as the American Recovery and Reinvestment Act of 2009, the plan entailed government spending of more than $800 billion on infrastructure, education, health, energy, tax incentives, and various social programs. Implemented in the midst of an economic crisis, it was the classic Keynesian response. Thirty-six of the thirty-seven top economists who responded to the survey said that the plan had been successful in its avowed objective of reducing unemployment. The University of Michigan economist Justin Wolfers cheered the consensus in his *New York Times* blog.[1] The virulent public debate about whether fiscal stimulus works, he complained, has become totally disconnected from what experts know and agree on.

Economists agree on many things that are often politically controversial. The Harvard economist Greg Mankiw listed some of them in 2009.[2] The following propositions garnered support from at least 90 percent of economists: import tariffs and quotas reduce general economic welfare; rent controls reduce the supply of housing; floating exchange rates provide an effective international monetary system; the United States should not restrict employers from outsourcing work to foreign countries; and fiscal policy stimulates the economy when there is less than full employment.

This consensus about so many important issues contrasts rather starkly with the general perception that economists rarely agree on anything. "If all the economists were laid end to end," George Bernard Shaw famously quipped, "they would not reach a conclusion." Frustrated by the conflicting and hedged advice that he was receiving from his advisers, President Dwight Eisenhower is said to have asked once for a "one-handed economist."

No doubt, there are many public-policy questions that economists debate vigorously. What should the top income-tax rate be? Should the minimum wage be raised? Should the fiscal deficit be reduced by raising taxes or cutting spending? Do patents stimulate or impede innovation? On these and many other issues, economists tend to be good at seeing both sides of the issue, and I suspect that a survey on such questions would reveal little consensus.

A consensus among economists can arise for both good and bad reasons. Sometimes a consensus is innocuous enough, as when you hear economists argue that one ignores the role of incentives at one's peril. Can anyone really disagree with that? Sometimes it is restricted to a particular episode and is based on evidence accumulated after the fact: yes, the Soviet economic system was hugely inefficient; yes, the Obama fiscal stimulus of 2009 did reduce unemployment.

But when a consensus forms around the universal applicability of a specific model, the critical assumptions of which are likely to be violated in many settings, we have a problem.

Consider some of the areas of widespread agreement that I listed above. The proposition that trade restrictions reduce economic welfare is certainly not generally valid, and it is violated when certain conditions—such as externalities or increasing returns to scale—are present. Moreover, it requires that economists make value judgments on distributional effects, which are better left to the electorate itself.

Likewise, the proposition that rent controls reduce the supply of housing is violated under conditions of imperfect competition. And the proposition that floating exchange rates are an effective system relies on assumptions about the workings of the monetary and financial system that have proved problematic; I suspect a poll today would find significantly less support for it.

Consider other issues of the day. The widely held presumption that minimum wages are damaging to employment carries considerably less weight today because of mounting evidence showing mixed results; there are models under which minimum wages either do not reduce employment or increase it. Even in the case of Brexit, where the weight of both evidence and theory predicts adverse economic results, economists would have been well advised to emphasize their uncertainty over their confidence.

Perhaps economists tend to agree that certain assumptions are more prevalent in the real world. Or they think that one set of models works better "on average" than another. Even so, as scientists, should they not adorn their endorsements with the appropriate caveats? Shouldn't they worry that categorical statements such as those above may prove to be misleading in at least some settings?

The problem is that economists often confuse a model for *the* model. When that happens, a consensus is certainly not something to cheer about.

Two kinds of mischief may then follow. First, there are errors of omission—cases in which blind spots in the consensus prevent economists from being able to see troubles looming ahead. A prominent example was the failure of economists to grasp the dangerous confluence of circumstances that produced the global financial crisis. As I argued earlier, the oversight was not due to the lack of models of bubbles, asymmetric information, distorted incentives, or bank runs. It was due to the fact that such models were neglected in favor of models that stressed efficient markets.

Then there are the errors of commission—cases in which economists' fixation on one particular model of the world makes them complicit in the administration of policies whose failure could have been predicted ahead of time. Economists' advocacy of neoliberal "Washington Consensus" policies and of financial globalization falls into this category. What happened in both cases is that economists overlooked serious second-best complications, such as learning externalities and weak institutions, which blunted the reforms and, in some cases, caused them to backfire.

The Peculiar Science of Economics

The firestorm over the Reinhart-Rogoff analysis overshadowed what in fact was a salutary process of scrutiny and refinement of economic research. Reinhart and Rogoff quickly acknowledged the spreadsheet mistake they had made. The dueling analyses clarified the nature of the data, their limitations, and the difference that alternative methods of processing them made to the results. Ultimately, Reinhart and Rogoff were not that far apart from their critics on either what the evidence showed or what the policy implications were.

So, the silver lining in this fracas is that it showed that economics can progress by the rules of science. No matter how far apart their political views may have been, the two sides shared a common language about what constitutes evidence and—for the most part—a common approach to resolving differences.

Economics, unlike the natural sciences, rarely yields cut-and-dried results. Economics is really a toolkit with multiple models—each a different, stylized representation of some aspect of reality. The contextual nature of its reasoning means that there are as many conclusions as potential real-world circumstances. All economic propositions are "if-then" statements. One's skill as an economic analyst depends on the ability to pick and choose the right model for the situation. Accordingly, figuring out which remedy works best in a particular setting is a craft rather than a science.

One reaction I get when I say this is the following: "How can economics be useful if you have a model for every possible outcome?" Well, the world is complicated, and we understand it by simplifying it. A market behaves differently when there are many sellers than when there are a few. Even when there are a few sellers, the outcomes differ depending on the nature of strategic interactions among them. When we add imperfect information, we get even more possibilities. The best we can do is to understand the structure of behavior in each one of these cases, and then have an empirical method that helps us apply the right model to the particular context we are interested in. So, we have "one economics, many recipes," as the title of one of my books puts it.[3] Unlike the natural sciences, economics advances not by newer models superseding old ones but through a richer set of models that sheds ever-brighter light at the variety of social experience.

It is surprising, therefore, that very little research is devoted in economics to what might be called *economic diagnostics*: figuring out which among multiple plausible models actually applies in a particular, real-world setting. Economists understand well the theoretical and empirical predicates of, say, Fama's or Shiller's models—but they lack systematic tools to determine conclusively whether it is one or the other that best characterizes Wall Street today or mortgage markets in 2007, for example. When they engage the real world, this leads them to render universal judgments rather than conditional ones—picking one model over the other instead of navigating among them as the circumstances require. The profession places a large premium on developing new models that shed light on as yet unexplained phenomena, but there seems little incentive for research that informs how appropriate models and remedies can be selected in specific contexts. My colleagues and I have brought such ideas to bear on problems of growth policy in developing countries.[4] But clearly this ought to be part of a much more general research agenda. Over time, of course, good economists develop a knack for performing the needed diagnostics. Even then, the work is done instinctively and rarely becomes codified or expounded at any length.

Unfortunately, empirical evidence in economics is rarely reliable enough to settle decisively a controversy characterized by deeply divided opinion—certainly not in real time. This is particularly true in macroeconomics, where the time-series data are open to diverse interpretations. Those with strong priors in favor of financial market efficiency, such as Eugene Fama, for example, can continue to absolve financial markets from culpability for the crisis, laying the blame elsewhere. Keynesians and "classical" economists can continue to disagree on their interpretation of high unemployment.

But even in microeconomics, where it is sometimes possible to generate precise empirical estimates using randomized controlled trials, those estimates apply only locally to a particular setting. The results must be extrapolated—using judgment and a lot of hand waving—in order to be applied more generally. New economic evidence serves at best to nudge the views—a little here, a little there—of those inclined to be open-minded.

"One thing that experts know, and that non-experts do not," the development economist Kaushik Basu has said, "is that they know less than non-experts think they do."[5] The implications go beyond not overselling any particular research result. Journalists, politicians, and the general public have a tendency to attribute greater authority and precision to what economists say than economists should really feel comfortable with. Unfortunately, economists are rarely humble, especially in public. And it does not help that what gets academic economists ahead in their careers is cleverness, not wisdom. Professors at top universities distinguish themselves not by being right about the real world but by devising imaginative theoretical twists or developing novel evidence. If these skills also render them perceptive observers of real societies and provide them with sound judgment, it is hardly by design.

So, economics is both science and craft. Ironically, it is the neglect of the craft element—aiming to elevate economics' status as science—that occasionally turns it into snake oil.

Discontent within Economics

It should be no surprise, therefore, that economics has never been short of critics. Ever since the late nineteenth century, when economics, increasingly embracing mathematics and statistics, developed scientific pretensions, its practitioners have been accused of a variety of sins. The charges—including hubris, neglect of social goals beyond incomes, excessive attention to formal techniques, and failure to predict major economic developments such as financial crises—have usually come from outsiders, or from a heterodox fringe. But lately it seems that even the field's leaders are unhappy.

Paul Krugman, a Nobel laureate who also writes a newspaper column, has made a habit of slamming the latest generation of models in macroeconomics for neglecting old-fashioned Keynesian truths.[6] Paul Romer, one of the originators of new growth theory, has accused some leading names, including the Nobel laureate Robert Lucas, of what he calls "mathiness"—using math to obfuscate rather than clarify.[7] Richard Thaler, a distinguished behavioral economist at the University of Chicago, has taken the profession to task for ignoring real-world behavior in favor of models that assume people are rational optimizers.[8] And finance professor Luigi Zingales, also at the University of Chicago, has charged that his fellow finance specialists have led society astray by overstating the benefits produced by the financial industry.[9]

This kind of critical examination by the discipline's big names is healthy and welcome—especially in a field that has often lacked much self-reflection. But there is a disconcerting undertone to this new round of criticism that needs to be made explicit—and rejected. Economics is not the kind of science in which there could ever be one true model that works best in all contexts. The point is not "to reach a consensus about which model is right," as Romer puts it, but to figure out which model applies best in a given setting. And doing that will always remain a craft (or art, in Keynes's terms), not a science, especially when the choice must be made in real time.

The social world differs from the physical world because it is man-made and hence almost infinitely malleable. So, unlike the natural sciences, economics advances scientifically not by replacing old models with better ones but by expanding its library of models, with each shedding light on a different social contingency.

For example, we now have many models of markets with imperfect competition or asymmetric information. These models have not made their predecessors, based on perfect competition, obsolete or irrelevant. They have simply made us more aware that different circumstances call for different models. Similarly, behavioral models that emphasize heuristic decision-making make us better analysts of environments where such considerations may be important. They do not displace rational-choice models, which remain the go-to tool in other settings. A growth model that applies to advanced countries may be a poor guide in developing countries. Models that emphasize expectations are sometimes best for analyzing inflation and unemployment levels; at other times, models with Keynesian elements will do a superior job.

Jorge Luis Borges, the Argentine writer, once wrote a short story—a single paragraph in fact—that is perhaps the best guide to the scientific method.[10] In it, he described a distant land where cartography—the science of making maps—was taken to ridiculous extremes. A map of a province was so detailed that it was the size of an entire city. The map of the empire occupied an entire province. In time, the cartographers became even more ambitious: they drew a map that was an exact, one-to-one replica of the whole empire. As Borges wryly notes, subsequent generations could find no practical use for such an unwieldy map. So, the map was left to rot in the desert, along with the science of geography that it represented.

Borges's point still eludes many social scientists today: understanding requires simplification and abstraction from many real-world details. The best way to respond to the complexity of social life is not to devise ever-more elaborate models but to learn how different causal mechanisms work, one at a time, and then figure out which ones are most relevant in a particular setting.

We use one map if we are driving from home to work and another one if we are traveling to another city. Yet other kinds of maps are needed if we are on a bike, on foot, or planning to take public transport.

Navigating among economic models—choosing which one will work better—is considerably more difficult than choosing the right map. Practitioners use a variety of formal and informal empirical methods with varying skill. And, in my book *Economics Rules*, I criticize economics training for not properly equipping students for the empirical diagnostics that the discipline requires.

But the profession's internal critics are wrong to claim that the discipline has gone wrong because economists have yet to reach consensus on the "correct" models (their preferred ones, of course). Let us cherish economics in all its diversity—rational and behavioral, Keynesian and classical, first-best and second-best, orthodox and heterodox—and devote our energy to becoming wiser at picking which framework to apply when.

It is only when we maintain a healthy diversity of frameworks that we can understand some of the key problems of our time. Consider two issues rife with important policy challenges: inequality and the effects of technology and innovation.

Good and Bad Inequality

In the pantheon of economic theories, the trade-off between equality and efficiency used to occupy an exalted position. The American economist Arthur Okun, whose classic work on the topic is called *Equality and Efficiency: The Big Tradeoff*, believed that public policies revolved around managing the tension between those two values. As recently as 2007, when New York University economist Thomas Sargent, addressing the graduating class at the University of California, Berkeley, summarized the wisdom of economics in twelve short principles, the trade-off was among them.[11]

The belief that boosting equality requires sacrificing economic efficiency is grounded in one of the most cherished ideas in economics: incentives. Firms and individuals need the prospect of higher incomes to save, invest, work hard, and innovate. If taxation of profitable firms and rich households blunts those prospects, the result is reduced effort and lower economic growth. Communist countries, where egalitarian experiments led to economic disaster, long served as "Exhibit A" in the case against redistributive policies.

In recent years, however, neither economic theory nor empirical evidence has been kind to the presumed trade-off. Economists have produced new arguments showing why good economic performance is not only compatible with distributive fairness but may even demand it. For example, in high-inequality societies, where poor households are deprived of economic and educational opportunities, economic growth is depressed. Then there are the Scandinavian countries, where egalitarian policies evidently have not stood in the way of economic prosperity. In 2014, economists at the International Monetary Fund produced empirical results that seemed to upend the old consensus.[12] They found that greater equality is associated with faster subsequent medium-term growth, both across and within countries. Moreover, redistributive policies did not appear to have any detrimental effects on economic performance. We can have our cake, it seems, and eat it too. That is a striking result—all the more so because it comes from the IMF, an institution hardly known for heterodox or radical ideas.

Economics is a science that can claim to have uncovered few, if any, universal truths. Like almost everything else in social life, the relationship between equality and economic performance is likely to be contingent rather than fixed, depending on the deeper causes of inequality and many mediating factors. So, the emerging new consensus on the harmful effects of inequality is as likely to mislead as the old one was.

Consider, for example, the relationship between industrialization and inequality. In a poor country where the bulk of the workforce is employed in traditional agriculture, the rise of urban industrial opportunities is likely to produce inequality, at least during the early stages of industrialization. As farmers move to cities and earn higher pay, income gaps open up. And yet this is the same process that produces economic growth; all successful developing countries have gone through it. In China, rapid economic growth after the late 1970s was associated with a significant rise in inequality. Roughly half of the increase was the result of urban–rural earnings gaps, which also acted as the engine of growth.

Or consider transfer policies that tax the rich and the middle classes in order to increase the income of poor households. Many countries in Latin America, such as Mexico and Bolivia, undertook such policies in a fiscally prudent manner, ensuring that government deficits would not lead to high debt and macroeconomic instability. On the other hand, Venezuela's aggressive redistributive transfers under Hugo Chávez and his successor, Nicolás Maduro, were financed by temporary oil revenues, placing both the transfers and macroeconomic stability at risk. Even though inequality has been reduced in Venezuela (for the time being), the economy's growth prospects have been severely weakened.

Latin America is the only world region where inequality has declined since the early 1990s. Improved social policies and increased investment in education have been substantial factors. But the decline in the pay differential between skilled and unskilled workers—what economists call the "skill premium"—has also played an important role.[13] Whether this is good news or bad for economic growth depends on why the skill premium has fallen. If pay differentials have narrowed because of an increase in the relative supply of skilled workers, we can be hopeful that declining inequality in Latin America will not stand in the way of faster growth (and may even be an early indicator of it). But if the underlying cause is the decline in demand for skilled workers, smaller differentials would suggest that the modern, skill-intensive industries on which future growth depends are not expanding sufficiently.

In the advanced countries, the causes of rising inequality are still being debated. Automation and other technological changes, globalization, weaker trade unions, erosion of minimum wages, financialization, and changing norms about acceptable pay gaps within enterprises have all played a role, with different weights in the United States relative to Europe. Each one of these drivers has a different effect on growth. Though technological progress clearly fosters growth, the rise of finance since the 1990s has probably had an adverse effect, via financial crises and the accumulation of debt.

It is good that economists no longer regard the equality-efficiency trade-off as an iron law. We should not invert the error and conclude that greater equality and better economic performance always go together. After all, there really is only one universal truth in economics: it depends.

The Different Faces of Technological Innovation

We seem to be living in an accelerated age of revolutionary technological breakthroughs. Barely a day passes without the announcement of some major new development in artificial intelligence, biotechnology, digitization, or automation. Yet those who are supposed to know where it is all taking us can't make up their minds.

At one end of the spectrum are the techno-optimists, who believe we are on the cusp of a new era in which the world's living standards will rise more rapidly than ever. At the other end are the techno-pessimists, who see disappointing productivity statistics and argue that the new technologies' economy-wide benefits will remain limited. Then there are those—the techno-worriers?—who agree with the optimists about the scale and scope of innovation but fret about the adverse implications for employment or equity.

What distinguishes these perspectives from one another is not so much disagreement about the rate of technological innovation. After all, who can seriously doubt that innovation is progressing rapidly? The debate is about whether these innovations will remain bottled up in a few tech-intensive sectors that employ the highest-skilled professionals and account for a relatively small share of GDP, or spread to the bulk of the economy. The consequences of any innovation for productivity, employment, and equity ultimately depend on how quickly it diffuses through labor and product markets.

Technological diffusion can be constrained on both the demand and supply sides of the economy. Take the demand side first. In rich economies, consumers spend the bulk of their income on services such as health, education, transportation, housing, and retail goods. Technological innovation has had comparatively little impact to date in many of these sectors.

Consider some of the figures provided by the McKinsey Global Institute's report Digital America.[14] The two sectors in the United States that have experienced the most rapid productivity growth since 2005 are the ICT (information and communications technology) and media industries, with a combined GDP share of less than 10 percent.

By contrast, government services and health care, which together produce more than a quarter of GDP, have had virtually no productivity growth.

Techno-optimists, such as the McKinsey authors, look at such numbers as an opportunity: there remain vast productivity gains to be had from the adoption of new technologies in the lagging sectors. The pessimists, on the other hand, think that such gaps may be a structural, lasting feature of today's economies. For example, the economic historian Robert Gordon argues that today's innovations pale in contrast to past technological revolutions in terms of their likely economy-wide impact.[15] Electricity, the automobile, airplane, air-conditioning, and household appliances altered the way that ordinary people live in fundamental ways. They made inroads in every sector of the economy. Perhaps the digital revolution, impressive as it has been, will not reach as far.

On the supply side, the key question is whether the innovating sector has access to the capital and skills it needs to expand rapidly and continuously. In advanced countries, neither constraint typically binds much. But when the technology requires high skills—technological change is "skill-biased," in economists' terminology—its adoption and diffusion will tend to widen the gap between the earnings of low- and high-skill workers. Economic growth will be accompanied by rising inequality, as it was in the 1990s.

The supply-side problem faced by developing countries is more debilitating. The labor force is predominantly low skilled. Historically, this has not been a handicap for late industrializers, so long as manufacturing consisted of labor-intensive assembly operations such as garments and automobiles. Peasants could be transformed into factory workers virtually overnight, implying significant productivity gains for the economy. Manufacturing was traditionally a rapid escalator to higher income levels.

But once manufacturing operations become robotized and require high skills, the supply-side constraints begin to bite. Effectively, developing countries lose their comparative advantage vis-à-vis the rich countries. We see the consequences in the premature deindustrialization of the developing world today. In a world of premature deindustrialization, achieving economy-wide productivity growth becomes that much harder for low-income countries. As we saw in an earlier chapter, it is not clear whether there are effective substitutes for industrialization.

The economist Tyler Cowen has suggested that developing countries may benefit from the trickle down of innovation from the advanced economies: they can consume a stream of new products at cheap prices.[16] This is a model of what Cowen calls "cellphones instead of automobile factories." But the question remains: What will these countries produce and export—besides primary products—to be able to afford the imported cellphones?

In Latin America, economy-wide productivity has stagnated despite significant innovation in the best-managed firms and vanguard sectors. The apparent paradox is resolved by noting that rapid productivity growth in the pockets of innovation has been undone by workers moving from the more productive to the less productive parts of the economy—a phenomenon that my coauthors and I have called "growth-reducing structural change."[17] This perverse outcome becomes possible when there is severe technological dualism in the economy and the more productive activities do not expand rapidly enough. Disturbingly, there is some evidence that growth-reducing structural change has been happening recently in the United States as well.[18]

Ultimately, it is the economy-wide productivity consequences of technological innovation, not innovation per se, that lifts living standards. Innovation can coexist side-by-side with low productivity (conversely, productivity growth is sometimes possible in the absence of innovation, when resources move to the more productive sectors). Techno-pessimists recognize this. The optimists might not be wrong, but to make their case, they need to focus on how the effects of technology play out in the economy as a whole.

In Praise of Foxy Scholars

We live in a complicated world, so we are forced to simplify it. We categorize people around us as friends or foes, classify their motives as good or bad, and ascribe events with complex roots to straightforward causes. Such shortcuts help us navigate the complexities of our social existence. They help us form expectations about the consequences of our and others' actions, and thereby facilitate decision-making.

But, because such "mental models" are simplifications, they are necessarily wrong. They may serve us well as we navigate our daily challenges, but they leave out many details and can backfire when we find ourselves in an environment in which our categorizations and ready-made explanations fit less well. The term *culture shock* refers to situations in which our expectations about people's behavior turn out to be so wrong that we find ourselves jolted by the experience.

And yet, without these shortcuts we would be either lost or paralyzed. We have neither the mental capacity nor the understanding to decipher the full web of cause-and-effect relations in our social existence. So, our daily behavior and reactions must be based on incomplete, and occasionally misleading, mental models.

The best that social science has to offer is in fact not much different. Social scientists—and economists in particular—analyze the world using simple conceptual frameworks that they call "models."

The virtue of such models is that they make explicit the chain of cause and effect, and therefore render transparent the specific assumptions on which a particular prediction rests.

Good social science turns our unexamined intuitions into a map of causal arrows. Sometimes it shows how those intuitions lead to surprising, unanticipated results when extended to their logical conclusions.

Fully general frameworks, such as economists' beloved Arrow-Debreu model of general equilibrium, are so broad and encompassing that they are totally unhelpful for real-world explanation or prediction. Useful social-science models are invariably simplifications. They leave out many details to focus on the most relevant aspect of a specific context. Applied economists' mathematical models are the most explicit example of this. But, whether formalized or not, simplified narratives are social scientists' bread and butter.

Stylized historical analogies often play a similar role. For example, international-relations scholars use the famous meeting between Neville Chamberlain and Adolf Hitler in Munich in 1938 as a model of how appeasing a power bent on expansionism can be futile (or dangerous).

But, as inevitable as simplification is for explanation, it is also a trap. It is easy to get wedded to particular models and fail to recognize that changed circumstances require a different model. Like other humans, social scientists are prone to overconfidence in their preferred model of the day. They tend to exaggerate the support for the model and discount new evidence that contradicts it—a phenomenon known as "confirmation bias."

In a world of diverse and changing circumstances, social scientists can do real harm by applying the wrong model. Neoliberal economic policies, predicated on well-functioning markets, misfired in developing countries—just as planning models, presuming competent and capable bureaucrats, failed in an earlier era. The efficient-markets theory led policy makers astray by encouraging them to undertake excessive financial deregulation. It would be costly to apply the analogy of Munich in 1938 to a specific international conflict when the underlying situation is more reminiscent of Sarajevo in 1914.

So how should we choose among alternative simplifications of reality? Rigorous empirical tests may eventually settle questions such as whether the US economy today is suffering more from Keynesian lack of demand or from policy uncertainty. Yet often we need to make decisions in real time, without the benefit of decisive empirical evidence. My research on growth diagnostics (with Ricardo Hausmann, Andrés Velasco, and others) is an example of this style of work, showing how one can identify in a specific context the more binding among a multitude of growth constraints.[19] Unfortunately, economists and other social scientists get virtually no training in how to choose among alternative models. Neither is such an aptitude professionally rewarded. Developing new theories and empirical tests is regarded as science, while the exercise of good judgment is clearly a craft.

The philosopher Isaiah Berlin famously distinguished between two styles of thinking, which he identified with the hedgehog and the fox.[20] The hedgehog is captivated by a single big idea, which he applies unremittingly. The fox, by contrast, lacks a grand vision and holds many different views about the world—some of them even contradictory.

We can always anticipate the hedgehog's take on a problem—just as we can predict that market fundamentalists will always prescribe freer markets, regardless of the nature of the economic problem. Foxes carry competing, possibly incompatible theories in their heads. They are not attached to a particular ideology and find it easier to think contextually. In the terminology of Daniel Drezner, foxes are "thought leaders" while hedgehogs are the true public intellectuals.[21]

Scholars who are able to navigate from one explanatory framework to another as circumstances require are more likely to point us in the right direction. The world needs fewer hedgehogs and more foxes.

CHAPTER 7

Economists, Politics, and Ideas

F or people who work in the world of ideas, economists are oddly silent on the role of ideas in shaping behavior and social outcomes. They emphasize "interests" instead—the raw, selfish motive of advancing one's own standing in material, social, and political arenas. Yet without ideas—about how the world works, what objectives we should pursue, and which strategies are available to pursue our ends—the concept of self-interest is empty and useless. Identities, norms, values, worldviews, opportunities, and constraints are all shaped by ideas in the air—and not just those of economists!

Taking ideas seriously helps us solve many conundrums in social and political life. Why do elites block economic reform in some societies, for fear that it may undermine their political power, while championing it in others? Why did intellectuals and political parties on the left turn into cheerleaders for globalization, rendering them incapable of responding to the eventual backlash? What compelled America's white middle class to vote against its apparent economic self-interest in the 2016 presidential elections? Equally important, taking ideas seriously helps us escape the iron cage of vested interests as we move forward to reform our economics and politics.

Economics and Political Economy

There was a time when we economists steered clear of politics. We viewed our job as describing how market economies work, when they fail, and how well-designed policies can enhance efficiency. We analyzed trade-offs between competing objectives (say, equity versus efficiency) and prescribed policies that meet desired economic outcomes, including equity. It was up to politicians to take our advice or not, and up to bureaucrats to implement it.

Then some of us became more ambitious. Frustrated by the reality that much of our advice went unheeded (so many free-market solutions still waiting to be taken up!) we turned our analytical toolkit on the behavior of politicians and bureaucrats themselves. We began to examine political behavior using the same frameworks that we use for consumer and producer decisions in a market economy. Politicians became income-maximizing suppliers of policy favors; citizens became rent-seeking lobbies and special interests; and political systems became marketplaces in which votes and political influence are traded for economic benefits.

Thus was born the field of rational-choice political economy and a style of theorizing that many political scientists readily emulated. The apparent payoff was that we could now explain why politicians did so many things that apparently violated economic rationality. Indeed, there was no economic malfunction for which the two words *vested interests* could not account.

Why are so many industries closed off to real competition? Because politicians are in the pockets of the incumbents who reap the rents.[1] Why do governments erect barriers to international trade? Because the beneficiaries of trade protection are concentrated and politically influential, while consumers are diffuse and disorganized.[2] Why do political elites block reforms that would spur economic growth and development? Because growth and development would undermine their hold on political power.[3] Why are there financial crises? Because banks capture the policy-making process so that they can take excessive risks at the expense of the general public.[4] In the aftermath of the financial crisis, for example, many economists laid the blame on the power of big banks. It is because politicians are beholden to financial interests, they said, that the regulatory environment allowed those interests to reap huge rewards at great social expense.

The most widely held theory of politics is also the simplest: the powerful get what they want. Financial regulation is driven by the interests of banks, health policy by the interests of insurance companies, and tax policy by the interests of the rich. Those who can influence government the most—through their control of resources, information, access, or sheer threat of violence—eventually get their way.

It's the same globally. Foreign policy is determined, it is said, first and foremost by national interests—not affinities with other nations or concern for the global community. International agreements are impossible unless they are aligned with the interests of the United States and, increasingly, other rising major powers. In authoritarian regimes, policies are the direct expression of the interests of the ruler and his cronies.

This is a compelling narrative, one with which we can readily explain how politics so often generates perverse outcomes. Whether in democracies, dictatorships, or in the international arena, those outcomes reflect the ability of narrow, special interests to achieve results that harm the majority. In order to change the world, we need to understand it. And this mode of analysis seemed to transport us to a higher level of understanding of economic and political outcomes.

But there was a deep paradox in all of this. The more we claimed to be explaining, the less room was left for improving matters. If politicians' behavior is determined by the vested interests to which they are beholden, economists' advocacy of policy reforms is bound to fall on deaf ears. The more complete our social science, the more irrelevant our policy analysis.

It helps here to draw an analogy between human sciences and natural sciences, not to suggest that one is like the other but to clarify the differences. Consider the relationship between science and engineering. As scientists' understanding of the physical laws of nature grows more sophisticated, engineers can build better bridges and buildings. Improvements in natural science enhance, rather than impede, our ability to shape our physical environment.

The relationship between political economy and policy analysis is not at all like this. By making politicians' behavior an inherent part of the model—endogenizing it, in economists' jargon—political economy disempowers policy analysts. It is as if physicists came up with theories that not only explained natural phenomena but also determined which bridges and buildings engineers would build. There would then scarcely be any need for engineering schools.

If it seems to you that something is wrong with this, you are on to something. In reality, our contemporary frameworks of political economy are replete with unstated assumptions about the system of ideas underlying the operation of our societies and political systems. Make those assumptions explicit, and the decisive role of vested interests evaporates. Policy design, political leadership, and human agency come back to life.

The Primacy of Ideas

John Maynard Keynes once famously said that "even the most practical man of affairs is usually in the thrall of the ideas of some long-dead economist." He probably didn't put it nearly strongly enough. The ideas that have produced, for example, the unbridled globalization and financial excess of the last few decades have emanated from economists who are (for the most part) very much alive. Those who chalk up the global financial crisis of 2008–2009 to the power of big banks conveniently overlook the legitimizing role played by economists themselves. It was economists and their ideas that made it respectable for policy makers and regulators to believe that what is good for Wall Street is good for Main Street.

Interests are not fixed or predetermined. They are themselves shaped by ideas—beliefs about who we are, what we are trying to achieve, and how the world works. Our perceptions of self-interest are always filtered through the lens of ideas. In truth, we don't have "interests." We have *ideas* about what our interests are.

Consider a struggling firm that is trying to improve its competitive position. One strategy is to lay off some workers and outsource production to cheaper locations in Asia. Alternatively, the firm can invest in skills training and build a more productive workforce with greater loyalty and hence lower turnover costs. It can compete on price or on quality. The mere fact that the firm's owners are self-interested tells us little about which of these strategies will be followed. What ultimately determines the firm's choice is a whole series of subjective evaluations of the likelihood of different scenarios, alongside a calculation of their costs and benefits.

Similarly, imagine that you are a despotic ruler in a poor country. What is the best way to maintain your power and preempt domestic and foreign threats? Do you build a strong, export-oriented economy? Or do you turn inward and reward your military friends and other cronies, at the expense of almost everyone else? Authoritarian rulers in East Asia embraced the first strategy; their counterparts in the Middle

East opted for the second. They had different conceptions of where their interests lie.

Or consider China's role in the global economy. As the People's Republic becomes a major power, its leaders will have to decide what kind of international system they want. Perhaps they will choose to build on and strengthen the existing multilateral regime, which has served them well in the past. But perhaps they will prefer bilateral, ad hoc relations that allow them to extract greater advantage in their transactions with individual countries. We cannot predict the shape that the world economy will take just from observing that China and its interests will loom larger.

We could multiply such examples endlessly. Are German governments' domestic political fortunes best served by stuffing austerity down Greece's throat, at the cost of another debt restructuring down the line, or by easing up on its conditions, which might give Greece a chance to grow out of its debt burden? Are US interests at the World Bank best served by directly nominating an American as president or by cooperating with other countries to select the most suitable candidate, American or not?

The fact that we debate such questions passionately suggests that we all have varying conceptions of where self-interest lies. Our interests are in fact hostage to our ideas.

So, where do those ideas come from? Policy makers, like all of us, are slaves to fashion. Their perspectives on what is feasible and desirable are shaped by the zeitgeist, the "ideas in the air." This means that economists and other thought leaders can exert much influence—for good or ill. Economists love theories that place organized special interests at the root of all political evil. In the real world, they cannot wriggle so easily out of responsibility for the bad ideas that they have so often spawned. With influence comes accountability.

Making the Role of Ideas Explicit

Any political-economy analysis in which organized interests do not figure prominently is likely to remain vacuous and incomplete. But it does not follow from this that interests are the ultimate determinant of political outcomes. There is in fact no well-defined mapping from interests to outcomes. This mapping depends on many unstated assumptions about the *ideas* that political actors have about: (1) their objectives, (2) how the world works, and (3) the set of tools they have at their disposal to further their interests. Importantly, these ideas are subject to both manipulation and innovation, making them part of the political game. There is, in fact, a useful analogy between inventive activity in technology, which economists now routinely make endogenous in their models, and investment in persuasion and policy innovation in the political arena. Once their fluid nature is recognized, vested interests become much less determining and the space of possible outcomes much wider.

While hidden assumptions play a role in all economic models, the failure to recognize the role of ideas in shaping interests (and their pursuit) has especially serious implications in political economy. Taking ideas into account allows us to provide a more convincing account of both stasis and change in political-economic life. It provides a way of bridging the sharp divide between policy analysis (what should be done) with political economy (what actually happens). It also yields an explanation for many mysteries in the real world: Why do people support policies that do not appear to be in their "interest"? Why do many reforms turn out to benefit the elites who previously blocked them? Why do apparently similar groups define their interests so differently? Why do vested interests that once appeared rock solid sometimes suddenly dissipate?

Let's take a look at the ways in which ideas make their way, more often than not implicitly, into established ways of thinking about political economy.

Every rational-choice model is built on the purposive behavior of individual decision makers. Typically, behavior is determined by assuming individuals solve what economists would call a well-defined optimization problem. At least three components must be specified in such an optimization exercise: an objective function (like a consumer utility function), a set of constraints (such as a budget constraint), and a set of choice variables (like consumption levels). Political-economy models in the rational-choice mold translate this framework into the political arena. Political agents—voters, lobbies, elites, congressmen—are represented as rational individuals who solve explicit optimization problems. This means they maximize a utility function defined over consumption, rents, or political benefits; they operate within constraints imposed by the rules of the game, both economic and political; and they choose a set of actions—which in various models may include votes, political contributions, rebellion, and suppression—that maximize their objection function given the constraints.

For example, and in simpler terms, business lobbies decide how much they should spend in political contributions in return for tariff protection, taking into account that politicians value societal welfare alongside the contributions.[5] Or a dictator decides whether to develop his economy so as to maximize his intertemporal stream of rents, taking into account that his decision affects both economic and political outcomes, including his longevity in power.[6]

Ideas enter this framework in several distinct ways that are rarely recognized. In fact, each of the three components of the optimization problem—preferences, constraints, and choice variables—rely on an implicit set of ideas.

1. *Preferences* are formed by ideas about who we are and what objectives we should pursue;

2. *Constraints* are shaped by our ideas of how the world works;

3. *Choice variables* are determined by ideas about what tools we have at our disposal.

I will discuss each of these in turn below and in the next chapter, providing examples from our present political-economic predicament to illustrate them. I emphasize that I am not contesting rationality or the utility of the basic optimizing framework in the political arena. My goal is to explore the role of ideas in shaping how interests are defined and pursued, discuss economists' contributions—both good and bad—and in turn open up space for new, more useful ideas.

Preferences: Who Are We?

Self-interest presumes the idea of a "self"—that is, a conception of who I am and what my purpose is. In many economic applications, the objectives we pursue are clear. It is reasonable to assume households want to maximize their consumer surplus and producers their profits, although these assumptions are not always entirely uncontroversial. In the political sphere, the choice of what is to be maximized is much less evident: depending on context, honor, glory, reputation, respect, income, power, durability in office, and "good of the country" are all plausible. As Jon Elster has written in a critique of rational political-economy frameworks attempting to explain historical political developments, the nobility in seventeenth-century France may have been interested in honor and glory as much as in material benefits.[7] Much human behavior is driven by abstract ideals, sacred values, or conceptions of loyalty that cannot be reduced to economic ends. Studies by anthropologists and psychologists suggest "humans will kill and die not only to protect their own lives or defend kin and kith, but for an idea—the moral conception they form of themselves, of 'who we are'"[8]—a point that should not be controversial in an age of suicide bombings.

How we evaluate different social states and judge whether they advance our "interests" depends crucially on how we define ourselves. We might view ourselves as a member of a social class ("middle class"), ethnic group ("white majority"), religion ("evangelical"), nation ("global citizen"), demographic cohort ("baby boomer"), profession ("educator"), or a myriad of other possible identities. As Amartya Sen has suggested, we might even combine all these identities in varying degrees.[9]

In political science, a well-established line of research has long held that interests of political actors are socially constructed rather than determined by well-defined material facts. In this "constructivist" tradition, conceptions of interests arise endogenously from norms, ideologies, and causal beliefs.[10] Interests, in fact, are "one form of idea."[11] In international law, a parallel discussion pits "legal realists," who argue that behavior among states is determined exclusively or largely by national interests, against scholars who see a significant role for norms of justice or law.[12]

Economists have rarely ventured as far as some of these other disciplines above in acknowledging the nuances of self-interest and identity, but the role of ideas in determining preferences has crept into various strands of research in economics. For example, the partisan-politics literature in macroeconomics endows political parties with explicit ideologies, typically represented as different preference weights on inflation versus unemployment.[13] These differences in preferences are typically imposed from outside the model, with little explanation. More recently there has been some work, both at the macro and micro levels, that looks at how ideologies are shaped and develop. These studies examine the formation of political preferences through exposure to societal outcomes, media, or early childhood experiences.[14]

The work of George Akerlof and Rachel Kranton on the economics of identity is particularly relevant here.[15] Akerlof and Kranton consider models where individuals associate themselves with specific social categories and their desired behavior derives from the attributes of those categories. Workers, for example, may acquire identities that moderate the incentive compatibility constraint vis-à-vis their employers, leading them to behave in greater conformity with the objectives of their firms. In turn, employers may seek to alter such identities to enhance workplace performance. Such models could explain a range of "anomalous" political action, including voting against immediate material interests. But the possible application of this approach to political phenomena has not yet received much attention.

In each of these frameworks, ideas play a crucial role. Instead of remaining implicit or a sideshow, they determine preferences directly, and therefore shape patterns of political behavior. This perspective requires social scientists to engage with the questions of where ideas come from and how they are spread and internalized.

Interests are shaped by identity, and identities are shaped in turn by our social and political interactions. Successful political leaders know that identities can be molded for political ends. Consider how the wealthy in the United States have been spared a popular revolt against inequality despite the vast increase in income concentration in recent decades.

How the Rich Rule

It is hardly news that the rich have more political power than the poor, even in democratic countries where everyone gets a single vote in elections. But two political scientists, Martin Gilens and Benjamin Page, have recently produced some stark findings for the United States that have dramatic implications for the functioning of democracy—in the United States and elsewhere.[16] The authors' research builds on prior work by Gilens, who painstakingly collected public-opinion polls on nearly two thousand policy questions from 1981 to 2002. The pair then examined whether America's federal government adopted the policy in question within four years of the survey, and tracked how closely the outcome matched the preferences of voters at different points of the income distribution.

When viewed in isolation, the preferences of the "average" voter— that is, a voter in the middle of the income distribution—seem to have a strongly positive influence on the government's ultimate response. A policy that the average voter would like is significantly more likely to be enacted. But, as Gilens and Page note, this gives a misleadingly upbeat impression of the representativeness of government decisions. The preferences of the average voter and of economic elites are not very different on most policy matters. For example, both groups of voters would like to see a strong national defense and a healthy economy. A better test would be to examine what the government does when the two groups have divergent views.

To carry out that test, Gilens and Page ran a horse race between the preferences of average voters and those of economic elites—defined as individuals at the top tenth percentile of the income distribution—to see which voters exert greater influence. They found that the effect of the average voter drops to insignificant levels, while that of economic elites remains substantial.

The implication is clear: when the elites' interests differ from those of the rest of society, it is their views that count—almost exclusively. (As Gilens and Page explain, we should think of the preferences of the top 10 percent as a proxy for the views of the truly wealthy, say, the top 1 percent—the genuine elite.) Gilens and Page report similar results for organized interest groups, which wield a powerful influence on policy formation. As they point out, "it makes very little difference what the general public thinks" once interest-group alignments and the preferences of affluent Americans are taken into account.

These disheartening results raise an important question: How do politicians who are unresponsive to the preferences of the vast majority of their constituents get elected and, more importantly, reelected, while doing the bidding mostly of the wealthiest individuals?

Part of the explanation may be that most voters have a poor understanding of how the political system works and how it is tilted in favor of the economic elite. As Gilens and Page emphasize, their evidence does not imply that government policy makes the average citizen worse off. Ordinary citizens often do get what they want, by virtue of the fact that their preferences frequently are similar to those of the elite. This correlation of the two groups' preferences may make it difficult for voters to discern politicians' bias.

But another, more pernicious, part of the answer may lie in the strategies to which political leaders resort in order to get elected. A politician who represents the interests primarily of economic elites must find other means of appealing to the masses. Such alternatives are provided by the politics of nationalism, sectarianism, and identity—a politics based on cultural values and symbolism rather than bread-and-butter interests. When politics is waged on these grounds, elections are won by those who are most successful at "priming" our latent cultural and psychological markers, not those who best represent our economic interests.

Karl Marx famously said that religion is "the opium of the people." What he meant is that religious sentiment could obscure the material deprivations that workers and other exploited people experience in their daily lives. In much the same way, the rise of the religious right and, with it, culture wars over "family values" and other highly polarizing issues (for example, immigration) have served to insulate American politics from the sharp rise in economic inequality since the late 1970s. Right-wing media outlets and think tanks have spun tales that led voters with stagnating incomes to attribute their hardship to minorities—African Americans, immigrants, women on welfare—that the government has supposedly favored over them.[17] As a result, conservatives have been able to retain power despite their pursuit of economic and social policies that are inimical to the interests of the middle and lower classes.

As I discussed in chapter 4 in the context of developing nations, identity politics is malignant because it tends to draw boundaries around a privileged in-group and requires the exclusion of outsiders—those of other countries, values, religions, or ethnicities. This can be seen most clearly in illiberal democracies such as Russia, Turkey, and Hungary. In order to solidify their electoral base, leaders in these countries appeal heavily to national, cultural, and religious symbols. In doing so, they typically inflame passions against religious and ethnic minorities. For regimes that represent economic elites (and are often corrupt to the core), it is a ploy that pays off handsomely at the polls.

Widening inequality in the world's advanced and developing countries thus inflicts two blows against democratic politics. Not only does it lead to greater disenfranchisement of the middle and lower classes but it also fosters among the elite a poisonous politics of sectarianism.

Constraints: Models of How the World Works

Let's turn next to the second set of ideas that enter the "optimization problem" outlined at the beginning of this chapter: ideas about how the world works. Investors, consumers, workers, and policy makers all operate under certain working assumptions about causal relationships around them. Their worldviews shape their perception of the consequences of their and others' actions in both economic and political domains. These ideas may fall on either side of some of the biggest controversies in the history of economic thought: Does the economy work better under laissez-faire or planning? Are economic growth and development more rapid under free trade or under protection? Does macroeconomic stability require Keynesian countercyclical policies or Hayekian nonintervention? Each of these positions presumes a particular model of how the economy works and therefore has different implications for political behavior. In recent decades, a succession of economic ideas (think of Keynesianism, monetarism, rational expectations, and the "Washington consensus") have served to change both elites' and nonelites' understanding of "economic reality" and thereby altered the political equilibrium.

A rent-extracting autocrat is likely to tax his subjects to the hilt when he believes they have little choice but to pay up; the same autocrat will be more restrained when he believes subjects can evade the tax or mount an effective opposition. Which of these two models is the correct one? "Elasticity pessimism," the belief that economic activities tend to be unresponsive to prices, lay behind the widespread consensus in support of the *dirigiste* economic development policies of the 1950s and 1960s. Pratap Mehta and Michael Walton describe the Nehruvian cognitive map that shaped India's development path in the decades following independence: the need for a big investment push, suspicions over the private sector, emphasis on the leading role of capital goods, and export pessimism (the fear that expansion of exports will run against serious limits) all derived from ideas about how a market system worked (or failed to do so).[18] As research demonstrated that the poor were as responsive to price incentives as the rich, policies in the developing world began to move in a more market-oriented direction.[19]

Economics is all about sharpening our ideas about the "right model" in the relevant context, a point on which I will elaborate below. Yet actors in our political-economy frameworks live in worlds where these questions have been effectively resolved. They believe that they know how the world works, if not precisely, at least probabilistically. Even if they disagreed for a time, adherents of this view argue, agents would eventually reach agreement on the "right model" as events and reactions to policy choices unfold. In practice, however, people often downplay evidence that seems inconsistent with their model of the world. Anomalous outcomes are dismissed as a fluke or as the result of insufficiently vigorous application of their preferred policy. Individuals with different prior beliefs may draw sharply different conclusions from the same piece of news. Observing a sudden rise in unemployment, a Keynesian might strengthen his belief that monetary policy is too tight, while a monetarist might infer monetary policy is even looser than he thought and is discouraging employment creation by generating expectations of future inflation.[20] Furthermore, even if all actors are rational and perfectly calculating, beliefs about the true model need not converge when there is sufficient variability in the external environment.[21]

A more realistic representation may be that cognitive and other limitations force political agents to live in a world of deep uncertainty with respect to their understanding of causal relationships.[22] Their view of the world could be wrong and could remain so even in the face of new evidence if that evidence is just used to confirm past beliefs. Conversely, new information may present realities previously not considered. For instance, voters may discover that an office holder has a long criminal track record, a possibility that may not have entered their calculus earlier. An interesting new empirical literature has begun to document how the provision of such information can influence voters' behavior.[23]

Consider the experience of the global economic and financial crisis in recent years and the extent to which it has altered beliefs. Many observers, such as Simon Johnson and James Kwak, have argued that the policies that produced the crisis were the result of powerful banking and financial interests getting their way, which seems like a straight-forward application of the theory of special interests.[24] Still, without the wave of ideas "in the air" that favored financial liberalization and self-regulation and emphasized the impossibility (or undesirability) of government regulation, these vested interests would not have got-ten nearly as much traction as they did. After all, powerful interests rarely get their way in a democracy by nakedly arguing for their own self-interest. Instead, they seek legitimacy for their arguments by say-ing these policies are in the public interest. The argument in favor of financial deregulation was not that it was good for Wall Street but that it was good for Main Street.

Other observers have argued that the financial crisis was a result of excessive government intervention to support housing markets, especially for lower-income borrowers. These arguments were also grounded on certain ideas—about the social value of homeowner-ship and the inattentiveness of the financial sector to those with lower incomes. Charles Calomiris and Stephen Haber suggest that it was the alliance between banking interests and community groups, the lat-ter seeking to increase home ownership among low-income groups, which played the critical role.[25] Again, ideas apparently shaped these groups' and politicians' views of how the world works—and therefore their interest in acting in ways that precipitated the crisis. Had commu-nity groups been more attentive to the problems of indebtedness, they may have been less interested in expanding home ownership among the poor. Finally, although all parties have observed the same Great Recession taking place, relatively few have altered their fundamental beliefs about whether the financial sector is over- or underregulated as a result.

A Class of Its Own

The very rich, F. Scott Fitzgerald famously wrote, "are different from you and me." Their wealth makes them "cynical where we are trustful," and makes them think "they are better than we are." If these words ring true today, perhaps it is because when they were written, in 1926, inequality in the United States had reached heights comparable to today.

We have seen before how the rich and the political elite can manipulate group identities to shape nonelites' political preferences. But where do the rich get their ideas about what is in their own best interest?

When inequality in the advanced countries was more moderate, the gap between the super-rich and the rest of society seemed less colossal—not just in terms of income and wealth but also in terms of attachments and social purpose. The rich had more money, of course, but they somehow still seemed part of the same society as the poor, recognizing that geography and citizenship made them share a common fate. Their mental map of how the world works made them take a broader interest in society.

Mark Mizruchi has shown how the American corporate elite in the postwar era had "an ethic of civic responsibility and enlightened self-interest."[26] They cooperated with trade unions and favored a strong government role in regulating and stabilizing markets. They understood the need for taxes to pay for important public goods such as the interstate highway and safety nets for the poor and elderly. Business elites were not any less politically powerful back then. But they used their influence to advance an agenda that was broadly in the national interest.

By contrast, today's super-rich are "moaning moguls," to use James Surowiecki's evocative term.[27] Exhibit A for Surowiecki is Stephen Schwarzman, the chairman and CEO of the private equity firm the Blackstone Group, whose wealth exceeds $10 billion. Schwarzman acts as if "he's beset by a meddlesome, tax-happy government and a whiny, envious populace." He has suggested that "it might be good to raise income taxes on the poor so they had 'skin in the game,' and that proposals to repeal the carried-interest tax loophole—from which he personally benefits—were akin to the German invasion of Poland." Other examples from Surowiecki, "the venture capitalist Tom Perkins and Kenneth Langone, the cofounder of Home Depot, both compared populist attacks on the wealthy to the Nazis' attacks on the Jews."

Surowiecki thinks that the change in attitudes has much to do with globalization. Large American corporations and banks now roam the globe freely, and are no longer so dependent on the US consumer. Their ideas about how the world works has changed radically. The health of the American middle class is of little interest to them these days. Moreover, Surowiecki argues, socialism has gone by the wayside, and there is no need to coopt the working class anymore.

Yet if corporate moguls think that they no longer need to rely on their national governments, they are making a huge mistake. The reality is that the stability and openness of the markets that produce their wealth have never depended more on government action. In periods of relative calm, governments' role in writing and upholding the rules by which markets function can become obscured. It may seem as if markets are on autopilot, with governments an inconvenience that is best avoided.

But when economic storm clouds gather on the horizon, everyone seeks shelter under their home government's cover. It is then that the ties that bind large corporations to their native soil are fully revealed. Here we can repeat Mervyn King's apt phrase in the context of finance: "global banks are global in life, but national in death."

Consider how the US government stepped in to ensure financial and economic stability during the global financial crisis of 2008–2009. If the government had not bailed out large banks, the insurance giant AIG, and the auto industry, and if the Federal Reserve had not flooded the economy with liquidity, the wealth of the super-rich would have taken a severe blow. Many argued that the government should have focused on rescuing homeowners. The government chose to support the banks instead—a policy from which the financial elite benefited the most.

Even in normal times, the super-rich depend on government support and action. It is largely the government that has financed the fundamental research that produced the information-technology revolution and the firms (such as Apple and Microsoft) that it has spawned. It is the government that enacts and enforces the copyright, patent, and trademark laws that protect intellectual property rights, guaranteeing successful innovators a steady stream of monopoly profits. It is the government that subsidizes the higher-education institutions that train the skilled work force. It is the government that negotiates trade agreements with other countries to ensure that domestic firms gain access to foreign markets.

If the super-rich believe that they are no longer part of society and have little need of government, it is not because this belief corresponds to objective reality. It is because the prevailing story line of our time portrays markets as self-standing entities that run on their own fuel.

This is a narrative that afflicts all segments of society, the middle class no less than the rich.

There is no reason to expect that the super-rich will act less selfishly than any other group. But it is not so much their self-interest that stands in the way of greater equality and social inclusion. The more significant roadblock is the missing recognition that markets cannot produce prosperity for long—for anyone—unless they are backed by healthy societies and good governance.

Economists once again have a big role to play here. When they emphasize market efficiency too much, at the expense of market failures, they feed and reinforce these incomplete views. Contrary to popular perception, economics is not a paean to free markets: it is a smorgasbord of models of how the world works, some calling for more government, others for less. Economists have a lot to say about which of these models may be more relevant in a particular context. Yet economists often fail to make a productive contribution to public debates for reasons discussed in the previous chapter.

Policy Choices: What Tools Do We Have at Our Disposal?

We have seen how ideas about who we are and how the world works shape perceived interests—of elites as much as ordinary people—and how economics contributes, for good or ill. I turn in the next chapter finally to the third sense in which ideas mold interests, by expanding our policy options and strategies.

Much of politics is about strategy: setting the agenda, making alliances, issuing promises (or threats), expanding or restricting the menu of options, and building or spending political capital. Regardless of whether they aim to enrich themselves or further a broader set of interests, political actors must continually ask: "What can be done?" As social scientists, our inclination is to remain grounded in our current reality. But the closer we stick to it, the more likely that we fail to imagine alternative arrangements. In the language of game theory, we restrict the strategy space in arbitrary ways; we overstructure the political game by limiting the policy choices on the menu. Yet new ideas about what can be done—innovative policies—can unlock what otherwise might seem like the iron grip of vested interests. [28]

The formal parallelism between behavior in the political arena and consumer behavior in the marketplace is least useful here. Consumers in a market have well-defined choices to make: how much to consume of each available good, given prices and their budget constraint. The standard utility maximization problem does not do great injustice to their strategy space. By contrast, political agents design their own strategy space. The available instruments are up for grabs and limited only by their political imagination.

CHAPTER 8

Economics as Policy Innovation

We economists care a lot about efficiency. So, when we see politicians make patently inefficient policy choices, we are puzzled. How do we explain the mystery? We take refuge, once again, in vested interests. Political systems are stuck in suboptimal situations, we argue, because powerful special interests block any progress toward better outcomes.

This line of argument is fine as far as it goes, but it also produces a deeply depressing implication. Short of war, revolution, or other similar cataclysms that dislodge powerful interests, it leaves us with very little leeway to address our major problems—inequality, exclusion, low growth.

Luckily, this is a very incomplete picture of politics. It leaves out the role of ideas as policy innovation. As we shall see in this chapter, vested interests can be overcome with new policy ideas. Such ideas can help the existing order's challengers sidestep political constraints. Sometimes these ideas are faulty, or advance the cause of groups that are narrowly self-interested. At other times, they can really move society forward.

The Political Economy of Inefficiency

Political-economy frameworks that "explain" policy inefficiency rest on a number of building blocks: (1) policy preferences of actors are determined by their interests; (2) the balance of political power determines whose interests matter (more); and (3) prevailing political institutions (or "rules of the game") determine the specific political equilibrium that arises.

These three postulates can explain redistribution from less powerful to more powerful groups; he who controls the levers of power also controls who gets what. But they do not explain inefficiency per se. Inefficiency implies we could increase the incomes of the powerless without reducing the incomes of the powerful—or, for that matter, increase the incomes of both. If all elites want is to extract income from society and are powerful enough to get their way, why do they have to do it by generating inefficiency?

To generate inefficiency, we need to add to our framework one or both of two additional features, each of which restricts the policy options available to the political elite: (4) lump-sum transfers or efficient redistributive mechanisms are unavailable; and (5) political power itself requires stasis, such that outcomes that move the economy closer to the efficiency frontier may reduce the power of elites.

The first of these assumptions rules out myriads of compensatory policies that can move the equilibrium from an inefficient to an efficient one. For example, most forms of economic liberalization, such as removing a tax or an import tariff, do not benefit all groups, unless accompanied by compensation. Ruling out compensation of politically powerful groups that lose out from liberalization is an easy way to generate inefficient outcomes. Accordingly, the typical practice in the literature on the political economy of trade policy is to assume away not only lump-sum transfers but also producer subsidies, so as to leave the door open for policies that restrict trade (which are in fact third-best for redistributive purposes).[1] Similarly, to explain why productivity-enhancing privatizations of state-owned enterprises do not take place, we might argue that powerful insiders (workers, managers) block the reform when there is no possibility to compensate them for losses they would experience in a privatized firm. Such restrictions are often rationalized by appealing to the inability to commit to compensation, an issue I will return to in the next chapter when I discuss compensation for trade agreements in the United States.

The other argument (feature 5 above) is that political elites avoid efficient policies for fear that such policies may undercut their political power and hence their ability to determine future policies. Under this scenario, the only feasible move to the efficient frontier involves traveling to a point on it such that the elites end up worse off. This type of argument has been invoked in the work of Daron Acemoglu and James Robinson, to explain, for example, why many states have blocked policies that would foster industrialization and economic growth during the nineteenth century in Europe.[2] Because economic growth uproots people from their traditional rural base and facilitates collective political action, it can destabilize entrenched elites. Forward-looking elites will prefer to ensure their power is not challenged, even if that means more inefficiency and less growth.

A different mechanism that produces a similar result is the dynamic inconsistency of compensation policies. In my model with Raquel Fernandez, reform is impeded by individual-specific uncertainty combined with the pattern of information revelation over time when reform is implemented.[3] Beneficiaries of today's inefficient policies cannot be made to accept a reform-now-and-compensation-later package, because they know reform will reveal the identity of a large group of winners and shift future political power to those winners. After the reform, the beneficiaries will have no need (or incentive) to carry out their promise of compensation.

The claim that elites block enhanced economic opportunities so that they can maintain their own power makes sense in many circumstances. But it too implies an unreasonable restriction on feasible strategies. In particular, it denies elites the imagination to devise policy arrangements that would allow them to take advantage of enhanced economic opportunities *without* losing power. It's not clear why we should rule out such strategies in general. Policy innovations and new political ideas can expand the strategy space in the desired direction.

I use the term *innovation* deliberately, as there is an apt analogy here with technological innovation. Just as we think of technological ideas as those that relax resource constraints, we can think of political ideas as those that relax political constraints, enabling those in power to make themselves (and possibly the rest of society) better off without necessarily undermining their political power. Economists recognize the importance of technological innovation and have made it the centerpiece of their models of long-term growth. In political-economy models, by contrast, the working assumption is that there is no room for discovery. Many political innovations are likely to remain ephemeral, inconsequential, or soon forgotten. But some, as with general-purpose technology, may prove substantial and durable. Think of political parties, independence of judiciary, or indeed democracy.

Technological change need not make everyone better off. Similarly, policy innovation could leave the nonelites worse off. Some ideas could be bad from the standpoint of society at large and yet gain currency: imagine elites successfully persuading nonelites that they should work harder in this life so they can have redemption in the next, or (closer to home) that an extremely low rate of capital taxation actually benefits them.

Practical economists and policy makers do spend considerable effort generating new policy ideas that seek, not always successfully, to work around political constraints. Perhaps the most telling examples of political innovation come from the real world, not the textbooks. Let's look at some historical and contemporary examples.

Economic Reform without Losing Power

Let's go back to the puzzle of why rulers often hold their economies back. If they fear losing their hold on power, they can perhaps devise economic development strategies that in fact strengthen, rather than weaken, them. Acemoglu and Robinson provide several examples. Consider why the Japanese elite decided to spur industrialization and economic development after the Meiji restoration circa 1868. Acemoglu and Robinson note that "the drive for modernization in Japan took a special form, strengthening the centralized government and increasing the entrenchment of bureaucratic elites." In other words, they developed an economic strategy that minimized the probability of their replacement while still fostering industrialization. This is similar to what happened in Britain and Germany where "the nonindustrial elites maintained their political power despite the process of industrialization." In Britain, "by adopting a strategy of gradual concessions, [elites] were able to control the political equilibrium and maintain power for at least a century following the onset of the political impact of industrialization . . . [and] the long history of Britain as a trading nation and mercantile power meant that many aristocrats had relatively diversified wealth . . ." In Germany, "the Junkers forged the coalition of 'Iron and Rye' with the rising industrial class to secure their economic interests."[4]

What stands out in these instances is the purposive strategy pursued by elites to mitigate their concern over loss of power as a side effect of economic change. State-directed industrialization, gradual concessions to the rising industrial classes, diversification into commerce and industry, alliance with industrial interests, and similar choices ensured elites could benefit from industrialization while staying on top of the political ladder. The question becomes in turn: Why were such strategies not used elsewhere too? Was it a lack of strategic ideas, or were there more fundamental, structural reasons? Whatever the answer to this broader question, these examples highlight the role of—and space for—policy innovation in relaxing political constraints that might have otherwise appeared irremovable.

Dual-Track Reform in China

During the 1970s, China was a centrally planned economy in which administered prices were a mechanism of generating rents and transfers to groups favored by the Communist regime. Price liberalization and the removal of obligatory grain deliveries to the state would generate significant efficiency gains in the countryside, where the bulk of the population lived. But it would come at the expense of depriving the state of its tax base, and urban workers of their cheap rations of food. By the standards of basic political-economy frameworks, these strong redistributive consequences provide an adequate explanation of why efficiency-enhancing reforms were resisted by the Chinese leadership.

But the Chinese government was able to devise a shortcut. Starting in the late 1970s, it made use of policy innovations such as two-track pricing and special economic zones that effectively delinked market-oriented incentives from their usual distributive implications. Consider, for example, how agriculture was reformed. Instead of abolishing the planned grain deliveries at fixed prices, the state simply grafted a market system on top of the centralized allocation system. Once the planned deliveries were made at state-set prices, farmers were free to sell additional amounts at any price the market would bear. As Lawrence Lau, Yingyi Qian, and Gerard Roland show, this system delivers allocative efficiency under fairly nonrestrictive conditions.[5] But from a political-economy perspective, the main virtue of the dual-track approach was that it shielded the prevailing stream of rents from the effects of the reform. The state did not lose its revenue, and urban workers were not denied their cheap food rations.

China's special economic zones functioned similarly. Rather than liberalize its trade regime in the standard way, which would have decimated the country's inefficient state enterprises, China allowed firms in special economic zones to operate under near-free-trade rules while maintaining trade restrictions elsewhere until the late 1990s. This enabled China to insert itself in the world economy while protecting employment and rents in the state sector. The Chinese Communist Party was strengthened and enriched, rather than weakened, as a result.

Democratization in South Africa

The black majority demanding democracy from the minority apartheid regime in South Africa faced a classic political-economy problem. Both sides understood that once the African National Congress (ANC) obtained power, it would come under strong pressure from the black majority it represented to expropriate (or at least severely tax) the white elite. For the latter to accede to political reform, it had to have credible guarantees against expropriation. In view of the international sanctions and the economic decline they faced, the elites would have been better off under democracy—but only provided that moderate future taxation could be assured. In the absence of such guarantees, it remained in the elites' interest to keep suppressing the black majority even at substantial economic cost to themselves and the country.

Nelson Mandela was keenly aware of the problem: "Especially in the first few years of the democratic government," he said in 1991, "we may have to do something to show that the system has got an inbuilt mechanism which makes it impossible for one group to suppress the other."[6] In the run-up to the democratic transition of 1994, South Africa's federal institutions were specifically designed to prevent the expropriation of the rich white minority by the poor black majority. Two key provisions were critical. First, critical redistributive services were left in the hands of provincial authorities. Second, borders ensured at least one important province (Western Cape) would remain in the hands of the white minority. Robert Inman and Daniel Rubinfeld argue these two arrangements together created a "hostage game" in which the incentives of a black national government to tax the white elites were moderated by the implicit threat of the local authorities in the Western Cape to respond by reducing service provision to the blacks in their province.[7] Creative manipulation of the rules enabled both a political transition and a movement closer to the efficiency frontier—at least for some period of time.

Other Examples

One can multiply these examples. During the 1980s and 1990s, reformist technocrats in Latin America overcame opposition from powerful insider groups by packaging liberalization and privatization (with strong redistributive effects) along with disinflation programs perceived by most—elites included—as inevitable and necessary.[8] In the United States, Trade Adjustment Assistance and other measures that operate as social insurance and compensation are the usual sweeteners offered to labor groups to buy their support for international trade agreements.[9] (However, this bargain has eroded over time, as I discuss in the next chapter.) The US Congress allowed the auctioning of radio frequencies only when political strings were devised—limiting the auctions to commercial wireless services and granting special rights to specific groups (women, minorities, small businesses)—to ensure that Congressional members would derive specific advantages from the move. Wayne Leighton and Edward López write: "in the end, everyone with a decision-making role in Congress got something, either more revenues or more political oversight."[10]

Such strategies represent policy innovations that overcome political constraints, which might have appeared insurmountable at the outset. They enable the capture of efficiency gains in ways that conserve the power of insiders and elites and protect their rents. Sometimes they enable radical political change, as in the South African case. At other times, they are designed to preclude political change, as in China. And even though I have focused on large-scale policy innovations that changed the course of nations, one can easily come up with a long list of others that are less revolutionary: the income tax, old-age pensions, the most-favored-nation principle in international trade, bank deposit insurance, work requirements for welfare recipients, conditional cash transfers, central bank independence, and marketable pollution trading. What these all have in common is that they unblock resistance to change to allow society to move closer to the efficient frontier.

In cases like these, does greater efficiency always justify helping elites?

Policy Ideas for Dictators?

It might seem obvious that economists should lend their expertise to help develop policy ideas for political leaders. Working even with some of the authoritarian leaders in the developing world, the ideas of economics can greatly expand the range of possibilities with which those in power develop their countries. This can greatly benefit the populations of these countries where there otherwise could have been little improvement at all. But what if these leaders are in charge of truly odious regimes?

Some years ago, a Harvard colleague wrote to me that Saif al-Islam el-Qaddafi, a son of Libya's then-ruler, would be in town and wanted to meet me. He is an interesting fellow, my colleague said, with a doctorate from the London School of Economics and Political Science (LSE); I would enjoy talking to him, and I might be able to help his thinking on economic matters.

The meeting, as it turned out, was a letdown. I was first briefed by a former Monitor Company employee, who gently intimated that I should not expect too much. Saif himself held photocopies of pages from one of my books on which he had scribbled notes. He asked me several questions—about the role of international NGOs, as I recall—that seemed fairly distant from my areas of expertise. I don't imagine he was much impressed by me; nor was I much taken by him. As the meeting ended, Saif invited me to Libya and I said—more out of politeness than anything else—that I would be happy to come.

Saif never followed up; nor did I (in the intervening years, Qaddafi's regime was overthrown and Said himself was jailed). But if a real invitation had come, would I have traveled to Libya, spent time with him, and possibly met his father and his cronies? Would I have been tempted by arguments such as, "We are trying to develop our economy, and you can really help us with your knowledge"? In other words, would I have followed in the footsteps of several of my Harvard colleagues who traveled to Libya to exchange views with and advise its dictator—and were paid for their services?

These scholars have been pilloried in the media in recent weeks for supposedly having cozied up to Qaddafi. Sir Howard Davies chose to resign as director of the LSE, which awarded Saif his doctorate (which some allege was plagiarized) and took money for the school from the Libyan regime.

There is a strong sentiment that academics and institutions that collaborated with such an odious regime—often with the encouragement of their governments, no doubt—suffered a grave lapse of judgment. But it is much easier to reach such judgments with hindsight. Were the moral overtones of dealing with the Qaddafis so obvious before the Arab revolutions spread to Libya? Or to pose the question more broadly, is it so clear that policy advisers should always steer clear of dictatorial regimes?

Universities all over the world are falling over each other trying to deepen their engagement with China. Most academics would jump at the chance to have a meeting with China's president Xi Jinping. I haven't heard much criticism of such contacts, which tend to be viewed as normal and unproblematic. And yet few would deny that China's is a repressive regime that deals with its opponents harshly. Memories of Tiananmen are not that distant, and the Chinese regime has, if anything, hardened in recent years. Who is to say how the Chinese leadership would respond to a future pro-democracy uprising that threatened to undermine the regime?

Or what about a country like Ethiopia? I have had intensive economic-policy discussions with the late Prime Minister Meles Zenawi in Addis Ababa. I must confess to having enjoyed these talks more than most meetings I have in Washington, DC, and other democratic capitals. I had no illusions about Meles's commitment to democracy—or lack thereof. But I also believed that he is trying to develop his economy, and I offered policy advice because I believed it may benefit ordinary Ethiopians.

The conundrum that advisers to authoritarian regimes face is akin to a long-standing problem in moral philosophy known as the dilemma of "dirty hands." A terrorist is holding several people hostage, and he asks you to deliver water and food to them. You may choose the moral high ground and say, "I will never deal with a terrorist." But you will have passed up an opportunity to assist the hostages. Most moral philosophers would say that helping the hostages is the right thing to do in this instance, even if doing so also helps the terrorist.

But choosing an action for the greater good does not absolve us from moral culpability. Our hands *do* become dirty when we help a terrorist or a dictator. The philosopher Michael Walzer puts it well: "It is easy to get one's hands dirty in politics." He immediately adds, however, that this getting one's hands dirty in this way is "often the right thing to do."[11]

In the end, an adviser to authoritarian leaders cannot escape the dilemma. Often, leaders seek the engagement only to legitimize their rule, in which case the foreign adviser should simply stay away. But when the adviser believes his work will benefit those whom the leader effectively holds hostage, he has a duty not to withhold advice.

Even then, he should be aware that there is a degree of moral complicity involved. If the adviser does not come out of the interaction feeling somewhat tainted and a bit guilty, he has probably not reflected enough about the nature of the relationship.

Where Do Policy Ideas Come From?

What determines the development and use of innovative political strategies? Why are some political systems blessed with a greater abundance of policy innovations? What explains the timing of their emergence?

Just as in the case of technological innovation, we might not be able to provide full answers to such questions. Innovation occurs, in large part, as a result of serendipity, as fundamental scientific discoveries yield unanticipated practical benefits or as experimentation and trial and error result in new products and processes. Similarly, we must presume there is a strong idiosyncratic element in political leadership and political creativity.

Nevertheless, as the economic literature on research and development and endogenous growth indicates, certain systematic elements are also in play.[12] For example, technological innovation responds to market incentives—the pursuit of monopoly profits through the acquisition of temporary advantages over competitors. Likewise, policy ideas that relax political constraints can be thought of as the consequence of both idiosyncratic processes and purposive behavior. Here are some sources of new ideas that come up repeatedly in the historical experience.

Political Entrepreneurship

Inefficiency creates opportunities for political entrepreneurship. As long as there are unexploited efficiency gains to be had, political agents have *some* incentive to engage in such search, regardless of the specific motives animating them. Economists, for example, develop proposals that they think will enhance economic performance. Sometimes (although not always, as Acemoglu and Robinson emphasize[13]), these proposals take political feasibility into account. But ultimately, political entrepreneurs are the ones who arbitrage between academic ideas and political inefficiencies. It would be nice to know the circumstances under which such arbitrage actually takes place and political entrepreneurs are actually able to implement their policy innovations; for now, there seems to be little research addressing this question.

In their book, Leighton and López place special emphasis on political entrepreneurship in making policy reform possible.[14] For new ideas to overcome vested interests, they write, it must be the case that "entrepreneurs notice and exploit those loose spots in the structure of ideas, institutions, and incentives."[15] They provide four case studies of this process: spectrum license auctions, airline deregulation, welfare reform, and housing finance. In their words: "[T]he public face of political change may be that of a madman, an intellectual, or an academic scribbler. But whatever form these leaders may take, they are political entrepreneurs—people whose ideas and actions are focused on producing change."[16] As these authors stress, political entrepreneurship can be socially harmful, as when the pursuit of individual rents comes at the expense of overall inefficiency. But the returns from enhancing economic performance can be very large as well.

Learning by Doing

Entrepreneurship is linked to learning. Just as firms travel down their cost curves as a result of accumulated experience, public organizations such as bureaucracies can learn about opportunities to reap efficiency gains. A large literature examines the potential trade-off between learning and obsolescence as organizations age.[17] Similarly, politicians might learn from their past successes and failures. The evolutionary approach to economics, based on trial and error by boundedly rational agents, provides a useful complementary perspective on learning, which also remains unexploited in political economy.[18]

Technological learning often spills over to other firms, depressing the incentives for technological innovation. An interesting possibility is that political learning by doing is characterized by a similar externality. Political incumbents may be deterred from experimentation because they will bear the full cost of failed policy experiments, but will share the rents resulting from any successes with potential challengers who act as copycats. In this framework, more contestable political systems, allowing freer entry, may have ambiguous effects on political ideas. More competition means more entrepreneurs vying for new ideas. But it also means more copycats—political opponents waiting in the wings—reducing the incentive for experimentation and learning about the strategies that relax political constraints.

Policy Mutations

By "policy mutation," I refer to unplanned policy experimentation that arises along the margins of existing policies. Such experimentation often results from the inability of policy makers to implement prevailing rules to the letter, for administrative or other reasons. As with random mutations, these variations on generally accepted practice can generate new and improved policies by demonstrating better practical results. For example, the idea for dual-track policies in China arose not from the planners themselves but from black markets in the Chinese countryside where farmers sold grain illegally. Planners were simply wise enough to understand that these markets-at-the-margin enriched farmers without harming the state, as long as the plan quotas themselves were enforced, and then built public policy on that understanding. Similarly, experiments with "supersaver fares" in California and Texas greatly facilitated US airline deregulation during the 1970s by revealing the sizable price benefits of greater competition and freer entry.[19]

James Leitzel has written insightfully on the reformist consequences of what he calls "rule evasion."[20] As he notes, "evasive behavior in essence presents an experiment, an alternative way of arranging society."[21] Leitzel discusses two reasons why rule evasion paves the ground for new policies. First, the evasion typically becomes common knowledge and conveys a sense that the existing policy is a failure. Second, it creates incentives for reform either by suggesting an alternative to current policy (say, legalizing black markets) or creating a constituency for the reform. In terms of the argument in this paper, it is a source of ideas for policy makers about what can work better within political constraints.

Crises

Times of crises are occasions for reconsidering existing policies. This is both because prevailing interests may lose some of their legitimacy and because incumbents may be open to trying new remedies. The need for a new narrative is greater and so is the willingness to experiment. "In moments of uncertainty," writes Mark Blyth, "crisis-defining ideas not only tell agents 'what has gone wrong' but also 'what is to be done.'"[22]

In the United States, the Great Depression proved a veritable laboratory for novel institutional arrangements. Franklin D. Roosevelt uttered a famous call for "bold, persistent experimentation" in 1932: "It is common sense to take a method and try it: If it fails, admit it frankly and try another. But above all, try something."[23] To a much lesser extent, the inflationary crisis of the 1970s played a similar role, preparing the groundwork for new ideas in macroeconomics such as rational expectations and central bank independence. The recent financial crisis has made taxation and control of international capital flows more palatable, although the extent to which financial interests have been weakened remains debated.

While the association between crises and new ideas seems plausible, much remains to be explained. Why are some crises much more prone to new ideas? What explains the type of ideas that take hold? The Great Depression spawned the New Deal in the United States, fascism in some parts of Europe, and socialism in some other parts of Europe. Were these outcomes preordained by the structure of interests? To what extent did political entrepreneurship and ideas play an autonomous role?

Emulation

Perhaps the single most important source of ideas and policy innovation are practices that prevail elsewhere. The fact that a policy has worked—or at least is perceived to have worked—somewhere can be a powerful reason to copy it. Social security privatization in Chile, microfinance in Bangladesh, conditional cash grants in Mexico, and special economic zones in China are some examples of policy innovation that gained adherents around the world following implementation in their native settings. Much legal and regulatory reform in the developing world is modeled after existing models in North America or western Europe. The appeal of "imported ideas" is clear. Ready-made policies eliminate or reduce the cost of homegrown innovation and experimentation. The perception of their success elsewhere can also act as a counterweight to powerful vested interests at home.

Of course, there is no guarantee that policy emulation will result in success. Context matters. Imported ideas can backfire because of ill fit with either the local economic or political landscape. Furthermore, emulation can be driven by bad motives as well as good ones. It may be used to provide aid donors with cover in case of failure, as a signal for new governments that they are the "good guys," and by domestic lobbies to legitimize their own self-interested agenda.[24]

Paul DiMaggio and Walter Powell have coined the term "isomorphic mimicry" to denote the pressures that organizations face to become similar, even as they struggle to change.[25] My colleague Matt Andrews documents how reform in poor countries through "isomorphic mimicry" results in the semblance of change, with little real progress achieved: a bureaucracy gets reorganized to look like those from advanced countries, but bureaucratic efficiency hardly improves.[26] In a paper with Sharun Mukand, we develop a formal model of the incentives for governments to mimic other countries' policies: implementing policies with a poor fit is costly, but so is experimentation—and an imperfectly informed electorate may be more likely to interpret domestic experimentation as an attempt at rent seeking, while being willing to accept emulation.[27]

What Do We Gain by Considering the Role of Ideas?

I have tried to show that, for all the emphasis placed on them in political economy, vested interests play a considerably less significant role than appears at first sight. Indeed, because of their neglect of ideas, political-economy frameworks often do a poor job of accounting for policy change. There is frequently an after-the-fact feel to this brand of theorizing: if reform happens despite vested interests, it must be because those interests were not sufficiently well entrenched to begin with or reform didn't hurt them. Conventional models of policy stasis are incomplete if they sidestep the ideas that political agents have about strategies they can pursue. And they cannot fully shed light on reform when it does occur.

Taking ideas seriously renders the notion of interests slippery and ephemeral. From the conventional political-economy standpoint, it is puzzling to observe instances in which elites resist reforms strenuously until the change actually happens, and then benefit from the reforms. The Korean military dictator President Park Chung-Hee threw the country's leading businessmen in jail when he came to power in 1961; they were released only after Park extracted promises from them that they would each undertake specific industrial investments. Given how the Korean economy prospered, these businessmen were hardly worse off for those investments.

Similarly, the Chinese Communist leadership was among the main beneficiaries of the dual-pricing regime and other market-oriented policy innovations that it had refused to consider until Mao's death. The critical change in these instances was not a transformation in the structure of power but the implementation of new ideas by those in power. Indeed, reform often happens not when vested interests are defeated but when different strategies are used to pursue those interests, or when interests themselves are redefined.

It is instructive to contrast my argument with that of Acemoglu and Robinson, who argue that well-meaning reforms often fail or produce unintended consequences because they overlook the changes in political outcomes the reforms generate.[28] In much of policy advice, they write, politics is "largely absent from the scene." Acemoglu and Robinson maintain that "economic analysis needs to identify, theoretically and empirically, conditions under which politics and economics run into conflict, and then evaluate policy proposals taking this conflict and the potential backlashes it creates into account."[29]

I agree with them on the need to take politics into account. But Acemoglu and Robinson take vested interests largely as given, and as a result, they are rather pessimistic about what policy can achieve. In contrast, I have argued that successful policy ideas work precisely because they take politics into account. I suggest that it is possible to do better than simply avoid political conflicts; ideas can be useful to *relax* political constraints. Just as ill-conceived economic ideas can produce disastrous political effects, politically well-informed ideas can move us closer to the efficiency frontier in a manner that is consistent with underlying political realities.

Raising the profile of ideas would also help alleviate the tension that exists today between political economy, on the one hand, and normative economics and policy analysis, on the other. Political economy seeks to explain political-economic outcomes. However, if policy outcomes are pinned down by the structure of interests, it is futile to make policy recommendations: there will be no takers for the recommendations, and such recommendations will be of no consequence. At best, they will constitute ideological fodder for vested interests, used to sweeten their exercise of naked power before the general public. When political economy becomes too enamored of vested interests at the expense of ideas, social science squeezes normative policy analysis out of useful existence. An explicit consideration of the role of ideas would free up some space for policy analysis.

Finally, a focus on ideas provides us with a new perspective on vested interests too. As social constructivists like to put it, "interests are an idea." Even if economic actors are driven purely by interests, they often have only a limited and preconceived idea of where their interests lie. This may be true in general, of course, but it is especially true in politics, where preferences are tightly linked to people's sense of identity and new strategies can always be invented. What the economist typically treats as immutable self-interest is too often an artifact of ideas about who we are, how the world works, and what actions are available.

All this is especially important as we move to an era when reforming the rules of how our economies work, in isolation and together, has become the paramount challenge. Problems of globalization, economic growth, and social inclusion require imaginative ideas and solutions. Democracies owe themselves a proper debate, so that they make their choices consciously and deliberately. I turn to specific proposals in the remaining chapters.

CHAPTER 9

What Will Not Work

The populist revolt of our time reflects the huge chasm that has opened up between the worldview of the world's intellectual and professional elites and that of ordinary voters. These two groups now live in different social worlds and orient themselves using different cognitive maps. Yet the intellectual consensus that shaped our contemporary political and economic landscape remains largely intact. Discussion in polite company rarely goes beyond a bit more worry about inequality, a bit more focus on compensating the losers. We need instead bolder, bigger ideas. Without them, we may find that the good things that the present consensus produced—a liberal, democratic order in particular—is swept away by the backlash wrought by its excesses.

If capitalism is to survive, it must be redesigned to address the multiple challenges of globalization, inequality (both national and global), rapid technological change, climate change, and democratic accountability under which it reels at present. In the remaining chapters I turn to some of the policy innovations that will be required. How can public policy be more effectively deployed to stimulate green technologies? How can the unequalizing forces of technological innovation be harnessed for greater equity and social inclusion? How can globalization be reformed to enhance both domestic and international equality, despite the apparent tension between the two? How can progressives develop a politically winning agenda that overcomes the appeal of populist demagogues?

I begin by discussing two key proposals around which today's conventional wisdom revolves: compensating the losers of globalization and enhanced global governance. Both of these ideas are largely dead ends. Neither offering compensation nor global governance, as conventionally understood, can move us in the right direction. Existing trade agreements and global finance rules do not provide a good model for the future. I will argue for a new model of "light" global governance more respectful of domestic policy priorities.

Too Late for Compensation

There is a new consensus these days among the world's business and policy elites about how to deal with the globalization backlash that populists such as Donald Trump have so ably exploited. Gone are confident assertions about how globalization benefits us all. Yes, we must accept that globalization produces both winners and losers, the elites concede. But the correct response is not to halt or reverse globalization but to ensure that the losers are compensated.

The new consensus is stated succinctly by Nouriel Roubini: the backlash against globalization "can be contained and managed through policies that compensate workers for its collateral damage and costs. Only by enacting such policies will globalization's losers begin to think that they may eventually join the ranks of its winners."[1]

This argument seems to make eminent sense, from both economic and political perspectives. Economists have long known that opening up to trade causes income redistribution and *absolute* losses for some groups even as it enlarges the national economic pie overall. Therefore, trade deals unambiguously enhance national well-being only to the extent that winners compensate losers. Compensation also ensures buy-in from broader constituencies and should be good politics.

Prior to the welfare state, the tension between openness and redistribution was resolved either by large-scale emigration of workers or by reimposing trade protection, especially in agriculture.[2] With the rise of the welfare state, the constraint became less binding, allowing for more trade liberalization. Today the advanced countries that are the most exposed to the international economy are also those where safety nets and social insurance programs—welfare states—are the most extensive.[3] Research in Europe has shown that losers from globalization within countries tend to favor more active social programs and labor-market interventions.[4]

If opposition to trade has not become politically salient in Europe today, it is in some part because such social protections remain strong there, despite having weakened in recent years. Even in Britain, where the reassertion of national autonomy has gone farthest, open trade policies are not controversial. In fact, pro-Brexit groups often buttressed their position by arguing the country would be in a position to adopt freer trade policies outside the EU. It is not much of an exaggeration to say that the welfare state and the open economy have been flip sides of the same coin during much of the twentieth century.

Compared to most European countries, the United States was a latecomer to globalization. Its large domestic market and relative geographical insulation provided considerable protection from imports until recently, especially from low-wage countries. It also traditionally had a weak welfare state.

When the United States opened itself up to imports from Mexico, China, and other developing nations more extensively after the 1980s, one might have expected the country to go the European route. Instead, under the sway of Reaganite and market-fundamentalist ideas, the country went in an opposite direction. As Larry Mishel, president of the Economic Policy Institute, puts it, "ignoring the losers was deliberate." In 1981, the "trade adjustment assistance (TAA) program was one of the first things Reagan attacked, cutting its weekly compensation payments."[5] The damage continued under subsequent, Democratic administrations. In the words of Mishel, "if free-traders had actually cared about the working class they could have supported a full range of policies to support robust wage growth: full employment, collective bargaining, high labor standards, a robust minimum wage, and so on." And all of this could have been done "before administering 'shocks' by expanding trade with low-wage countries."

Could the United States now reverse course and follow the newly emergent conventional wisdom? As late as 2007, political scientist Ken Scheve and economist Matt Slaughter called for "a New Deal for globalization" in the United States, which would link "engagement with the world economy to a substantial redistribution of income."[6] In the United States, they argued, this would mean adopting a much more progressive federal tax system.

Slaughter had served in a Republican administration, under President George W. Bush. It is an indication of how polarized the US political climate has become that it is impossible to imagine similar proposals coming out of Republicans these days. As President Trump's and his Congressional allies' determination to emasculate Obama's health insurance program shows, the conservatives' agenda is to scale back social protections rather than expand them.

Today's consensus around compensation presumes globalization's winners are motivated by enlightened self-interest—that they believe buy-in from the losers is essential to maintain open economic borders. An alternative perspective is that globalization, at least as presently construed, tilts the balance of political power toward those with the skills and assets to benefit from the global economy, undermining whatever organized influence the losers might have had in the first place. As Trump's presidency has already amply revealed, the inchoate discontent around globalization can be easily subverted to serve an altogether different agenda, more in line with elites' interests.

The politics of compensation is always subject to a problem that economists call time inconsistency. Before a new policy—say a trade agreement—is adopted, beneficiaries have the incentive to promise compensation. Once the policy is adopted, they have little interest to carry out the compensation they promised—either because reversal is costly all around or because underlying balance of power shifts toward them. Given the history of US trade agreements, this is one—but certainly not the only—reason promises of adjustment assistance have very little credibility today.

The time for compensation has come and gone. Even if compensation may have been a viable approach two decades ago, it no longer serves as a practical response to globalization's ills. If we are serious about bringing the losers along, we will need to consider changes in the rules of globalization itself. I will present my own proposals in the next chapter, but first let's look at another standard approach to these problems.

The False Promise of Global Governance

We hear it time and again: we have become too interconnected for policies that are purely national in scale. Global problems require global solutions. Only global governance can address the signal economic problems of our time—economic vulnerability, low growth, financial crises, inequality, and joblessness.

So commonplace are such assertions that we rarely question the logic behind them. And the call for greater international cooperation and coordination surely makes sense in certain policy domains. But what may be true for truly global problems such as climate change or health pandemics is largely incorrect in the sphere of economics. Unlike the atmosphere, the oceans, or the ozone layer, the world economy is not a global commons. Global governance can do only limited good to fix it—and it occasionally does some damage.

What makes, say, global warming a global rather than national problem is that the globe has a single atmosphere. It makes no difference where greenhouse gases are emitted. Domestic restrictions on carbon emissions provide no or little benefit at home, unless such policies are emulated by other countries as well. Similarly, investment in early warning systems against health pandemics that cross borders provide collective, global benefits, while the costs are paid by the governments that fund the investment. In both areas, nation-states left to their own devices would have little incentive to safeguard the global commons. Global cooperation is therefore key.

Good economic policies, by contrast, are different. Policies such as openness, financial and macroeconomic stability, full employment, investments in human capital, infrastructure, and innovation benefit the home economy first and foremost. The price for bad economic policies is paid primarily by domestic residents. The economic fortunes of individual nations are determined largely by what happens at home rather than abroad.

This is particularly true of trade policies. The case for removing trade barriers is that this enriches the home economy as a whole.

If open economy policies are desirable, it's because openness is in a nation's own self-interest—not because it helps others. Openness and other good policies that contribute to global economic prosperity rely on self-interest, not on global spirit.

Policies in one country do affect others as well, of course. We might be particularly concerned about instances where domestic economic advantage comes at the expense of other nations. Such cases are called "beggar-thy-neighbor" policies. The purest illustration occurs when a dominant supplier of a natural resource, such as oil, restricts supply on world markets so as to drive up world prices. In this instance, the exporter's gain is the rest of the world's loss. A similar mechanism operates with so-called "optimum tariffs," whereby a large country manipulates its terms of trade—lowering the price of what it buys from abroad—by placing trade restrictions on its imports. In such instances, there is a clear argument for global rules that limit or prohibit the use of such policies.

But the vast majority of cases in world trade and finance that preoccupy global policy makers are not of this kind. Typically when governments impose trade barriers, the last thing on their mind is to make imported goods cheaper; the point of protectionism is to raise domestic prices and increase profits and employment in relatively inefficient import-competing firms. Similarly, think of agricultural subsidies, bans on genetically modified organisms (GMOs) in Europe, the abuse of antidumping rules in the United States, or inadequate protection of investors' rights in the developing nations. These are all in essence "beggar thyself" policies, not "beggar-thy-neighbor" ones. Their economic costs are borne primarily at home, even though they may produce adverse effects on others as well. They are deployed not to extract advantages from other nations but because other competing objectives at home—such as distributional, administrative, public-health, or political concerns—dominate economic efficiency motives. For example, economists generally agree that agricultural subsidies are inefficient and that the benefits to European farmers come at large costs to everyone else in Europe, in the form of high prices, high taxes, or both. European democracies maintain these subsidies nevertheless, for domestic political motives.

The same is true for poor banking regulations or macroeconomic policies that aggravate the business cycle and generate financial instability and crises. As the global financial crisis showed, these can have momentous implications beyond a country's own borders. But if US regulators fell asleep on the job, this was not because their economy benefited while everyone else paid the price. The US economy was among those that suffered the most.

Perhaps the biggest policy letdown of our day is the failure of governments in advanced democracies to address rising inequality. This too has its roots in domestic politics—the hold on the policy process by financial and business elites and the narratives they have spun about the limits of redistributive policies. Sure, global tax havens are an example of beggar-thy-neighbor policies. But powerful countries such as the United States and European nations could have done much on their own to limit tax evasion—and the race to the bottom in corporate taxation—if they so desired.

So, the problems of our day have little to do with the lack of global cooperation. They are domestic in nature and cannot be fixed by rule making through international institutions, which are easily overwhelmed by the same special vested interests that undermine domestic policy. Too often global governance is another name for the pursuit of these interests' global agenda. This is perhaps clearest with trade agreements.

The Muddled Case for Trade Agreements

Global trade negotiations have been deadlocked for a long time. Trade negotiators have turned their attention to regional trade agreements instead. Until President's Trump's rejection of such arrangements, the United States was at the center of two mega deals that could shape the future path of world trade. The Trans-Pacific Partnership was further along, and involved eleven countries besides the United States that collectively produce as much as 40 percent of global output, but crucially not China. The Transatlantic Trade and Investment Partnership with the European Union had an even more ambitious reach, promising to join two giant regions that together cover half of world trade.

Trade agreements have long stopped being the province of experts and technocrats. So, it is not surprising that both initiatives have generated significant and heated public discussion. The perspectives of proponents and opponents are so polarized that it is hard not be utterly confused about the likely consequences. To appreciate what's at stake in these as well as other trade agreements, we must understand that these deals were motivated by a mix of objectives—some benign, and others less so from a global perspective.

On the economic front, the trade agreements' defenders tend to talk with both sides of their mouths. On the one hand, the reduction of trade barriers is said to promote economic efficiency and specialization. On the other hand, it is supposed to increase exports and jobs by increasing access to trade partners' markets. The first of these is the conventional comparative-advantage argument for trade liberalization; the second is a mercantilist argument.

The difficulty is that the comparative advantage and mercantilist goals are contradictory. In the comparative advantage perspective, the gains from trade arise from imports: exports are what a country must give up in order to afford those imports. And these gains accrue to all countries, as long as trade expands in a balanced fashion. In the mercantilist worldview, exports are good and imports are bad. Countries that expand their net exports gain, while the others lose.

From the comparative advantage vantage point, trade agreements do not create jobs; they simply reallocate them across industries. From the mercantilist vantage point, they can create jobs, but only to the extent that they destroy jobs in other countries. Therefore, it is inconsistent to claim, as the US and European governments were prone to do, that these agreements would simultaneously create jobs and be mutually beneficial.

On the political front, proponents argued that TPP and TTIP will enshrine good, liberal rules for world trade. Lower barriers and greater transparency in regulation are generally good things. But here too the reality was much more complex.

For the United States, a great draw of the TPP was that it would have enforced tighter intellectual property rules on other countries. Such rules tend to have uncertain impact on innovation while generating substantial rents for US patent and copyright holders. In the TTIP, the reduction of so-called nontariff barriers to trade between the United States and Europe would have almost certainly restricted the space for domestic regulatory action. Even if regulatory harmonization wouldn't have created a race to the bottom, the interests of investors and exporters would have cast a longer shadow than ever before over social and environmental goals.

Perhaps most worrisome were the Investor-State Dispute Settlement (ISDS) provisions of the agreements. These provisions establish a separate judicial track, outside a country's own legal system, that allows firms to sue governments for apparent rights violations under trade treaties. Proponents defended ISDS by saying that it wouldn't have had much consequence for countries, such as the United States, where there is good rule of law and would have promoted investment in countries, such as Vietnam, where there isn't. Even so, it is unclear why ISDS provisions were needed for the TTIP, which would have covered the advanced economies of North America and Europe.

In all these areas, the TPP and TTIP seemed to be not so much about liberalism as about corporate capture.

One of the most important, and equally ambiguous, objectives of these agreements related to a subject that would not have made any appearance in the texts: China. Both the United States and Europe would like China to play the trade game by their rules. Negotiating trade rules without China's participation could be viewed as a strategy of eventually coaxing China into a liberal global system. But it could also be considered as isolating China and erecting discriminating barriers against it in lucrative markets.

Finally, what especially grated on the opponents was the secrecy of the negotiations. The draft agreements were not open to public scrutiny, and the few outsiders who were allowed access to them were prohibited from divulging the contents. The stated goal was to facilitate negotiations. As Senator Elizabeth Warren put it, that got it exactly backwards. If transparency would make it harder to sell the final product to the public, it raises serious questions about the desirability of the treaty.

It would have made a lot of sense to subject the final text of trade agreements to an up-and-down vote without allowing amendments. But that could have been done while making draft tests public. The time for secrecy had past, if it ever existed.

In the end, there was much uncertainty about the economic and political consequences of these trade agreements and considerable room for concern. Proponents only discredited themselves by deriding the skeptics as protectionists. Open, informed debate about specific provisions is exactly what was called for. That would have been possible only if the negotiating texts were opened to public scrutiny.

Global Capital Rules

In a remarkable reversal, in 2012 the International Monetary Fund put its stamp of approval on capital controls, thereby legitimizing the use of taxes and other restrictions on cross-border financial flows. Not so long ago, the global institution had pushed hard for countries—rich or poor—to open up to foreign finance. Now it has endorsed the reality that financial globalization can be disruptive—inducing financial crises and inappropriate movements in the value of currencies.

So here we are with yet another twist in the never-ending saga of our love-and-hate relationship with capital controls.

Under the classical Gold Standard that prevailed until 1914, free capital mobility had been sacrosanct. The turbulence of the interwar period convinced many, including most famously John Maynard Keynes, that an open capital account is incompatible with macroeconomic stability. The new consensus was reflected in the Bretton Woods agreement of 1944, which enshrined capital controls in the IMF's Articles of Agreement. As Keynes said at the time, "what used to be heresy is now endorsed as orthodoxy."

By the late 1980s, policy makers had become enamored yet again with capital mobility. The European Union made capital controls illegal in 1992, and the Organization for Economic Cooperation and Development enforced free finance on its new members, paving the way for financial crises in Mexico and South Korea in 1994 and 1997, respectively. The IMF adopted the agenda wholeheartedly, and its leadership sought (unsuccessfully) to amend the articles of agreement

to give the organization formal powers over capital account management policies in its member states.

Yet the promise of free capital mobility did not hold up. By and large,
capital inflow bonanzas boosted consumption rather than investment
in recipient countries, exacerbating economic volatility and making
painful financial crises more frequent. Rather than exert discipline,
global financial markets have increased the availability of debt, weakening budget constraints of profligate governments and overextended
banks. The world witnessed financial crises in Asia, Brazil, Argentina,
Russia, Turkey, and eventually Europe and America.

As long as it was developing nations that were whiplashed by global
finance it was fashionable to say the fault lay with those countries
themselves. The IMF and Western economists argued that governments in Mexico, South Korea, Brazil, Turkey, and elsewhere had not
adopted the requisite policies—prudential regulations, fiscal restraint,
and monetary controls—needed to take advantage of capital flows
and prevent crises. The problem was with domestic policies, not with
financial globalization. The answer, therefore, lay not in controls on
cross-border financial flows but in domestic reforms.

Once the advanced countries themselves became the victim of
financial globalization in the global financial crisis of 2008, it became
much harder to sustain this line of argument. It became clearer that
the problem lay with instability in the global financial system itself—
the bouts of euphoria and bubbles, followed by sudden stops that are
endemic to financial markets that remain unsupervised and unregulated. The IMF's recognition that it is appropriate for countries to try
to insulate themselves from these syndromes is therefore welcome and
came none too soon.

But we should not exaggerate the IMF's change of heart. The IMF
still regards free capital mobility as an ideal and presumes countries

will eventually converge toward it. All that needs to happen is for countries to pass through the threshold conditions of adequate "financial and institutional development." The IMF treats capital controls as a last resort, to be deployed under a rather narrow set of circumstances—when other macro, financial, or prudential measures are unable to stem the tide of inflows, the exchange rate is decidedly overvalued, the economy is overheating, and foreign reserves are already adequate. It lays out an "integrated approach to capital account liberalization" and specifies a detailed sequence of liberalization. There is nothing remotely comparable on capital controls and how to render them more effective.

This reflects over-optimism on two fronts: first, about how well policy can be fine-tuned to target directly the underlying failures that make global finance unsafe; and second, about the extent to which convergence in domestic financial regulations will rule out the need for cross-border management of flows.

The first point can be best seen using an analogy with gun controls. Guns, like capital flows, have their uses, but they can also produce catastrophic consequences when used accidentally or placed in the wrong hands. The IMF's reluctant endorsement of capital controls resembles the attitude of gun control opponents: policies should target the behavior causing harm rather than bluntly restrict individual freedoms. As the gun lobby in America likes to say, "guns don't kill people; people kill people." The implication is that we should punish offenders rather than restrict circulation of guns. Similarly, in financial markets, we should ensure intermediaries fully internalize the risks they are taking rather than taxing or restricting certain types of transactions.

But as Avinash Dixit likes to say, the world is always second-best at best. An approach that presumes we can identify and directly regulate problematic behavior lacks realism in light of substantive and practical difficulties. Most societies control guns directly because we cannot perfectly monitor and discipline behavior, and the social costs of failure are high. Similarly, caution dictates direct regulation of cross-border flows.

As the advocates of capital mobility tirelessly point out, benefiting from financial globalization has a long list of prerequisites, including protection of property rights, sound contract enforcement, eradication of corruption, enhanced transparency and financial information, sound corporate governance, monetary and fiscal stability, debt sustainability, market-determined exchange rates, high-quality financial regulation, and prudential supervision. The illogic of presuming first-world institutions as a prerequisite to what is supposed to enable economic growth in the first place is too obvious to elaborate.

The list is not only long; it is also open ended. As the experience of the advanced countries with the global financial crisis has demonstrated, even apparently the most sophisticated regulatory and supervisory systems are far from being failsafe. Demanding that developing countries build the kind of institutions that will render capital flows safe therefore not only puts the cart before the horse but also is a fool's errand. Prudence dictates a more pragmatic approach that recognizes a permanent role for capital controls alongside other regulatory and prudential tools. Regulating or prohibiting certain transactions is a second-best strategy in a world where the ideal may not be attainable.

Moreover, access to external finance does little for growth in many developing countries where the economy is constrained by investment demand, rather than shortage of domestic saving. In these economies, it is the reluctance of the private sector to invest that is the main problem. The social return to investment may be high, but the private return is low because of externalities, high taxes, poor institutions, or any others among the wide array of factors that keep private appropriability of returns low.

Economies that suffer from low investment demand respond quite differently to capital inflows. It is consumption that is fueled rather than capital accumulation. In addition, the appreciation of the currency due to capital inflows aggravates the investment shortage. The profitability of tradable industries—the industries most likely to suffer from appropriability problems—takes a hit, and investment demand falls further. In these economies, capital inflows may well retard growth rather than stimulate it. Once again, appropriately formulated regulatory policies could restore first-best outcomes, but in practice this will rarely happen.

Such concerns have led emerging markets to experiment with a variety of capital controls. Many of these do not work very well. That is not because they fail to have an effect on the quantity or composition of flows but because such effects are quite small. As Brazil, Colombia, South Korea, and others have found out, limited controls that target specific markets such as bonds or short-term bank lending do not have sizable effects on the outcomes of interest—the exchange rate, monetary independence, or domestic financial stability. The uneasy implication is that capital controls may need to be blunt and comprehensive rather than surgical and targeted to be truly effective.

The second complication with presuming convergence toward free capital mobility is that even advanced countries with well-developed institutions are moving toward different models of financial regulation. Along the efficient frontier of financial regulation, one needs to consider the trade-off between financial innovation and financial stability. The more we want of one, the less we can have of the other. Some countries will opt for greater stability, imposing tough capital and liquidity requirements on their banks, while others may favor greater innovation and pursue a lighter regulatory touch.

Free capital mobility poses a severe difficulty here. Borrowers and lenders can resort to cross-border financial flows to evade domestic controls and erode the integrity of regulatory standards at home. To prevent such regulatory arbitrage, domestic regulators may be forced to take measures against financial transactions originating from jurisdictions with more lax regulations. A world in which finance is regulated in diverse ways by different sovereigns requires some traffic rules on managing the interface of national regulations. Presuming that free capital mobility is an ideal to which all will converge diverts us from the hard thinking that is needed.

Capital controls by themselves are no panacea, and they may often create worse problems than they solve, such as corruption or delay of needed reforms. But this is no different than in any other area of government action. We live in a second-best world where policy action is almost always partial (and partially effective), and well-intentioned reforms in one area may backfire in the presence of distortions elsewhere in the system. Treating capital controls as the last resort, always and everywhere, has little rationale in such a world; in effect, it makes a fetish out of financial globalization. We need case-by-case, hard-headed pragmatism instead, recognizing that capital controls sometimes deserve a prominent place.

Global Governance Light

We are entering a new phase of the world economy, in which achieving global cooperation will become increasingly more difficult. For one thing, the world is becoming more multipolar and less "hegemonic." The United States and western Europe are no longer able to lay down the rules and expect others will fall into line. Moreover, they are now burdened by high debt and low growth—and therefore preoccupied with domestic concerns. The continuing troubles of the eurozone will exert a particularly crippling effect on Europe's global role.

Compounding this trend, rising powers such as China and India place great value on national sovereignty and noninterference in domestic affairs. This makes them unwilling to surrender policy autonomy to international rules. It also makes them unlikely candidates for investing in global policy regimes, as the United States once did in the aftermath of the Second World War.

Therefore, global leadership and cooperation will remain in limited supply going forward. This change in the global context necessitates a carefully calibrated response in the governance of the world economy. It requires a thinner set of rules that recognizes the diversity of national circumstances and the demands for policy space. Yet discussions in the G20, World Trade Organization, and other multilateral fora proceed as if the right remedy is more of the same—more rules, more harmonization, and more discipline on national policies.

Going back to basics, the principle of "subsidiarity" provides the right way of thinking about issues of global governance. It tells us which kinds of policies should be coordinated or harmonized globally and which should be left largely to domestic decision-making. The principle demarcates areas where we need extensive global governance and areas where only a thin layer of global rules is adequate. We can think of this also as a choice between a WTO-type (thick) global regime versus GATT-type (thin) regime.

My previous discussion suggests economic policies come roughly in four different variants. At one extreme are domestic policies that create no (or very few) spillovers across national borders, such as education policies. These require no international agreement and can be safely left to domestic policy makers.

At the other end are policies that relate to "global commons," such as global climate. The characteristic of a global commons is that the outcome for each nation is determined not by domestic policies but by (the sum total of) other countries' policies. The classic case here is greenhouse gases. There is a very strong case for establishing strong and binding global rules in these policy domains, since it is in the interest of each country individually to neglect its share of the upkeep of the global commons. Failure to reach global agreement would condemn all to a collective disaster.

In between, there are two other types of policies that create spillovers of the type I mentioned previously. These must be treated differently. "Beggar-thy-neighbor" policies need to be regulated at the international level. At present the most important examples are systemically important countries running outsized trade surpluses, making it difficult for other countries to maintain full employment. China was emblematic until recently, but its external surpluses have shrunk in recent years. Germany, with a current account surplus approaching 9 percent of GDP, is the worst transgressor at present.

"Beggar thyself" policies are different. With these policies, the economic costs are borne primarily at home, even though they may produce effects on others. Examples, again, are agricultural subsidies, bans on GMOs, lax financial regulation, or weak property-rights protection. The case for global discipline is quite a bit weaker with beggar-thyself policies. It should not be up to the "global community" to tell individual nations how they ought to weight competing goals. Democracies, in particular, ought to be allowed to make their own "mistakes." And imposing costs on other nations is not a sufficient cause on its own for global regulation. Economists hardly complain when a country's trade liberalization harms nations that compete with it on world markets.[7]

Of course, there is no guarantee that domestic policies accurately reflect societal demands. Even democracies are frequently taken hostage by special interests. So, there could still be a case for global discipline for beggar-thyself policies. Even so, global rules must take a different and weaker form, focused on procedural requirements rather policy harmonization. I will say more about this in the next chapter.

Different types of policies call for different responses at the global level. At present, too much global political capital is wasted on harmonizing beggar-thyself policies (particularly in the areas of trade and financial regulation) and not enough on beggar-thy-neighbor policies (such as macroeconomic imbalances). Overambitious and misdirected efforts at global governance will not serve us well at a time when global cooperation is bound to be scarce.

CHAPTER 10

New Rules for the Global Economy

S uppose that the world's leading policy makers were to meet
again at the Mount Washington Hotel in Bretton Woods, New
Hampshire, to design a new global economic order. What are
some of the guiding principles of global economic governance on
which they might agree? Here are seven commonsense principles I first
proposed in 2011, which I think are more relevant than ever.[1]

1. Markets must be deeply embedded in systems of governance. The idea that
markets are self-regulating received a mortal blow in the global financial crisis and should be buried once and for all. Markets require other
social institutions to support them. They rely on courts, legal frameworks, and regulators. They depend on the stabilizing functions that
lenders-of-last-resort and countercyclical fiscal policy provide. They
need the political buy-in that redistributive taxation, safety nets, and
social insurance programs help generate. They need public investment
in infrastructure and R&D to innovate. What is true of domestic markets is true also of global ones.

2. Democratic governance and political communities are organized largely within nation-states, and are likely to remain so for the foreseeable future. The nation-state lives, and even if not entirely well, remains essentially the only game in town. The quest for extensive global governance is a fool's errand, both because national governments are unlikely to cede significant control to transnational institutions and because harmonizing rules would not benefit societies with diverse needs and preferences. The European Union is possibly the sole exception to this truism, but Brexit, the rise of populist parties, and the reassertion of national autonomy show the limits of the political dimensions of the European project.

Too often we waste international cooperation on overly ambitious goals, ultimately producing weak results that go little beyond the lowest common denominator among major states. When international cooperation does "succeed," it typically codifies the preferences of the more powerful states or, even more frequently, of international corporations and banks in those states. The Basle rules on capital requirements; the WTO's rules on subsidies, intellectual property, and investment measures; and investor–state dispute settlement (ISDS) arrangements typify this kind of overreaching. We can enhance both the efficiency and the legitimacy of globalization if we empower rather than cripple democratic procedures at home.

3. There is no "one way" to prosperity. Once we acknowledge that the core institutional infrastructure of the global economy must be built at the national level, it frees up countries to develop the institutions that suit them best. The United States, Europe, and Japan are all successful societies; they have each produced comparable amounts of wealth over the long term. Yet the regulations that cover their labor markets, corporate governance, antitrust, social protection, and even banking and finance have differed considerably. These differences enable journalists and pundits to anoint a succession of these "models"—a different one each decade—as the great success for all to emulate. Such fads should not blind us to the reality that none of these models can be deemed a clear winner in the contest of "capitalisms." The most successful societies of the future will leave room for experimentation and allow for further evolution of institutions over time. A global economy that recognizes the need for and value of institutional diversity would foster rather than stifle such experimentation and evolution.

4. Countries have the right to protect their own regulations and institutions. The previous principles may have appeared uncontroversial and innocuous. Yet they have powerful implications that clash with the received wisdom among boosters of globalization. One such implication is that we need to accept the right of individual countries to safeguard their domestic institutional choices. The recognition of institutional diversity would be meaningless if nations were unable to "protect" domestic institutions—if they did not have the instruments available to shape and maintain their own institutions.

We should therefore accept that countries can uphold national rules—tax policies, financial regulation, labor standards, or consumer health and safety—and can do so by raising barriers at the border if necessary, *when trade demonstrably threatens domestic practices enjoying broad popular support.* If globalization's advocates are right, then the clamor for protection will fail for lack of evidence or support. If they are wrong, there will be a safety valve in place to ensure that these contending values—the benefits of open economies and the gains from upholding domestic regulations—both receive a proper hearing in the domestic political debate.

5. Countries do not have the right to impose their institutions on others. Using restrictions on cross-border trade or finance to uphold values and regulations at home must be sharply distinguished from using them to impose these values and regulations on other countries. Globalization's rules should not force Americans or Europeans to consume goods that are produced in ways that most citizens in those countries find unacceptable. But they also should not allow the United States or the European Union to use trade sanctions or other kinds of pressure to alter the way that foreign nations go about their business in labor markets, environmental policies, or finance. Nations have a right to difference, not to impose convergence.

6. *The purpose of international economic arrangements must be to lay down the traffic rules for managing the interface among national institutions.* Relying on nation-states to provide the essential governance functions of the world economy does not mean we should abandon international rules. The Bretton Woods regime, after all, did have clear rules, even though these were limited in scope and depth. A completely decentralized free-for-all would not benefit anyone; one nation's decisions can affect the well-being of others. What we need are traffic rules that help vehicles of different size and shape and traveling at varying speeds navigate around each other, rather than impose an identical car or a uniform speed limit on all. We should strive to attain the maximum globalization that is consistent with maintaining space for diversity in national institutional arrangements.

7. *Nondemocratic countries cannot count on the same rights and privileges in the international economic order as democracies.* What gives the previous principles their appeal and legitimacy is that they highlight democratic deliberation—where it really occurs, within nation-states. When nation-states are not democratic, this scaffolding collapses. We can no longer presume a country's institutional arrangements reflect the

preferences of its citizenry. So, nondemocracies need to play by different, less permissive rules.

These principles support a different model of global governance, one that would be democracy enhancing rather than globalization enhancing. They would open up space for democracies to improve their functioning at home, without prejudging what the policy outputs ought to be or whether the result is greater economic integration. Global governance could then usefully contribute to democracy, through global norms and procedural requirements designed to enhance the quality of domestic policy making—instead of rules aimed at increasing global trade and investment.

Specific examples of such requirements are global disciplines pertaining to transparency, broad representation, accountability, and use of scientific/economic evidence in domestic proceedings. Disciplines of this type are already in use in global institutions to some extent. For example, the World Trade Organization's Agreement on Application of Sanitary and Phytosanitary Measures (the SPS Agreement) explicitly requires the use of scientific evidence when health concerns are at issue for imported goods. Procedural rules of this kind can be used much more extensively and to greater effect to improve domestic decision-making. Antidumping rules can be improved by requiring that consumer and producer interests that would be adversely affected by the imposition of import duties take part in domestic proceedings. Subsidy rules can be improved by requiring economic cost-benefit analyses that incorporate potential consequences of industrial policies for both static and dynamic efficiency.

The key point is this: problems rooted in failures of domestic deliberation—those produced by beggar-thyself policies—can be solved only through improved democratic decision-making. Global governance can make a very limited contribution here, and only if it focuses on enhancing domestic decision-making rather than constraining it. Otherwise, global governance becomes a yearning for technocratic solutions that override and undercut public deliberation. That, in turn, is a recipe for democratic malfunction and populist reactions.

Fair Trade and Free Trade

Many of the problems of the world economy are exemplified by the tensions between China and the Western economies, countries with very different social systems and approaches to economic management.

When China negotiated to join the World Trade Organization, there was a critical question: Is China a market economy, as the United States and the EU understood the term? As typically happens when diplomats face a thorny question, the decision was postponed. China's WTO accession agreement signed in December 2001 permitted the country's trade partners to deal with China as a "nonmarket economy" for a period of up to fifteen years. NME status in turn meant that it was a lot easier for importing countries to impose special tariffs on Chinese exports, in the form of antidumping duties. In particular, they could use production costs in more expensive countries as a proxy for true Chinese costs, increasing both the likelihood of a dumping finding and the estimated margin of dumping. Many countries, such as Argentina, Brazil, Chile, and South Korea, have already rewarded China with market-economy status—but not the United States and the European Union.[2]

The delay has simply postponed the escalation of the trade conflict between these giant economies. Unfortunately, the terms of this battle have ensured nothing was done to address the deeper flaw of the world trade regime. Regardless of whether China is given market economy status, prevailing antidumping measures are ill-suited to the task of addressing concerns over unfair trade. This is not because such concerns are ungrounded but because they go well beyond dumping. Antidumping facilitates protectionism of the worst kind, while doing nothing for countries that need legitimate policy space.

Economists have never been fond of the WTO's antidumping rules. From a strictly economic standpoint, pricing below costs is not a problem for the importing economy as long as the firms that engage in the strategy have little prospect of monopolizing the market. That is why domestic competition policies typically require evidence on anticompetitive practices or likelihood of successful predation. Under WTO rules, however, pricing below costs on the part of exporters is sufficient for imposing import duties, even when it is standard competitive practice—such as during economic downturns.

This and other procedural elements make antidumping the preferred route for firms to obtain protection from their foreign rivals when times are tough. The WTO does have a specific "safeguard" mechanism that enables countries to raise import tariffs temporarily when imports cause "serious injury" to domestic firms. But the procedural hurdles are higher for safeguards, and countries that use them must compensate exporters who are adversely affected.

The numbers speak for themselves. Since the WTO was established in 1995, in excess of three thousand antidumping duties have been put in place (with India, the United States, and the EU being the heaviest users). The corresponding number for safeguard measures is a mere 155 (with developing countries being the heaviest users). Clearly, antidumping is the trade remedy of choice.

But beyond the economics, the global trade regime must address issues of fairness in addition to economic efficiency. When domestic firms have to compete with, say, Chinese firms that are financially supported by a government with deep pockets, the playing field becomes tilted in ways that most people would consider unacceptable.[3] Certain types of competitive advantage undermine the legitimacy of international trade, even when (as with this example) they may confer aggregate economic benefits to the importing country. So, the antidumping regime is not without its political logic.

Trade policy makers are deeply familiar with this logic, which is why the antidumping regime exists in the form that it does, enabling relatively easy protection. What they have never taken on board is that the fairness argument extends beyond the dumping arena. If it is unfair for domestic firms to compete with foreign entities that are subsidized or propped up by their governments, is it not similarly unfair for domestic workers to compete with foreign workers who lack fundamental workers' rights such as collective bargaining or protections against abuse in the workplace? What about firms that despoil the environment, employ child workers, or provide hazardous employment conditions—are they not a source of unfair competition?

Such concerns about unfair trade lie at the heart of the antiglobalization backlash. Yet trade remedy laws allow little room for them beyond the narrow commercial realm of pricing below cost. Labor unions, human rights NGOs, consumer groups, or environmental groups do not have direct access to protection in the way that firms do.

Trade experts have long been wary of opening up the WTO regime to questions about labor and environmental standards or human rights, fearing the slippery slope of protectionism. But it is becoming increasingly clear that failure to take these issues on board does greater damage. Refusal to acknowledge that trade with countries with very different economic, social, and political models raises genuine legitimacy concerns undermines not only those trade relationships but the entirety of the trade regime.

We must distinguish between two different versions of an argument as to why trade may be problematic from a social or political perspective. Some suggest trade is problematic because it redistributes income. The basis for that claim is true, but trivial. Pretty much everything else that happens in a market economy redistributes income somehow. Technology and market competition are the source of endless churn in an economy. Moreover, plenty of other things, including skill-biased innovation and minimum wage laws, have vastly greater effects on income distribution than trade per se.

So it makes very little sense to set international trade apart and decouple it from other domains or approaches for dealing with inequality in labor markets at large (progressive tax systems, active labor market policies, employment-friendly macro policies, etc.). Imports from, say, France may adversely affect domestic firms that are displaced, but there's no reason to treat the people who lose out any differently than workers who are adversely affected by, say, technological innovation. There is a coherent justification for compensating the losers of free trade for reasons of solidarity and equity—but the justification would apply in the case of innovation too. Consequently, the preferred remedies should be the same as well.

There is a second, different social and political objection to trade—that trade violates norms embodied in our institutional arrangements. The suggestion here is that trade may undercut the social bargains struck within a nation and embedded in its laws and regulations. Think for example of workers that must compete with countries where bargaining rights are severely repressed by authoritarian governments. These workers are effectively told that they must either accept lowering their own standards of pay and bargaining or lose their jobs. In such cases compensating the losers would be beside the point, because what is at stake is the surreptitious modification of the rules of the game—the undermining of domestic social bargains through the back door. Trade is not merely a market relationship but an intervention into domestic institutions and an instrument for reconfiguring them to the detriment of certain groups. Responding to such an injury by directly curtailing the trade flows that have the alleged effect would have a legitimate basis. After all, this is no different than keeping imports out that violate, say, domestic health and safety regulations, which most countries already do.

And this brings us back to fair trade. The notion of fair trade is much derided by economists who view it as a thinly disguised cover for self-interested protectionism. But it is already enshrined in trade laws (in the form of antidumping and safeguard remedies), although in a skewed, corporation-friendly way.

So rather than abandon the fair trade concept, we should broaden it, as it exists in trade law, to include *social* dumping. Just as countries can impose duties on goods that are sold below costs, they should be allowed to restrict imports that demonstrably threaten damage to domestic regulatory arrangements. I discuss what such a process may look like in my book *Globalization Paradox*. I would argue that this would not open the trade regime to more protectionist abuse than current antidumping practices already do!

The benefit of thinking about fair trade along these lines is that it allows the drawing of a clear line between trade flows that threaten legitimate domestic political arrangements and those that don't. For example, there is a clear distinction between situations where a trade partner's low wages are due to low productivity versus the abuse of worker rights (including, say, the absence of collective bargaining, or freedom of association.). Both may generate distributional implications at home—but there is a problem of unfair trade only in the second case.

Economists should be more willing to accept that trade may fail to pass the fairness or legitimacy test in certain circumstances. Paradoxically, this would strengthen their defense of international trade in the bulk of cases where the test is easily passed. It would enable them to speak to popular concerns about fairness in trade without undermining the general case for trade.

Advocates of globalization lecture the rest of the world incessantly about how countries must change their policies and institutions to expand their international trade and to become more attractive to foreign investors. This way of thinking confuses means for ends. Globalization should be an instrument for achieving the goals that societies seek: prosperity, stability, freedom, and quality of life. Whether globalization sets off a race to the bottom or not, we can break the deadlock between the proponents and opponents of globalization by acknowledging a simple proposition: social dumping that undermines democratically legitimated domestic practices is not acceptable.

The principle rules out extremism on both sides. It prevents globalizers from gaining the upper hand in cases in which international trade and finance are a backdoor for eroding widely accepted standards at home. Similarly, it prevents protectionists from obtaining benefits at the expense of the rest of society when no significant public purpose is at stake. In less clear-cut cases, in which different values must be traded off against each other, the principle forces internal deliberation and debate—the best way to handle difficult political questions.

One can imagine the questions that a domestic political debate may raise. How much social or economic disruption does the trade in question threaten? How much domestic support is there for the practices, regulations, or standards at stake? Are the adverse effects felt by particularly disadvantaged members of society? How large are the compensating economic benefits, if any? Are there alternative ways of achieving the desired social and economic objectives without restricting international trade or finance? What does the relevant evidence—economic and scientific—say on all these questions?

If the policy process is transparent and inclusive, these kinds of questions will be generated naturally by the forces of competition among interest groups, both pro- and antitrade. To be sure, there are no fail-safe mechanisms for determining whether the rules in question enjoy "broad popular support" and are "demonstrably threatened" by trade. Democratic politics is messy and does not always get it "right." But when we have to trade off different values and interests, there is nothing else on which to rely.

Removing such questions from the province of democratic deliberation and passing them on to technocrats or international bodies is the worst solution. It ensures neither legitimacy nor economic benefits. International agreements *can* make an important contribution, but their role is to reinforce the integrity of the domestic democratic process rather than to replace it.

By refusing to acknowledge the possibility of social dumping—and failing to put in place remedies to it—the trade technocracy has instead opened the door to populists and demagogues on trade. It has allowed trade in general to come under attack instead of the specific problematic flows that probably constitute a very small share of overall imports. It is a clear instance of trade purists doing damage to their cause.

Some regional trade agreements do take social dumping concerns on board, but I think trying to "improve" other countries' labor, environmental, or social standards through trade agreements is generally ineffective—and also misguided to the extent that it puts commercial interests in the driver's seat of what is a deeper developmental problem. There is an important difference, often eluded in fair trade discussions, between using trade policy to prevent the undermining of domestic standards and the use of trade policy to export our standards to other countries. The first is legitimate; the second much less so.

Even if we care about human rights, labor standards, and environmental safeguards in other countries, we should pursue these goals in other international forums, dedicated specifically to these goals, and not through trade deals. If Vietnam has a labor problem, let us not delude ourselves that we can fix it through TPP. And if that problem threatens to undercut our own labor standards, let's deal with that as an instance of social dumping, through domestic trade remedies.

I recognize that such considerations leave me at odds with all the established strands of thinking on trade. Populists such as President Donald Trump have correctly identified the malaise with trade and have capitalized on it. But they greatly exaggerate the real-world significance of the "fairness" concern and seem determined to fix a surgical problem with a sledgehammer.

Meanwhile, economists rightly point out that trade is only weakly implicated in the major economic problems of the day—deindustrialization and income inequality. They are correct that the distributional consequences of trade are better addressed with safety net programs and nontrade remedies. But they have systematically downplayed these consequences—especially when the requisite compensatory programs have remained on paper. And they seem unable to grasp the valid core of the public concern on social dumping.

Finally, progressive voices and their allies affiliated with the labor movement in the United States have been keenly aware of the potential of social dumping. But they want to fight it with revamped global governance measures that are at best ineffective and, at worst, the cause of populist backlash in the countries subject to them.

Responding to the economic and political crisis of our day requires that we restore a healthy balance between an open global economy and the prerogatives of the nation-state. That in turn requires that we be honest about trade's consequences, in particular the stresses it generates for our social compacts alongside the economic opportunities.

None of this implies, for example, that democracies should not trade with nondemocracies or countries with labor abuses. The point is that commercial logic is not the only factor that should govern their economic relationships. We cannot escape, and therefore must confront the dilemma that the gains from trade sometimes come at the expense of strains on domestic social arrangements. Public discussion and deliberation are the only way that democracies can sort out the contending values and trade-offs at stake. Trade disputes with China and other countries are an opportunity for airing—rather than repressing—these issues, and a step forward to ultimately democratizing the world's trade regime.

Conflict between North and South?

Fair trade of this sort isn't antitrade—quite the opposite. Globally, the principle of fairness should include leeway for poorer countries to grow their economies. That means not saddling them with the restrictive rules on intellectual property, industrial policies, capital-account regulations, and investor rights, as current regional trade agreements typically do. For progressives who worry both about inequality in the rich nations and poverty in the rest of the world, the good news is that it is indeed possible to advance on both fronts. But to do so, we must transform our approach to trade deals in some drastic ways.

The world's trade regime is currently driven by a peculiarly mercantilist logic: you lower your barriers in return for me lowering mine. This logic of "exchange of market access" has little economic justification, but has been remarkably successful in promoting trade expansion.

Now that the world economy is already very open, it has run its useful course and causes more problems than it solves.

The principles I laid out above would replace it with a different logic, that of "exchange of policy space." Poor and rich nations alike need to carve out greater space for pursuing their respective objectives: the former to restructure their economies and promote new industries and the latter to address domestic concerns over inequality and distributive justice. Progressives should not buy into a false and counterproductive narrative that sets the interests of the global poor against the interests of rich nations' lower and middle classes. With sufficient institutional imagination, the trade regime can be reformed to the benefit of both sides of the equation.

National Citizens, Global Consciousness

Recognizing the centrality of nation-states and the futility of global governance is compatible with reorienting national interests, over time, in a more global direction. Progress along such a path would require national citizens to recognize that their interests extend beyond their state's borders. National governments are accountable to their own citizens, at least in principle. So, the more global these citizens' sense of their interests becomes, the more globally responsible national policy will be.

This may seem like a pipedream, but something along these lines has already been happening for a while. The global campaign for debt relief for poor countries was led by nongovernmental organizations that successfully mobilized young people in rich countries to put pressure on their governments. Multinational companies are well aware of the effectiveness of such citizen campaigns, having been compelled to increase transparency and change their ways on labor practices around the world. Some governments have gone after foreign political leaders who committed human-rights crimes, with considerable domestic popular support. Nancy Birdsall, the president of the Center for Global Development, cites the example of a Ghanaian citizen providing testimony to the US Congress in the hope of convincing American officials to pressure the World Bank to change its position on user fees in Africa.

The greatest potential upside to such bottom-up efforts to "globalize" national governments can be found in environmental policies, particularly those aimed at mitigating climate change—the most intractable global problem of all. Interestingly, some of the most important initiatives to stem greenhouse gases and promote green growth are the products of local political pressures. World Resources Institute president Andrew Steer notes that more than fifty developing countries are now implementing costly policies to reduce climate change. From the perspective of national interest, that makes no sense at all, given the global-commons nature of the problem.

Some of these policies are driven by the desire to attain a competitive advantage, as is the case with China's support for green industries. But when voters are globally aware and environmentally conscious, good climate policy can also be good politics.

Consider California, which in early 2012 launched a cap-and-trade system that aims to reduce carbon emissions to 1990 levels by the year 2020. While global action remained stalled on capping emissions, environmental groups and concerned citizens successfully pushed for the plan over the opposition of business groups, and the state's Republican governor at the time, Arnold Schwarzenegger, signed it into law in 2006. If it proves a success and remains popular, it could become a model for the entire country.

Global polls such as the World Values Survey indicate that there is still a lot of ground that needs to be covered: self-expressed global citizenship tends to run 15–20 percentage points behind national citizenship. But the gap is smaller for young people, the better educated, and the professional classes. Those who consider themselves to be at the top of the class structure are significantly more globally minded than those who consider themselves to be from the lower classes.

As I have already noted, "global citizenship" will always remain a poor metaphor, because there will never be a world government administering a worldwide political community. But the more we each think of ourselves as globally minded and express our preferences as such to our governments, the less we will need to pursue the chimera of global governance.

CHAPTER 11

Growth Policies for the Future

Global arrangements that open up space for national policy autonomy must be complemented by domestic policies that put that space to good use. That means pursuing economic strategies that are at once productivity enhancing and socially inclusive. We face considerable uncertainty as to what will work in a global environment marked by significant economic and technological dualism, both within and among nations. But the good news is that there is no shortage of good ideas. I begin with the challenges facing developing nations, and then turn to the advanced economies.

Will Developing Nations Lead the World Economy?

The future of the global economy lies more and more in the hands of poor nations. The United States and Europe struggle on as wounded giants, the casualty of their financial excess and political paralysis. They seem condemned to years of low growth at best, widening inequality, and possible social strife.

Much of the rest of the world is meanwhile brimming with energy and hope. China is already the world's largest economy, and emerging and developing countries account for more than half of the world's output. Africa, long synonymous with economic failure, has been christened the land of "lions on the move" by McKinsey.

As is often the case, it is fiction that best reflects the changing mood. Gary Shteyngart's 2010 comic novel "Super Sad True Love Story" is as good a source as any to what may lie ahead.[1] Set in the near future, the novel unfolds against the background of a United States that has slid into financial ruin and single-party dictatorship, and that finds itself embroiled in yet another pointless foreign adventure—this one in Venezuela. All the real work in corporations is done by skilled immigrants, Ivy League colleges have taken on the names of their Asian counterparts to survive, the economy is beholden to China's central bank, and "yuan-pegged US dollars" have replaced regular currency as the safe asset of choice.

But can developing countries really carry the world economy? Much of the optimism about their economic prospects is the result of extrapolation. The decade that preceded the global financial crisis was in many ways the best that the developing world had ever experienced. Growth spread far beyond a few Asian countries, and for the first time since the 1950s the vast majority of poor nations experienced what economists call convergence—a narrowing of the income gap with rich countries.

But this was a special time with lots of tailwind. Commodity prices were high, which especially benefited African and Latin American countries. External finance was plentiful and cheap. Many countries in Africa hit bottom and rebounded from long periods of civil war and economic decline. And, of course, there was generally rapid growth in the advanced countries themselves, fueling world trade volumes to unprecedented heights. Not all these conditions hold in the post-crisis environment.

In principle, low growth in the advanced countries need not handicap the performance of poor nations. Growth ultimately depends on supply-side factors—investment in and acquisition of new technologies. The stock of technologies that are available for poor countries to adopt does not disappear when growth in the advanced countries is sluggish. So, the growth potential is determined by lagging countries' ability to close the gap with the technology frontier—not by how rapidly the frontier itself is advancing.

The bad news is that we still lack an adequate understanding of when this potential is realized and convergence takes place. We do not have a good fix on the kind of policies that generate self-sustaining growth. Even unambiguously successful cases have been subject to conflicting interpretations. The Asian economic miracle is ascribed by some to freer markets, while others think it was state intervention that did the trick. Too many growth accelerations have eventually fizzled out.

The optimists think that this time *is* different. They believe the reforms of the 1990s—improved macroeconomic policy, greater openness, and more democracy—have set the developing world on course for sustained growth. Growth will be easy for poor countries with young populations with access to cheap technologies from abroad, many analysts predict.

My reading of the evidence leads me to be more cautious. It is certainly cause for celebration that inflationary policies have been banished and governance has by and large improved throughout much of the developing world. But by and large these are things that enhance an economy's resilience to shocks and prevent economic collapse. Igniting and sustaining high growth requires something on top: production-oriented policies that stimulate ongoing structural change and foster employment in new economic activities—manufacturing industries in particular. Growth that relies on capital inflows or commodity booms tends to be short-lived. Real growth requires devising the system of carrots and sticks that coax the private sector to invest in new industries that they would not have otherwise, and doing so with minimal corruption and adequate competence.

If history is a guide, the range of countries that are able to pull this off will remain narrow. The process of premature deindustrialization I have discussed earlier will contribute strong headwinds. So, while there may be fewer economic collapses on account of better macroeconomic management, high growth will likely remain episodic and exceptional. On average, this may make for a somewhat better performance than the past but one that is not as stellar as what the optimists expect.

The big question for the world economy is whether advanced countries in economic distress will be able to make room for the faster-growing developing nations. Much of the latter's growth will come by making inroads in manufacturing and service industries in which the rich countries have been traditionally dominant. The employment consequences in the North will be problematic, especially in the context of a shortage of high-paying jobs. Considerable social conflict may become unavoidable, threatening political support for economic openness. Re-designing the world's trade rules to provide adequate policy space for rich and poor nations alike, along the lines I have discussed, will be critical.

The Structural Transformation Gap

Consider the challenges faced by the world's poorest region, Sub-Saharan Africa. Long viewed as an economic basket case, Sub-Saharan

Africa has been experiencing its best growth performance since the immediate post-independence years. Natural-resource windfalls have helped, but the good news extends beyond resource-rich countries. Countries such as Ethiopia, Rwanda, and Uganda, among others, have grown at East Asian rates since the mid-1990s. Africa's business and political leaders are teeming with optimism about the continent's future.

The question is whether this performance can be sustained. So far, growth has been driven by a combination of external resources (aid, debt relief, or commodity windfalls) and the removal of some of the worst policy distortions of the past. Domestic productivity has been given a boost by an increase in demand for domestic goods and services (mostly the latter), increased public investment, and more efficient use of resources. The trouble is that it is not clear from whence future productivity gains will come.

The underlying problem is the weakness of these economies' structural transformation. East Asian countries grew rapidly by replicating, in a much shorter time frame, what today's advanced countries did following the Industrial Revolution. They turned their farmers into manufacturing workers, diversified their economies, and exported a range of increasingly sophisticated goods. Little of this process is taking place in Africa. As researchers at the African Center for Economic Transformation in Accra, Ghana, put it, the continent is "growing rapidly, transforming slowly."

In principle, the region's potential for labor-intensive industrialization is great. A Chinese shoe manufacturer, for example, pays its Ethiopian workers one-tenth what it pays its workers back home. It can raise Ethiopian workers' productivity to half or more of Chinese levels through in-house training. The savings in labor costs more than offset other incremental costs of doing business in an African environment, such as poor infrastructure and bureaucratic red tape.

But the aggregate numbers tell a worrying story. Fewer than 10 percent of African workers find jobs in manufacturing, and among those only a tiny fraction—as low as one-tenth—are employed in modern, formal firms with adequate technology. Distressingly, there has been very little improvement in this regard, despite the high growth rates. In fact, Sub-Saharan Africa is *less* industrialized today than it was in the 1980s. Private investment in modern industries, especially nonresource tradables, has not increased and remains too low to sustain structural transformation. The rapid digitization and automation of many traditionally labor-intensive industries will make it even harder for Africa to make its mark in manufacturing. Once shoes can be produced cheaply with 3D printing technologies, the winners will be countries like Germany, not Ethiopia.

As in all developing countries, farmers in Africa are flocking to the cities. But, as a study from the Groningen Growth and Development Center shows, rural migrants do not end up in modern manufacturing industries, as they did in East Asia, but in services such as retail trade and distribution.[2] Though such services have higher productivity than much of agriculture, they are not technologically dynamic in Africa and have been falling behind the world frontier.

Consider Rwanda, a much-heralded success story where GDP has increased by a whopping 9.6 percent per year, on average, since 1995 (with per-capita incomes rising at a 5.2 percent annual pace). As Xinshen Diao of the International Food Policy Research Institute shows, this growth was led by nontradable services, in particular construction, transport, and hotels and restaurants. The public sector dominates investment, and the bulk of public investment is financed by foreign grants. Foreign aid has caused the real exchange rate to appreciate, compounding the difficulties faced by manufacturing and other tradables.

None of this is to dismiss Rwanda's progress in reducing poverty, which reflects reforms in health, education, and the general policy environment. Without question, these improvements have raised the country's potential income. But improved governance and human capital do not necessarily translate into economic dynamism. What Rwanda and other African countries lack are the modern, tradable industries that can turn the potential into reality by acting as the domestic engine of productivity growth.

The African economic landscape's dominant feature—an informal sector comprising microenterprises, household production, and unofficial activities—absorbs the growing urban labor force and acts as a social safety net. But the evidence suggests it cannot provide the missing productive dynamism. Studies show that very few microenterprises grow out of informality, just as the bulk of successful established firms do not start out as small, informal enterprises.

Optimists say that the good news about African structural transformation does not yet show up in macroeconomic data. They may well be right. But if they are wrong, Africa may confront some serious difficulties in the decades ahead.

Half of Sub-Saharan Africa's population is under twenty-five years of age. According to the World Bank, each year an additional five million are turning fifteen, "crossing the threshold from childhood to adulthood." Given the slow pace of positive structural transformation, the Bank projects that over the next decade only one in four African youth will find regular employment as a salaried worker, and that only a small fraction of those will be in the formal sector of modern enterprises.

Two decades of economic expansion in Sub-Saharan Africa have raised a young population's expectations of good jobs without greatly expanding the capacity to deliver them. These are the conditions that make social protest and political instability likely. Economic planning based on simple extrapolations of recent growth will exacerbate the discrepancy. Instead, African political leaders may have to manage expectations downward, while working to increase the rate of structural transformation and social inclusion.

Back to Fundamentals in Developing Nations

For developing economies, the three key growth fundamentals are as follows: the acquisition of skills and education by the workforce; the improvement of institutions and governance; and structural transformation from low-productivity to high-productivity activities (as typified by industrialization). East Asian–style rapid growth has typically required a heavy dose of structural transformation for a number of decades, with steady progress on education and institutions over the years providing the longer-term underpinnings of convergence with advanced economies.

Premature industrialization rules out the traditional path of specialization in a sequence of export-oriented manufactures. So, developing nations must rely more on the longer-term fundamentals of education and institutions. These do generate growth—and indeed are indispensable to it ultimately. But they generate 2–3 percent growth per capita at best, and not East Asia's 7–8 percent growth.

Compare India with China. China grew by building factories and filling them up with peasants with little education. The transformation generated an instant boost in productivity. India's comparative advantage lies in relatively skill-intensive services—such as IT—which can absorb no more than a tiny slice of the country's largely unskilled labor force. It will take many decades for the average skill level in India to rise to the point where it can pull overall productivity of the economy significantly higher. So, the medium-term growth potential of India lies much below China's record of recent decades. A significant boost in infrastructure spending and policy reforms can make a difference, but only so far.

On the other hand, being the porpoise rather than the hare in the growth race can be an advantage too. Countries that rely on the steady, economy-wide accumulation of skills and on improved governance may not grow as fast, but they may be more stable, less prone to crises, and more likely to converge with advanced countries eventually. China's economic achievements are undeniable. But it remains an authoritarian country where the Communist Party retains its political monopoly. So, the challenges of political and institutional transformation China faces are immeasurably greater than India's. The uncertainty that confronts a long-term investor is correspondingly higher.

Cheap external finance, plentiful capital inflows, and commodity booms helped hide many such blemishes and fueled growth across the emerging markets over the last decade and a half. In the years ahead, the world economy will not be as supportive. It will be easier to tell apart those countries that have truly strengthened their economic and political fundamentals from those that have coasted on false narratives and the strength of investor appetite for emerging markets.

What the World Needs from Developing Nations

In 2001 Goldman Sachs's Jim O'Neill famously coined the term *BRIC* to characterize the world's four largest developing economies—Brazil, Russia, India, and China.[3] Nearly two decades later, just about the only thing that these four have in common is that they are the only ones ranked among the world's fifteen biggest (measured in purchasing-power adjusted dollars) that are not members of the Organization of Economic Cooperation and Development (OECD).

The countries have very different economic structures: Russia and Brazil rely on commodities, India on services, and China on manufacturing. Brazil and India are democracies, while China and Russia are decidedly not. And as Joe Nye has written, Russia is a superpower in decline while China and (less markedly) the others are on the rise.

Yet in a strange case of life imitating fantasy, BRICS—the original four countries now joined by South Africa—have formed a grouping of their own with regular meetings and policy initiatives. Their most ambitious effort to date is the establishment of a development bank in 2014.

The "New Development Bank" focuses on infrastructure development. Infrastructure investment in developing countries, BRICS leaders have said, is constrained by "insufficient long-term financing and foreign direct investment." They have pledged to make an initial capital contribution to the bank that would be "substantial and sufficient for the bank to be effective in financing infrastructure." A second initiative, announced in Durban in 2013, is the creation of a $100 billion contingent reserve facility to deal with "short-term liquidity pressures."[4]

That the world's biggest developing economies are regularly talking to each other and coming up with common initiatives can be cause only for celebration. Nonetheless, it is disappointing that they have chosen to focus on infrastructure finance as their first major collaboration. This approach represents a 1950s view of economic development, which has long been superseded by a more variegated perspective that recognizes a multiplicity of constraints—everything from poor governance to market failures—of varying importance in different countries. One might even say that today's global economy suffers from too much, rather than too little, cross-border finance.

What the world needs from BRICS is not another development bank but greater leadership on the global issues of the day. The BRICS nations are home to around half of the world's population and the bulk of unexploited economic potential. If the global community fails to confront the serious challenges it faces—from the need for a sound global economic architecture to addressing climate change—they are the ones that will pay the dearest price. Yet these countries have so far played rather unimaginative and timid roles in international forums such as the Group of 20 or the World Trade Organization. When they have asserted themselves, it has been largely in pursuit of narrow national interests.

The world economy has lived so far under a set of ideas and institutions emanating from the advanced countries of the West. The United States gave us the doctrine of liberal, rule-based multilateralism; the system had many blemishes, but these served only to highlight the lofty principles against which, by and large, the regime operated. From Europe came democratic values, social solidarity, and for all its current problems, the most impressive feat of institutional engineering of the century, the European Union. These old powers neither have the legitimacy nor the power to sustain the global order into the future.

The new rising powers must demonstrate what they stand for and which values they will articulate and disseminate. They must develop their vision of a new global economy, beyond complaints about the asymmetric power structure. Unfortunately, it is not yet clear whether they have the inclination to rise above their immediate interests to address the globe's common challenges.

Their own development experience makes countries like China, India, and Brazil resistant to market fundamentalism and natural advocates for institutional diversity and pragmatic experimentalism in the world economy. They can build on this experience to articulate a new global narrative that emphasizes the real economy over finance, policy diversity over harmonization, national policy space over external constraints, and social inclusion over technocratic elitism. They must stop being supplicants, and act like real leaders, understanding that others too, including advanced countries, face challenges that sometimes require policies that put the domestic economy before the global one. And they must work to uphold the corner-stone principles of the world economy that have served it so well in the last sixty years: nondiscrimination and multilateralism.

Ultimately, though, BRICS must also lead by example. China's and Russia's human-rights practices and their suppression of political dissent are incompatible with global leadership. These authoritarian regimes must reform themselves at home if they are to exert any kind of moral claim abroad.

The Return of Public Investment

The idea that public investment in infrastructure—roads, dams, and power plants—is an indispensable driver of economic growth has always held powerful sway over the minds of policy makers in poor nations. It lay behind early development assistance programs following the Second World War, as the World Bank and bilateral donors funneled resources to newly independent nations to finance large infrastructure projects. It is also the thinking that motivates the new Asia Infrastructure Investment Bank (AIIB), a China-led initiative that aims to fill the region's supposedly $8 trillion infrastructure gap. China's massive One Belt, One Road (OBOR) plan is an attempt at once to project the country's growing power and to maintain its high economic growth rate.

This kind of public investment–driven growth model—often derisively called "capital fundamentalism"—has long been out of fashion among development experts. Since the 1970s, economists have been advising policy makers to deemphasize the public sector, physical capital, and infrastructure and to prioritize private markets, human capital (skills and training), and reforms in governance and institutions. From all appearances, development strategies have been transformed wholesale as a result.

Yet look at countries that are still growing very rapidly—despite the global economic headwinds of late—and you will find public investment is doing a lot of the work.

In Africa, Ethiopia is the most astounding success story of the last decade. Its economy has expanded at an average annual rate above 10 percent since 2004, registering significant improvements in poverty and health outcomes. The country is resource-poor and did not benefit from commodity booms, unlike many of its peers in the continent. Economic liberalization and structural reforms of the type typically recommended by the World Bank and other donors did not play much of a role either.

High growth was the result of a massive increase in public investment, which rose from 5 percent of GDP in the early 1990s to 19 percent in 2011—the third highest in the world according to the World Bank. The Ethiopian government went on a spending spree, building roads, railways, power plants, and an agricultural extension system that significantly enhanced productivity in rural areas where most of the poor reside. Expenditures were financed in part by foreign aid and in part by heterodox policies (such as financial repression) that channeled private saving to the government.

In India, rapid growth is also underpinned by a substantial increase in overall investment, which now stands at around one-third of GDP. Much of this increase has come from private sources, as the shackles on the business sector were gradually relaxed since the early 1980s. But the public sector continues to play an important role. The government has had to step in as both private investment and total factor productivity growth have faltered in recent years. These days it is public investment on infrastructure that helps maintain India's growth momentum. "I think two sectors holding back the economy are private investments and exports," says the government's chief economic adviser Arvind Subramanian. "That is why . . . public investment is going to fill in the gap."[5]

Turning to Latin America, Bolivia is one of the rare mineral exporters that has managed to avoid the fate of others in the current downturn of the commodity cycle. Its growth rate is expected to remain at or above 4 percent in a region that is barely growing. Much of that has to do with public investment. The country's president Evo Morales sees public investment as the engine of the Bolivian economy. Since 2006, total public investment has more than doubled in relation to national income, from 6 percent in 2005 to 13 percent in 2014, and the government intends to push the ratio even higher in coming years.

We know that public investment hikes, just like commodity booms, end all too often in tears. The economic and social returns go down and money dries up, preparing the stage for a debt crisis. An International Monetary Fund study finds that most public investment drives falter, after some early positive effects.[6] But much depends on local specificities. Public investment can enhance the economy's productivity for a substantial period of time, of a decade or more, as it clearly has done in Ethiopia. It can also catalyze private investment, and there is some evidence that it has done so in India in recent years.[7]

The potential benefits of public investment are not limited to developing countries. In fact, today it may be the advanced economies of North America and western Europe that stand to gain the most from a ramp up in domestic public investment. In the aftermath of the great recession, there are many ways in which these economies could put additional public spending to good use: to increase demand and employment, restore crumbling infrastructures, and enhance R&D, particularly in green technologies.

In policy debates such arguments are typically countered by objections related to fiscal balance and macroeconomic stability. But public investment is different from other types of public spending, such as expenditures on the government wage bill or social transfers. They serve to accumulate assets rather than consume them. As long as the return to those assets exceeds the cost of funds, public investment in fact strengthens the government's balance sheet.

We do not fully know how the experiments in Ethiopia, India, or Bolivia will eventually turn out. Caution is warranted before one extrapolates lessons to other cases. Nevertheless, they are useful examples for other countries, including developed ones, which are in search of growth strategies in a global environment that threatens to turn even more hostile.

Inclusive Growth in the Developed World

The developed world needs new ideas—perhaps even more so than developing nations, which can always emulate yesterday's successes—to embark on a path of inclusive economic growth. We are getting a fresh policy take for sure with Donald Trump's ascendancy to the US presidency. But all indications as I write these lines are that he will lead us astray and make our problems worse.

Donald Trump's brand of flawed economic strategy was on full display even before he took office as president. Within weeks of the election, Trump had already claimed a victory. Through a mix of carrots and sticks, he was able to prevail on the heating and cooling firm Carrier to keep some of its operations alive in Indiana, "saving" around 1,000 American jobs. Touring the Carrier plant subsequently, he warned other US firms that he would impose stiff tariffs on them if they move plants overseas and ship products back home.

His Twitter account has produced a stream of commentary in the same vein. He has taken credit for Ford's decision keep a Lincoln plant in Kentucky and not move it to Mexico. He has threatened General Motors with import tariffs if it continues to import Chevrolet Cruzes from Mexico instead of making them in the United States. Trump has also gone after defense contractors for cost overruns, berating aerospace giants Boeing and Lockheed Martin, in particular, on different occasions for producing planes that are too expensive.

Trump's policy style is evidently a sharp break from his predecessors. It is highly personalized, temperamental, and particularistic. It relies on threats and bullying. It is prone to boasting and exaggeration about actual successes. It is a type of public spectacle, staged on Twitter. And it is deeply corrosive of democratic norms.

Economists tend to advocate an arms' length approach in the government's relationship to business. Public officials are supposed to insulate themselves from private firms, lest they become corrupted and engage in favoritism. This is a prized principle in the United States—but more often honored in the breach than in the observance. To take only the most obvious example, finance moguls have exerted an undeniable influence in shaping US government policy over the last three decades.

Yet a similar practice of close business–government interactions lies also behind many of America's successes. The history of US economic development is one of pragmatic partnerships and close collaboration between the public and private sector, rather than arms' length relationships and rigid rules. As historically minded economists and policy analysts such as Stephen Cohen, Brad de Long, and Michael Lind have reminded us, the United States is heir to a Hamiltonian tradition in which the federal government provides the investment, infrastructure, finance, and other support that private enterprise needs.[8]

US technological innovation owes as much to American entrepreneurs' and inventors' ingenuity as it does to specific government programs such as loan assistance or government purchases. As Harvard Business School professor Josh Lerner mentions, some of the most dynamic technology companies in the United States, including Apple and Intel, received financial support from the government before going public.[9] The electric car maker Tesla was a beneficiary of the same public loan guarantee program as Solyndra, the solar cell company that went bust in a public and spectacular manner.

As the last example illustrates, many public initiatives fail. However, the ultimate test is whether the social return on the portfolio as a whole is positive, taking successes together with the flops. Such broad evaluations tend to be rare. But one analysis found that US programs in energy efficiency had produced positive net benefits. Interestingly, the bulk of the benefits were attributable to three relatively modest projects.[10]

Sociologists Fred Block and Matthew Keller have provided perhaps the best analysis of the US "developmental state"—a reality that they say has been obscured in public discussion thanks to the reigning market fundamentalist ideology. They describe how a "decentralized network of publicly funded laboratories" and an "alphabet soup" of different funding initiatives, such as the Small Business Innovation Research (SBIR) program, work with private firms and help them commercialize their products.[11] They and their colleagues have documented the extensive role of both federal and state governments in supporting the collaborative networks on which innovation rests—whether in biotech, green technologies, or nanotech.[12]

Such industrial policies, based on close collaboration and coordination between the public and private sectors, have of course been the hallmark of East Asian economic policy making. It is difficult to imagine China's transformation into a manufacturing powerhouse—and the attendant success of its export-oriented model—without the helping and guiding hand the Chinese government provided. It is ironic that the same people who extol Chinese gains from globalization are often alarmed that a US administration may copy the Chinese approach and explicitly endorse industrial policies.

Unlike China, of course, the United States purports to be a democracy. And industrial policy in a democracy requires transparency, accountability, and institutionalization. The relationship between the government and private firms must be calibrated carefully. Government agencies need to be close enough to private enterprises to elicit the requisite information about the technological and market realities on the ground. For example, what are the fundamental reasons for the loss in manufacturing jobs in, say, autos and how can the government help, if at all? But they cannot get so close to private firms that they are captured and end in their pocket, or, in the other extreme, simply order them around.

And that is where industrial policy a la Trump fails to pass the test. On the one hand, his appointments to key economic positions indicate he has little intention to sever government ties to Wall Street and big finance. On the other hand, his policy-making-by-tweet suggests he doesn't have much interest in building the institutionalized dialog, with all the required safeguards, sound industrial policy requires.

So, we can expect his administration's industrial policy to vacillate between cronyism and bullying, doing little good for American workers or the economy as a whole.

Green Industrial Policies

The future of our planet depends on the world economy's rapid transition to "green growth" based on clean technologies—modes of production that emit substantially fewer greenhouse gases. Yet carbon remains badly mispriced, thanks to both fossil fuel subsidies and the absence of taxes needed to address global climate change externalities.

In this context, subsidies that promote the development of green technologies—wind, solar, bio-energy, geothermal, and hydrogen and fuel cell technologies, among others—are doubly necessary. First, they nudge pioneers to invest in uncertain, risky ventures where their research and development efforts generate social learning of great value. Second, they counter the effects that the mispricing of carbon has on the direction of technical change. These two considerations provide mutually reinforcing reasons for why the world would be collectively better off if governments nurtured and supported green technologies.

Government support for green industries has in fact become rampant, both in advanced and emerging economies. Look around those economies and you will find a bewildering array of government initiatives designed to encourage renewable energy use and stimulate green technology investment. Even though full pricing of carbon would be a far better way to address climate change, it appears most governments would rather deal with the problem through subsidies and regulations that increase the profitability of investments in renewable energy sources. Often, the motive seems to be to give the domestic industry a leg up in global competition.

Normally, we consider these competitive motives to have a beggar-thy-neighbor nature. Market-share considerations are zero-sum from a global standpoint in traditional industries, and any resources invested in generating national gains come at the cost of global losses. However, in the context of green growth, national efforts to boost domestic green industries can be globally desirable, even if the motives are parochial and commercial. When cross-border spillovers militate against taxing carbon and subsidizing technological development in clean industries, boosting green industries for competitive reasons is a good thing, not a bad thing.

Industrial policy opponents rely on two arguments. The first is that governments do not have the information needed to make the right choices as to which firms or industries to support. The second is that once governments are in the business of supporting this or that industry, they invite rent seeking and political manipulation by well-connected firms and lobbyists. In the United States, the case of Solyndra—a solar cell manufacturer that folded after having received more than half a billion in loan guarantees from the US government—provides a recent illustration where both failures were apparently in play.

In reality, the first of these arguments—about lack of omniscience— is largely irrelevant, while the second—about political influence—can be overcome with appropriate institutional design. Good industrial policy does not rely on government's omniscience or ability to pick winners. Failures are an inevitable and necessary part of a well-designed industrial policy program.

While it is too early to pass a firm judgment on the US loan guarantee program, it is clear that the Solyndra case cannot be properly evaluated without taking into account the many successes the program has spawned. Tesla Motors, which received a $465 million loan guarantee in 2009, has seen its shares soar and is now a model company. An early evaluation of US Department of Energy programs in energy efficiency in 2001 found the net benefits amounted to $30 billion—an excellent return for an investment of roughly $7 billion over twenty-two years (in 1999 dollars).[13] Interestingly, much of the positive impact was due to three relatively modest projects in the building sector.

Intelligent industrial policy requires mechanisms that recognize errors and revise policies accordingly. Clear objectives, measurable targets, close monitoring, proper evaluation, well-designed rules, and professionalism provide useful institutional safeguards. As challenging as these may be in practice, they constitute a much less formidable requirement than that of picking winners.

An explicit industrial policy that is carried out self-consciously and designed with pitfalls in mind is more likely to overcome the typical informational and political barriers than one that is implemented, as is so often the case, surreptitiously and under the radar screen.

Where green industrial policy can get damaging is when national strategies take the form not of subsidizing domestic industries but of taxing or restricting market access to foreign green industries. The case of solar panels provides a cautionary tale. Trade disputes between China, on the one hand, and the United States and Europe, on the other, have attracted much attention. Luckily, this is the exception rather than the rule. Trade restrictions have so far played a small role relative to subsidies to domestic industry.

In practice, we are unlikely to get purely green industrial policy, focusing squarely on the development and diffusion of green technologies instead of competitiveness, commercial, employment, or mercantilist motives. Indirect, but politically salient, objectives such as "green jobs" will likely continue to present a more attractive platform for promoting industrial policy than alternative energy or clean technologies.

From a global standpoint, it would be far better if national competitiveness concerns were to lead to a subsidy war than a tariff war. The former expands the global supply of clean technologies while the latter restricts it. So far, that is largely what we have been getting, though there is no guarantee that we can extrapolate this trend into the future.

From Welfare State to Innovation State

A specter is haunting the world economy—the specter of job-killing technology. How this challenge is handled will determine the fate of the world's market economies and democratic polities, in much the same way that Europe's response to the rise of the socialist movement during the late nineteenth to early twentieth centuries shaped the course of subsequent history.

In the earlier period, governments diffused the threat of revolution from below that Karl Marx had prophesied by expanding political and social rights, regulating markets, erecting a welfare state that provided extensive transfers and social insurance, and smoothing the ups and downs of the macroeconomy. In effect, they reinvented capitalism to make it more inclusive and to give workers a stake in the system.

Today's technological revolutions call for another reinvention of similar magnitude. The potential benefits of ongoing discoveries and applications in robotics, biotechnology, digital technologies, and other areas are all around us and easy to see. Instead, many believe that the world economy may be at the cusp of another explosion in new technologies. The trouble is that the bulk of these new technologies are labor-saving. They entail the replacement of workers with low to moderate skills with machines and highly-skilled operatives.

There are of course some low-skill tasks that cannot be easily automated. Janitors, to cite a common example, cannot be replaced by robots—at least not as of yet. But few jobs are really protected from technological innovation. To continue with the same example, as the workplace gets digitalized and fewer workers are needed to run it, there will be less human-generated trash that needs to be cleaned up.

A world in which robots and machines do the work of humans need not be one where there is a lot of unemployment. But it is certainly one where the lion's share of the productivity gains accrues to the owners of the new technologies and the machines that embody them. The bulk of the workforce is condemned either to joblessness or low wages.

Indeed, something like this has been going on in the advanced countries for at least four decades. Skill- and capital-intensive technologies are the leading culprit behind the rise in inequality since the late 1970s. By all indications this trend is likely to continue. It will produce levels of inequality that are historically unprecedented, threating severe social and political conflict.

It doesn't have to be this way. With some creative thinking and institutional engineering, we can save capitalism from itself—once again.

The key is to recognize that disruptive new technologies produce large social gains and private losses simultaneously. These gains and losses can be repackaged in a manner that benefits everyone. Just as with the earlier reinvention of capitalism, there is a large role for the state here.

Consider how new technologies develop. Each potential innovator faces a large upside, but also a high risk. If the innovation is successful the innovator reaps a large gain, as does society at large. But if it fails, the innovator is out of luck. Among all the new ideas that are pursued, only a few eventually become commercially successful.

These risks are especially high at the dawn of a new innovation age. Achieving the socially desirable level of innovative effort then requires either foolhardy entrepreneurs—who are willing to take high risks— or the availability of risk capital on a sufficient scale.

Financial markets in the advanced economies provide risk capital through different sets of arrangements—venture funds, stock markets, private equity, and so on. But there is no reason why the state should not be playing this role on an even larger scale, enabling not only greater amounts of technological innovation but also channeling the benefits directly to society at large. As Mariana Mazzucato has pointed out, the state already plays a significant role in funding new technologies.[14] The Internet and many of the key technologies used in the iPhone have been spillovers of government subsidized R&D programs and US Department of Defense projects. But typically the government acquires no stake in the commercialization of such successful technologies, leaving the profits entirely to the firms and their private funders.

There is an even broader argument for a public stake in new technologies. Regardless of whether they are directly subsidized or not, private innovation relies on a wide range of public supports—highways and other public infrastructure, public education and universities, intellectual property rules, a legal system that can enforce contracts, macroeconomic and financial stability, and so on. Plant Silicon Valley's brightest minds in Southern Sudan, and they would hardly be as productive—or as rich.

Imagine that a government would set up a number of professionally managed public venture funds that would invest and take equity stakes in a large cross-section of new technologies. The resources needed would be raised by issuing bonds in financial markets. These funds would operate on market principles and have to provide periodic accounting to political authorities (especially when their overall rate of return falls below a threshold), but would be otherwise autonomous.

Designing the right institutions for public venture capital can be difficult. For a model of how such funds might operate independently of day-to-day political pressure, we can turn to central banks.

Society, through its agent—the government—would then end up as co-owner of the new generation of technologies and machines. The public venture funds' share of profits from the commercialization of new technologies would be returned to ordinary citizens in the form of a social innovation dividend. This income stream would supplement workers' earnings from the labor market. It would also allow them to reduce their working hours—finally approaching Marx's dream of a society in which technological advance enables individuals to "hunt in the morning, fish in the afternoon, rear cattle in the evening, criticize after dinner."

The welfare state was the innovation that democratized capitalism in the twentieth century. The twenty-first century requires an analogous shift to the "innovation state." The Achilles' heel of the welfare state was that it required a high level of taxation without stimulating a compensating investment in innovative capacity. An innovation state, along the lines sketched above, would reconcile equity with incentives for innovation.

Rethinking Democracy

The global dissemination of democratic norms from the advanced countries of the West to the rest of the world has been perhaps the most significant benefit of globalization. Yet not all is well with democracy. Today's democratic governments perform poorly and their future remains very much in doubt. In the advanced countries, dissatisfaction revolves around their inability to deliver effective economic policies for growth and inclusion. In the newer democracies of the developing world, failure to safeguard civil liberties and political freedom is an additional source of discontent.

A true democracy, one that combines majority rule with respect for the rights of the minority, requires two sets of institutions. First, we need institutions of *representation* such as political parties, parliaments, and electoral rules, designed to elicit popular preferences and turn them into policy action. Second, we need institutions of *restraint* such as the judiciary and media, which uphold fundamental rights like freedom of speech and prevent the government of the day from abusing its power. Elections without the rule of law are a recipe for the tyranny of majority.

Democracy in this sense—what many call "liberal democracy"—flourished only after the emergence of the nation-state and the popular mobilization and upheaval that the industrial revolution produced. So, it should not be a surprise that its crisis in the old democracies is a reflection of the stress that the nation-state finds itself under.

The attack on the nation-state comes both from below and from above. Forces of economic globalization have blunted the instruments of national economic policy and have weakened traditional mechanisms of inclusion through transfers and redistribution. Policy makers hide behind (real or imagined) competitive pressures emanating from the global economy to justify their lack of responsiveness to popular demands. And they cite the very same pressures when they must implement unpopular policies such as fiscal austerity. One consequence has been the rise of extremist groups in Europe and populist politicians like Donald Trump.

At the same time, regional separatist movements such as those in Catalonia and Scotland challenge the legitimacy of nation-states as they are currently configured and seek their breakup. Whether they do too much or too little, national governments face a crisis of representation.

In many developing nations, it is the institutions of restraint that are failing. Governments that come to power through the ballot box often become corrupt and power hungry. They replicate the practices of the elitist regimes they replaced, clamping down on the press and civil liberties and emasculating (or capturing) the judiciary. The result has been called "illiberal democracy" or "competitive authoritarianism."[15] Venezuela, Turkey, Egypt, and Thailand are some of the better-known recent examples.

When democracy fails to deliver economically or politically, it is perhaps not surprising that many people look for authoritarian solutions. Delegating economic policy to technocratic bodies in order to insulate them from the "folly of the masses" is the preferred approach of many economists. With its independent central bank and fiscal rules, the European Union has already travelled far along this road. In India, businessmen look wistfully at China and wish their leaders could act just as boldly and decisively—more autocratically—to address reform challenges. In countries like Egypt and Thailand, military intervention is viewed as a temporary necessity in order to put an end to the irresponsibility of elected leaders.

These autocratic responses are ultimately self-defeating, as they deepen the democratic malaise. In Europe, economic policy needs more democratic legitimacy, not less. This in turn can be achieved by either significantly strengthening democratic deliberation and accountability at the level of the union or increasing the policy autonomy of individual member states. In other words, Europe faces a choice between more political union and less economic union. As long as it delays making the choice, democracy will suffer.

In developing nations, military intervention undermines long-term prospects for democracy because it impedes the development of a democratic "culture"—habits of moderation and compromise among competing civilian groups. As long as the military remains the ultimate political arbiter, these groups focus their strategies on the military rather than each other.

Effective institutions of restraint do not emerge overnight. And it may seem like those in power would never want to create such institutions. But if there is some likelihood that I will be voted out of office and the opposition will take over, institutions of restraint protect me from others' abuses tomorrow—as much as they protect others from my abuses today. So, one prerequisite for illiberal democracies to turn into liberal ones over time is for the prospects of sustained political competition to remain strong.

Optimists believe that all these problems will be solved as new technologies and modes of governance render democracies centered on the nation-state as archaic as the horse-drawn carriage. Pessimists think that they pale in comparison to the external challenges that will be mounted by illiberal states like China and Russia, which play on the global stage by realpolitik rules. Either way, democracy will need to be reinvigorated if it is to have a future.

CHAPTER 12

It's the Politics, Stupid!

A s the world reels from Brexit, Trump's victory, and other shocks, it is dawning on economists and policy makers that they severely underestimated the political fragility of the current form of globalization. The popular revolt that appears to be underway is taking diverse, overlapping forms: reassertion of local and national identities, demand for greater democratic control and accountability, rejection of centrist political parties, and distrust of elites and experts.

This backlash was predictable. Some economists, including me, did warn about the consequences of pushing economic globalization beyond the boundaries of institutions that regulate, stabilize, and legitimize markets. Too much international economic integration, I wrote a full two decades ago, risks domestic disintegration.[1] Indeed, the push for hyperglobalization in trade and finance, intended to create seamlessly integrated world markets, tore domestic societies apart. Even two decades ago, it was easy to see that mainstream politicians' unwillingness to offer remedies for the insecurities and inequalities of our globalized age would create political space for demagogues with easy solutions. Back then, it was Ross Perot and Patrick Buchanan; today it is Donald Trump, Marine Le Pen, and sundry others.

The Abdication of the Left

The bigger surprise is the decidedly right-wing tilt the political reaction has taken. In Europe, it is predominantly nationalists and nativist populists that have risen to prominence, with the left advancing only in a few places such as Greece and Spain. In the United States, the right-wing demagogue Donald Trump has managed to displace the Republican establishment, while the leftist Bernie Sanders was unable to overtake the centrist Hillary Clinton.

As an emerging new establishment consensus grudgingly concedes, globalization accentuates class divisions between those who have the skills and resources to take advantage of global markets and those who don't. Income and class cleavages, in contrast to identity cleavages based on race, ethnicity, or religion, have traditionally strengthened the political left. So why has the left been unable to mount a significant political challenge to globalization?

One answer is that immigration has overshadowed other globalization "shocks." The perceived threat of mass inflows of migrants and refugees from poor countries with very different cultural traditions aggravates identity cleavages that far-right politicians are exceptionally well placed to exploit. So, it is not a surprise that rightist politicians from Trump to Marine Le Pen lace their message of national reassertion with a rich dose of anti-Muslim symbolism.

Latin American democracies provide a telling contrast. These countries experienced globalization mostly as a trade and foreign-investment shock, rather than as an immigration shock. Globalization became synonymous with so-called Washington Consensus policies and financial opening. Immigration from the Middle East or Africa remained limited and had little political salience. So, the populist backlash in

Latin America—in Brazil, Bolivia, Ecuador, and, most disastrously, Venezuela—took a left-wing form.

The story is similar in the main two exceptions to right-wing resurgence in Europe—Greece and Spain. In Greece, the main political fault line has been austerity policies imposed by European institutions and the International Monetary Fund. In Spain, most immigrants until recently came from culturally similar Latin American countries. In both countries, the far right lacked the breeding ground it had elsewhere.

But the experience in Latin America and southern Europe reveals perhaps a greater weakness of the left: the absence of a clear program to refashion capitalism and globalization for the twenty-first century. From Greece's Syriza to Brazil's Workers' Party, the left has failed to come up with ideas that are economically sound and politically popular, beyond ameliorative policies such as income transfers.

Economists and technocrats on the left bear a large part of the blame. Instead of contributing to such a program, they abdicated too easily to market fundamentalism and bought in to its central tenets. Worse still, they led the hyperglobalization movement at crucial junctures.

The enthroning of free capital mobility—especially of the short-term kind—as a policy norm by the European Union, the Organization for Economic Cooperation and Development, and the IMF was arguably the most fateful decision for the global economy in recent decades. As Rawi Abdelal has shown, this effort was spearheaded in the late 1980s and early 1990s not by free-market ideologues but by French technocrats such as Jacques Delors (at the European Commission) and Henri Chavranski (at the OECD), who were closely associated with the Socialist Party in France.[2] Similarly, in the United States, it was technocrats associated with the more Keynesian Democratic Party, such as Lawrence Summers, who led the charge for financial deregulation.

France's Socialist technocrats appear to have concluded from the failed Mitterrand experiment with Keynesianism in the early 1980s that domestic economic management was no longer possible, and that there was no real alternative to financial globalization. The best that could be done was to enact Europe-wide and global rules, instead of allowing powerful countries like Germany or the United States to impose their own.

The good news is that the intellectual vacuum on the left is being filled, and there is no longer any reason to believe in the tyranny of "no alternatives." Politicians on the left have less and less reason not to draw on "respectable" academic firepower in economics.

Consider just a few examples: Anat Admati and Simon Johnson have advocated radical banking reforms that would prevent the problem of "too big to fail." Thomas Piketty and Tony Atkinson have proposed a rich menu of policies to deal with inequality at the national level, including the taxation of wealth and rules that would make technological innovation more worker friendly. Mariana Mazzucato and Ha-Joon Chang have written insightfully on how to deploy the public sector to foster inclusive innovation. Brad DeLong, Jeffrey Sachs, and Lawrence Summers (the very same!) have argued for long-term public investment in infrastructure and the green economy. Joseph Stiglitz and José Antonio Ocampo have proposed reforms for the global economy to enhance the influence of developing nations, which complement the proposals in this book. There are enough elements here for building a programmatic economic response from the left.[3]

A crucial difference between the right and the left is that the right thrives on deepening divisions in society—"us" versus "them"—while the left, when successful, overcomes these cleavages through reforms that bridge them. Hence the paradox that earlier waves of reforms from the left—Keynesianism, social democracy, and the welfare state—both saved capitalism from itself and effectively rendered themselves super-fluous. Absent such a response again, the field will be left wide open for populists and far-right groups to make further gains. They will lead the world—as they always have—to deeper division and more frequent conflict.

The Politics of Anger

History never quite repeats itself, but its lessons are important nonetheless. We should recall that the first era of globalization, which reached its peak in the decades before the First World War, eventually produced an even more severe political backlash.

In the heyday of the gold standard, Jeffry Frieden argues, mainstream political actors had to downplay social reform and national identity because they gave priority to international economic ties.[4] The response took one of two fatal forms in the interwar period: socialists and communists chose social reform, while fascists chose national assertion. Both paths led away from globalization to economic closure (and far worse).

Today's backlash most likely will not go quite so far. As costly as they have been, the dislocations of the great recession and the euro crisis pale in significance compared to those of the Great Depression. Advanced democracies have built—and retain (despite recent setbacks)—extensive social safety nets in the form of unemployment insurance, retirement pensions, and family benefits. The world economy now has functional international institutions—such as the International Monetary Fund and the World Trade Organization—that it lacked prior to the Second World War. Global value chains have entrenched strong business lobbies for continued integration that even an instinctive protectionist like Donald Trump will find hard to overcome. Last but not least, truly extremist political movements such as fascism and communism have been largely discredited.

Still, the conflicts between a hyperglobalized economy and social cohesion are real, and mainstream political elites ignore them at their peril. The internationalization of markets for goods, services, and capital drives a wedge between the cosmopolitan, professional, skilled groups that are able to take advantage of it and the rest of society. Two types of political cleavage are exacerbated in the process: an identity cleavage, revolving around nationhood, ethnicity, or religion, and an income cleavage, revolving around social class. Populists derive their appeal from one or the other of these cleavages. Right-wing populists such as Trump engage in identity politics. Left-wing populists such as Bernie Sanders emphasize the gulf between the rich and the poor.

In both cases, there is a clear "other" toward which anger can be directed. You can barely make ends meet? It is the Chinese who have been stealing your jobs. Upset by crime? It is the Mexicans and other immigrants who bring their gang warfare into the country. Terrorism? Why, Muslims, of course. Political corruption? What do you expect when the big banks are bankrolling our political system? Unlike mainstream political elites, populists can easily point to the culprits responsible for the masses' ills.

Of course, establishment politicians are compromised because they have been at the helm all this time. But they are also immobilized by their central narrative, which smacks of inaction and helplessness. This narrative puts the blame for stagnant wages and rising inequality on technological forces beyond our control. It treats globalization and the rules that sustain it as inexorable and inevitable. The remedy it offers, investment in education and skills, promises few immediate rewards and would bear fruit years from now, at best.

In reality, today's world economy is the product of explicit decisions that governments have made in the past. It was a choice not to stop at the General Agreement on Tariffs and Trade and to build the much more ambitious—and intrusive—WTO. Similarly, it will be a choice in the future whether we adopt mega-trade deals such as the Trans-Pacific Partnership and the Transatlantic Trade and Investment Partnership.

It was the choice of governments to loosen regulations on finance and aim for full cross-border capital mobility, just as it was a choice to maintain these policies largely intact, despite a massive global financial crisis. And, as the late Anthony Atkinson reminds us in his masterful book on inequality, even technological change is not immune from government agency: There is much that policy makers can do to influence the direction of technological change and ensure that it leads to higher employment and greater equity.[5]

The appeal of populists is that they give voice to the anger of the excluded. They offer a grand narrative as well as concrete, if misleading and often dangerous, solutions. Mainstream politicians will not regain lost ground until they, too, offer serious solutions that provide room for hope. They should no longer hide behind technology or unstoppable globalization, and they must be willing to be bold and entertain large-scale reforms in the way the domestic and global economy are run.

If one lesson of history is the danger of globalization running amok, another is the malleability of capitalism. It was the New Deal, the welfare state, and controlled globalization (under the Bretton Woods regime) that eventually gave market-oriented societies a new lease on life and produced the postwar boom. It was not tinkering and minor modification of existing policies that produced these achievements but rather radical institutional engineering. Without bolder, bigger ideas we may find that the good things that the present consensus produced—a liberal, democratic order in particular—is swept away by the backlash wrought by its excesses.

Politicians of all stripes, take note.

ACKNOWLEDGMENTS

I want to thank my various publishers for their permission to use original material written for them. Kenneth Murphy deserves a special note of thanks: as editor-in-chief at Project Syndicate, he read and edited the PS columns that I have used here, improving them considerably along the way.

Andrew Wylie and Jacqueline Ko of the Wylie Agency steered the manuscript ably and efficiently in the right direction. Joe Jackson at Princeton University Press was a model editor. He gently goaded me to do more work on the manuscript than I had intended—and I am glad he did. The book is much better as a result of his efforts and suggestions. Jessica De Simone, my faculty assistant at the Kennedy School, provided invaluable help in preparing the manuscript.

I am very lucky to be in an environment as stimulating as the Kennedy School at Harvard, where students keep me energized while faculty colleagues keep me on my toes. A special word of thanks to David Ellwood, the School's former Dean, for not having given up on my return to the School and for making it happen.

My greatest debt, as always, is to my wife Pınar who somehow always knows best.

Sources

Project Syndicate columns by Dani Rodrik include the following: "New Rules for the Global Economy" (*PS*, January 10, 2011), https://www.project-syndicate.org/commentary/new-rules-for-the-global-economy?barrier=accessreg; "National Governments, Global Citizens" (*PS*, March 12, 2013), https://www.project-syndicate.org/commentary/how-to-globalize-a-national-authority-by-dani-rodrik?barrier=accessreg; "The False Economic Promise of Global Governance" (*PS*, August 11, 2016), https://www.project-syndicate.org/commentary/global-governance-false-economic-promise-by-dani-rodrik-2016-08?barrier=accessreg; "What the World Needs from the BRICS" (*PS*, April 10, 2013), https://www.project-syndicate.org/commentary/the-brics-and-global-economic-leadership-by-dani-rodrik?barrier=accessreg; "Global Capital Rules" (*PS*, December 13, 2012), https://www.project-syndicate.org/commentary/the-imf-s-timid-embrace-of-capital-controls-by-dani-rodrik?barrier=accessreg; "The Muddled Case for Trade Agreements" (*PS*, June 11, 2015), https://www.project-syndicate.org/commentary/regional-trade-agreement-corporate-capture-by-dani-rodrik-2015-06?barrier=accessreg; "Fairness and Free Trade" (*PS*, May 12, 2016), https://www.project-syndicate.org/commentary/china-market-economy-status-debate-by-dani-rodrik-2016-05?barrier=accessreg; "No Time for Trade Fundamentalism" (*PS*, October 14, 2016), https://www.project-syndicate.org/commentary/protectionism-for-global-openness-by-dani-rodrik-2016-10?barrier=accessreg; "Don't Cry over Dead Trade Agreements" (*PS*, December 8, 2016), https://www.project-syndicate.org/commentary/no-mourning-dead-trade-agreements-by-dani-rodrik-2016-12?barrier=accessreg; "Will Greece Make It?" (*PS*, June 10, 2011), https://www.project-syndicate.org/commentary/will-greece-make-it?barrier=accessreg; "Europe's Next Nightmare" (*PS*,

November 9, 2011), https://www.project-syndicate.org/commentary /europe-s-next-nightmare?barrier=accessreg; "The Truth About Sovereignty" (*PS*, October 8, 2012), https://www.project-syndicate.org /commentary/why-economic-integration-implies-political-unification -by-dani-rodrik?barrier=accessreg; "Europe's Way Out" (*PS*, June 12, 2013), https://www.project-syndicate.org/commentary/saving-the-long -run-in-the-eurozone-by-dani-rodrik?barrier=accessreg; "Reforming Greek Reform" (*PS*, February 13, 2015), https://www.project-syndicate .org/commentary/greek-exports-reform-by-dani-rodrik-2015-02? barrier=accessreg; "Greece's Vote for Sovereignty" (*PS*, July 7, 2015), https://www.project-syndicate.org/commentary/greece-referendum -nationalism-democracy-by-dani-rodrik-2015-07?barrier=accessreg; "The Poverty of Dictatorship" (*PS*, February 9, 2011), https://www .project-syndicate.org/commentary/the-poverty-of-dictatorship? barrier=accessreg; "No More Growth Miracles" (*PS*, August 8, 2012), https://www.project-syndicate.org/commentary/no-more-growth -miracles-by-dani-rodrik?barrier=accessreg; "The Growing Divide Within Developing Economies" (*PS*, April 11, 2014), https://www .project-syndicate.org/commentary/dani-rodrik-examines-why-informal -and-traditional-sectors-are-expanding--rather-than-shrinking?barrier= accessreg; "Back to Fundamentals in Emerging Markets" (*PS*, August 13, 2015), https://www.project-syndicate.org/commentary/emerging -market-growth-by-dani-rodrik-2015-08?barrier=accessreg; "Economists and Democracy" (*PS*, May 11, 2011), https://www.project-syndicate .org/commentary/economists-and-democracy?barrier=accessreg; "Saif Qaddafi and Me" (*PS*, April 12, 2011), https://www.project -syndicate.org/commentary/saif-qaddafi-and-me?barrier=accessreg; "Milton Friedman's Magical Thinking" (*PS*, October 11, 2011), https:// www.project-syndicate.org/commentary/milton-friedman-s-magical -thinking?barrier=accessreg; "Free Trade Blinders" (*PS*, May 9, 2012), https://www.project-syndicate.org/commentary/free-trade-blinders? barrier=accessreg; "The New Mercantilist Challenge" (*PS*, January 9, 2013), https://www.project-syndicate.org/commentary/the-return-of -mercantilism-by-dani-rodrik?barrier=accessreg; "The Tyranny of Political Economy" (*PS*, February 8, 2013), https://www.project-syndicate .org/commentary/how-economists-killed-policy-analysis-by-dani -rodrik?barrier=accessreg; "In Praise of Foxy Scholars" (*PS*, March 10, 2014), https://www.project-syndicate.org/commentary/dani-rodrik-on -the-promise-and-peril-of-social-science-models?barrier=accessreg; "The Perils of Economic Consensus" (*PS*, August 14, 2014), https:// www.project-syndicate.org/commentary/dani-rodrik-warns-that -agreement-among-economists-can-create-an-illusion-of-certain -knowledge?barrier=accessreg; "Good and Bad Inequality" (*PS*, December 11, 2014), https://www.project-syndicate.org/commentary/equality -economic-growth-tradeoff-by-dani-rodrik-2014-12?barrier=accessreg; "Economists vs. Economics" (*PS*, September 10, 2015), https://www .project-syndicate.org/commentary/economists-versus-economics -by-dani-rodrik-2015-09?barrier=accessreg; "Straight Talk on Trade" (*PS*, November 15, 2016), https://www.project-syndicate.org/commentary /trump-win-economists-responsible-by-dani-rodrik-2016-11?barrier =accessreg; "Ideas over Interests" (*PS*, April 26, 2012), https://www .project-syndicate.org/commentary/ideas-over-interests?barrier= accessreg; "The Right Green Industrial Policies" (*PS*, July 11, 2013), https://www.project-syndicate.org/commentary/the-right-green -industrial-policies-by-dani-rodrik?barrier=accessreg; "Rethinking Democracy" (*PS*, June 11, 2014), https://www.project-syndicate.org /commentary/dani-rodrik-examines-the-root-causes-of-political -malaise-in-advanced-and-developing-countries?barrier=accessreg; "A Class of Its Own" (*PS*, July 10, 2014), https://www.project-syndicate .org/commentary/dani-rodrik-explains-why-the-super-rich-are

-mistaken-to-believe-that-they-can-dispense-with-government? barrier=accessreg; "How the Rich Rule" (*PS*, September 10, 2014), https://www.project-syndicate.org/commentary/dani-rodrik-says -that-widening-inequality-drives-economic-elites-toward-sectarian -politics?barrier=accessreg; "From Welfare State to Innovation State" (*PS*, January 14, 2015), https://www.project-syndicate.org/commentary /labor-saving-technology-by-dani-rodrik-2015-01?barrier=accessreg; "The Return of Public Investment" (*PS*, January 13, 2016), https:// www.project-syndicate.org/commentary/public-infrastructure-investment -sustained-growth-by-dani-rodrik-2016-01; "The Politics of Anger" (*PS*, March 9, 2016), https://www.project-syndicate.org/commentary /the-politics-of-anger-by-dani-rodrik-2016-03; "A Progressive Logic of Trade" (*PS*, April 13, 2016), https://www.project-syndicate.org /commentary/progressive-trade-logic-by-dani-rodrik-2016-04?barrier= accessreg; "Innovation Is Not Enough" (*PS*, June 9, 2016), https://www .project-syndicate.org/commentary/innovation-impact-on-productivity -by-dani-rodrik-2016-06?barrier=accessreg; "The Abdication of the Left" (*PS*, July 11, 2016), https://www.project-syndicate.org/commentary /anti-globalization-backlash-from-right-by-dani-rodrik-2016-07; "How Much Europe Can Europe Tolerate?" (*PS*, March 14, 2017), https://www.project-syndicate.org/commentary/juncker-white-paper -wrong-question-by-dani-rodrik-2017-03?barrier=accessreg; "The Myth of Authoritarian Growth" (*PS*, August 2010), https://www.project -syndicate.org/commentary/the-myth-of-authoritarian-growth?barrier= accessreg; "It's Too Late for Compensation" (*PS*, April 2017), https:// www.project-syndicate.org/commentary/free-trade-losers-compensation -too-late-by-dani-rodrik-2017-04; "The Trade Numbers Game" (*PS*, February 2016), https://www.project-syndicate.org/commentary/tpp -debate-economic-benefits-by-dani-rodrik-2016-02?barrier= accessreg; "Can Macron Pull It Off?" (*PS*, May 2017), https://www.project

-syndicate.org/commentary/macron-germany-eurozone-fiscal-union
-by-dani-rodrik-2017-05.

Other sources include: "Who Needs the Nation State?" (*Economic Geography* 89[1], January 2013: 1–19); "The Future of Democracy in Europe" (in Luuk van Middelaar and Philippe Van Parijs, eds, *After the Storm: How to Save Democracy in Europe*, Tielt (Belgium): Lannoo, 2015); "The Elusive Promise of Structural Reform" (first published in *The Milken Institute Review*, Second Quarter, 2016); "Is Liberal Democracy Feasible in Developing Countries?" (first published in *Studies in Comparative International Development*, 50th Anniversary Issue, 2016. Courtesy of Springer.); "Work and Human Development in a Deindustrializing World" (originally an occasional paper for the Human Development Report 2015 "Work for Human Development" published by United Nations Development Programme in December 2015. More information at: hdr.undp.org); "Economics: Science, Craft, or Snake Oil?" (first published in *The Institute Letter*, Institute for Advanced Study, Fall 2013); "When Ideas Trump Interests: Preferences, World Views, and Policy Innovations" (first published in *The Journal of Economic Perspectives* 28[1], Winter 2014: 189–208); "It's Time to Think for Yourself on Free Trade" (*Foreign Policy*, January 27, 2017), http://foreignpolicy.com/2017/01/27/its-time-to-think-for-yourself-on-free-trade/.

NOTES

1. On NAFTA, see Shushanik Hakobyan and John McLaren, "Looking for Local Labor-Market Effects of NAFTA," *Review of Economics and Statistics*, vol. 98(4), October 2016: 728–741. On the China trade shock, see David H. Autor, David Dorn, and Gordon H. Hanson, "The China Shock: Learning from Labor-Market Adjustment to Large Changes in Trade," *Annual Review of Economics*, vol. 8, October 2016: 205–240. Hakobyan and McLaren find NAFTA reduced wage growth in the most affected industries by 17 percentage points relative to other industries. Autor et al. document large, sustained wage and employment effects in hard-hit communities, without corresponding gains elsewhere.

2. A recent academic study uses all the bells and whistles of modern trade theory to produce the estimate that NAFTA's overall gains amount to a "welfare" gain of 0.08 percent for the United States. Trade volume impacts are much larger: a doubling of US imports from Mexico. (Lorenzo Caliendo and Fernando Parro, "Estimates of the Trade and Welfare Effects of NAFTA," *Review of Economic Studies*, vol. 82(1), 2015: 1–44.) What is equally interesting is that fully half of the miniscule 0.08 percent gain for the United States is not an efficiency gain but a benefit due to terms-of-trade improvement. That is, Caliendo and Parro estimate that the world prices of what the United States imports fell relative to what it exports. These are not efficiency gains but income transfers from other countries (here principally Mexico and Canada). These gains came at the expense of other countries.

3. Christina Starmans, Mark Sheskin, and Paul Bloom, "Why People Prefer Unequal Societies," *Nature: Human Behaviour*, vol. 1, April 2017: 82.

4. Zack Beauchamp, "If You're Poor in Another Country, This Is the Scariest Thing Bernie Sanders Has Said," *Vox*, April 5, 2016, http://www.vox.com/2016/3/1/11139718/bernie-sanders-trade-global-poverty.

5. Dani Rodrik, "Growth Strategies," in *Handbook of Economic Growth*, P. Aghion and S. Durlauf, eds., vol. 1A, North-Holland, 2005: 967–1014.

6. Dani Rodrik, "Mexico's Growth Problem," *Project Syndicate*, November 13, 2014, https://www.project-syndicate.org/commentary/mexico-growth-problem-by-dani-rodrik-2014-11?barrier=accessreg.

7. Dani Rodrik, *The Globalization Paradox: Democracy and the Future of the World Economy*, W. W. Norton, New York, 2011.

8. The "political trilemma of the world economy" was first discussed in Dani Rodrik, "How Far Will International Economic Integration Go?" *Journal of Economic Perspectives*, Winter 2000. I elaborate on it in historical perspective in my book *The Globalization Paradox*.

9. Jeffry A. Frieden, *Global Capitalism: Its Rise and Fall in the Twentieth Century*, W. W. Norton, New York, 2007.

10. Dani Rodrik, "Premature Deindustrialization," *Journal of Economic Growth*, vol. 21, 2015: 1–33.

11. Carl J. Green, "The New Protectionism," *Northwestern Journal of International Law & Business*, vol. 3, 1981: 1.

12. John Gerard Ruggie, "International Regimes, Transactions, and Change: Embedded Liberalism in the Postwar Economic Order," *International Organization*, vol. 36(2), Spring 1982: 379–415.

13. "IMF Sees Subdued Global Growth, Warns Economic Stagnation Could Fuel Protectionist Calls," IMF News, October 4, 2016, http://www.imf.org/en/News/Articles/2016/10/03/AM2016-NA100416-WEO.

CHAPTER 2: How Nations Work

1. John Rentoul, "Theresa May's conference speech: What she said... and what she really meant," *The Independent*, October 5, 2016, http://www.independent.co.uk/voices/theresa-may-conference-speech-what-she

-said-what-she-meant-john-rentoul-a7346456.html; Roger Cohen, "Theresa May's 'Global Britain' Is Baloney," *New York Times*, January 20, 2017, https://www.nytimes.com/2017/01/20/opinion/theresa -mays-global-britain-is-baloney.html?_r=0; Bagehot, "May's revolutionary conservatism," *Economist*, October 8, 2016, http://www.economist.com /news/britain/21708223-britains-new-prime-minister-signals-new -illiberal-direction-country; Philip Murphy, "Theresa May's rejection of Enlightenment values," Letters Section, *The Guardian*, October 9, 2016, https://www.theguardian.com/politics/2016/oct/09/theresa-may -rejection-of-enlightenment-values.

2. Leon Trotsky, "Nationalism and Economic Life," *Foreign Affairs*, vol. 12, 1933: 395.

3. Peter Singer, *One World: The Ethics of Globalization*, Yale University Press, New Haven, CT, 2002, p. 12.

4. Amartya Sen, *The Idea of Justice*, Harvard University Press, Cambridge, MA, 2009, p. 143.

5. James A. Anderson and Eric van Wincoop, "Trade Costs," *Journal of Economic Literature*, vol. 42, 2004: 691–751.

6. Stanley Hoffman, "Obstinate or Obsolete? The Fate of the Nation-State and the Case of Western Europe," *Daedalus*, vol. 95(3), 1966: 862–915.

7. Raymond Vernon, "Sovereignty at Bay: The Multinational Spread of US Enterprises," *Thunderbird International Business Review*, vol. 13(4), 1971: 1–3.

8. Dani Rodrik, "Is Global Equality the Enemy of National Equality?" HKS Working Paper, January 2017.

9. François Bourguignon and Christian Morrisson, "Inequality Among World Citizens: 1820–1992," *American Economic Review*, vol. 92, 2002: 727–744.

10. Charles Tilly, *Coercion, Capital, and European States, AD 990–1992*, Blackwell, Cambridge, MA, 1992; Ernest Gellner, *Nations and Nationalism*, Cornell University Press, Ithaca, New York, 1983; Steven Pinker, *The Better Angels of our Nature: Why Violence Has Declined*, Viking, New York, 2011; Elie Kedourie, *Nationalism*, 4th ed., Blackwell, New York, 1993;

Benedict Anderson, *Imagined Communities: Reflections on the Origin and Spread of Nationalism*, revised ed., Verso, London, 2006.

11. Quoted in Elie Kedourie, *Nationalism*, 7.

12. John Agnew, "Putting Politics into Economic Geography," in *The Wiley-Blackwell Companion to Economic Geography*, T. J. Barnes, J. Peck, and E. Sheppard, eds., Wiley-Blackwell, Malden, MA, 2012.

13. Dani Rodrik, *The Globalization Paradox: Democracy and the Future of the World Economy*, W. W. Norton, New York, 2011.

14. Anne Marie Slaughter, *A New World Order*, Princeton University Press, Princeton, NJ, 2004.

15. John Ruggie, "Reconstituting the Global Public Domain—Issues, Actors, and Practices," *European Journal of International Relations*, vol. 10, 2004: 499–531; Frederick Mayer and Gary Gereffi, "Regulation and Economic Globalization: Prospects and Limits of Private Governance," *Business and Politics*, vol. 12(3), 2010: 1–25.

16. Joshua Cohen and Charles F. Sabel, "Global Democracy?" *International Law and Politics*, vol. 37, 2005: 779.

17. Peter A. Hall and David Soskice, *Varieties of Capitalism: The Institutional Foundations of Comparative Advantage*, Oxford University Press, Oxford, UK, 2001.

18. Roberto Mangabeira Unger, *Democracy Realized: The Progressive Alternative*, Verso, New York, 1998.

19. Richard Freeman, "Labor Market Institutions Around the World," Discussion Paper No. 844, London School of Economics, Centre for Economic Performance, London, January 2008.

20. Elie Kedourie, *Nationalism*, 46.

21. Alexander Gerschenkron, *Economic Backwardness in Historical Perspective*, Belknap Press of Harvard University Press, Cambridge, MA, 1962.

22. Alberto Alesina and Enrico Spolaore, *The Size of Nations*, MIT Press, Cambridge, MA, 2003.

23. Anne-Célia Disdier and Keith Head, "The Puzzling Persistence of the Distance Effect on Bilateral Trade," *Review of Economics and Statistics*, vol. 90(1), 2008: 37–48.

24. Matias Berthelon and Caroline Freund, "On the Conservation of Distance in International Trade," *Journal of International Economics*, vol. 75(2), July 2008: 311.

25. The following account, based on Keith Hampton, "Netville: Community on and Offline in a Wired Suburb," in *The Cybercities Reader*, S. Graham Routledge, ed., London, 2004: 256–262, was taken from Dani Rodrik, *The Globalization Paradox*.

26. Bernardo S. Blum and Avi Goldfarb, "Does the Internet Defy the Law of Gravity?" *Journal of International Economics*, vol. 70(2), 2006: 384–405.

27. Charles Duhigg and Keith Bradsher, "How the U.S. Lost Out on iPhone Work," *New York Times*, January 21, 2012, http://www.nytimes.com/2012/01/22/business/apple-america-and-a-squeezed-middle-class.html?pagewanted=all.

28. Edward Leamer, "A Flat World, a Level Playing Field, a Small World After All, or None of the Above? A Review of Thomas L. Friedman's *The World is Flat*," *Journal of Economic Literature*, vol. 45(1), 2007: 83–126.

29. Kevin Morgan, "The Exaggerated Death of Geography: Learning, Proximity, and Territorial Innovation Systems," *Journal of Economic Geography*, vol. 4, 2004: 3–21.

30. Josiah Ober, "Wealthy Hellas," Presidential Address, Transactions of the American Philological Association, vol. 140, 2010: 241–286.

31. Elie Kedourie, *Nationalism*, 47.

32. Kelvin Lancaster, *Consumer Demand: A New Approach*, Columbia University Press, New York, 1971; Avinash K. Dixit and Joseph E. Stiglitz, "Monopolistic Competition and Optimum Product Diversity," *American Economic Review*, vol. 27, 1977: 217–238.

33. Michael P. Devereux, Ben Lockwood, and Michela Redoano, "Do Countries Compete Over Corporate Tax Rates?" *Journal of Public Economics*, vol. 92(5), June 2008: 1210–1235. See also S. M. Ali Abbas and Alexander Klemm, with Sukhmani Bedi and Junhyung Park, "A Partial Race to the Bottom: Corporate Tax Developments in Emerging and Developing Economies," IMF Working Paper WP/12/28, Washington, DC, January 2012, on developing economies.

34. Dani Rodrik, "Is Global Equality the Enemy of National Equality?" HKS Working Paper, January 2017.

35. "'Mrs. May, We Are All Citizens of the World,' Says Philosopher," BBC News, October 29, 2016.

CHAPTER 3: Europe's Struggles

1. Olivier Blanchard and Daniel Leigh, "Growth Forecast Errors and Fiscal Multipliers," IMF Working Paper, January 2013.

2. Olivier Blanchard, "Greece: Past Critiques and the Path Forward," IMF Blog, July 9, 2015, https://blog-imfdirect.imf.org/2015/07/09/greece-past -critiques-and-the-path-forward/.

3. Jan Babecký and Nauro F. Campos, "Does Reform Work? An Econometric Survey of the Reform-Growth Puzzle," *Journal of Comparative Economics*, vol. 39(2), 2011: 140–158. For a more recent study with similar results, see Pasquale Marco Marrazzo and Alessio Terzi, "Wide-Reaching Structural Reforms and Growth: A Cross-Country Synthetic Control Approach," unpublished paper, Harvard, CID, April 2017.

4. Steven N. Durlauf, Paul A. Johnson, and Jonathan R. W. Temple, "Growth Econometrics," Working Paper no. 61, Vassar College Economics, October 2004, https://economics.vassar.edu/docs/working-papers/VCEWP61.pdf.

5. Zsolt Darvars, "Is Greece Destined to Grow?" *Bruegel*, June 15, 2015, http://bruegel.org/2015/06/is-greece-destined-to-grow/.

6. Ricardo Hausmann, Lant Pritchett, and Dani Rodrik, "Growth Accelerations," *Journal of Economic Growth*, vol. 10(4), 2005: 303–329.

7. This argument was developed in Arvind Subramanian and Dani Rodrik, "From 'Hindu Growth' to Productivity Surge: The Mystery of the Indian Growth Transition," *IMF Staff Papers*, vol. 52(2), 2005, on which the rest of this paragraph is based.

8. Ricardo Hausmann, Dani Rodrik, and Andrés Velasco, "Growth Diagnostics," in *The Washington Consensus Reconsidered: Towards a New Global Governance*, J. E. Stiglitz and N. Serra, eds., Oxford University Press, New York, 2008.

9. Theodore Pelagidis, "Why Internal Devaluation is Not Leading to Export-Led Growth in Greece," *Brookings Online*, September 12, 2014,

http://www.brookings.edu/blogs/up-front/posts/2014/09/12-internal-devaluation-export-growth-greece-pelagidis.

10. "Pour l'économiste Thomas Piketty: Macron, c'est 'l'Europe d'hier'," *Le Point*, February 20, 2017, http://www.lepoint.fr/presidentielle/pour-l-economiste-thomas-piketty-macron-c-est-l-europe-d-hier-19-02-2017-2105950_3121.php#section-commentaires.

11. "Emmanuel Macron proposes Nordic economic model for France," *Financial Times*, February 23, 2017, https://www.ft.com/content/3691a448-fa1d-11e6-9516-2d969e0d3b65.

12. "Merkel rules out eased eurozone spending rules to help Macron," *Financial Times*, May 8, 2017, https://www.ft.com/content/2d3004a2-33ee-11e7-bce4-9023f8c0fd2e.

13. "Macron calls for radical reform to save euro," *Financial Times*, September 24, 2015, https://www.ft.com/content/6d327720-62c5-11e5-a28b-50226830d644.

14. Peter Foster, "Jean-Claude Juncker Faces Dissent Over EU's 'Five Pathways to Unity' Survival Blueprint after Brexit," *The Telegraph*, March 1, 2017, http://www.telegraph.co.uk/news/2017/02/28/jean-claude-juncker-faces-dissent-eu-survival-blueprint/.

CHAPTER 4: Work, Industrialization, and Democracy

1. Dani Rodrik, "Unconditional Convergence in Manufacturing," *Quarterly Journal of Economics*, vol. 128(1), February 2013: 165–204.

2. Jaana Remes and Luis Rubio, "The Two Mexicos," *Project Syndicate*, April 1, 2014, https://www.project-syndicate.org/commentary/jaana-remes-and-luis-rubio-take-issue-with-flattering-headlines-heralding-a-new-emerging-market-success-story.

3. Dani Rodrik, "Premature Deindustrialization," *Journal of Economic Growth*, vol. 21, November 2015: 1–33.

4. James C. Scott, *Two Cheers for Anarchism*, Princeton University Press, Princeton, NJ, and Oxford, 2012: 91–92.

5. Dani Rodrik, "Institutions for High-Quality Growth: What They Are and How to Acquire Them," *Studies in Comparative International Development*, vol. 35(3), Fall 2000.

6. Dani Rodrik, *One Economics, Many Recipes*, Princeton University Press, Princeton, NJ, 2007.

7. The evidence that democracy leads to higher growth is generally considered to be weak. However, the paper Daron Acemoglu, Suresh Naidu, Pascual Restrepo, and James A. Robinson, "Democracy Does Cause Growth," NBER Working Paper No. 20004, March 2014, makes a strong case that it does.

8. Sharun Mukand and Dani Rodrik, "The Political Economy of Liberal Democracy," Harvard Kennedy School, March 2017, Figure 1.

9. Larry Diamond, "Facing Up to the Democratic Recession," *Journal of Democracy*, vol. 26(1), January 2015: 141–155.

10. Fareed Zakaria, "The Rise of Illiberal Democracy," *Foreign Affairs*, November/December 1997.

11. Mukand and Rodrik, "Political Economy of Liberal Democracy."

12. See, for example, Carles Boix, *Democracy and Redistribution*, Cambridge University Press, New York, 2003; Daron Acemoglu and James A. Robinson, "Foundations of Societal Inequality," *Science*, vol. 326(5953), 2009: 678–679; and Ben W. Ansell and David J. Samuels, *Inequality and Democratization: An Elite-Competition Approach*, Cambridge University Press, 2014.

13. T. H. Marshall, "Citizenship and Social Class," in Jeff Manza and Michael Sauder, eds., *Inequality and Society*, W. W. Norton, New York, 2009 [originally published in 1949].

14. Richard J. Goldstone, "The South African Bill of Rights," *Texas International Law Journal*, vol. 32(3), Summer 1997.

15. Edmund Fawcett, *Liberalism: The Life of an Idea*, Princeton University Press, Princeton, NJ, and London, 2014, p. 144.

16. Gerhard Lehmbruch, "A Non-Competitive Pattern of Conflict Management in Liberal Democracies: The Case of Switzerland, Austria and Lebanon," International Political Science Association, Seventh World Congress, Brussels, September 18–23, 1967.

17. *Report on Tunisia*, Freedom House, 2011, https://freedomhouse.org/report/freedom-world/2011/tunisia.

18. Samuel P. Huntington, *Political Order in Changing Societies*, Yale University Press, New Haven, CT, 1968, p. 5.

19. Lehmbruch, "Non-Competitive Pattern."

20. Paul Collier, *Wars, Guns and Votes*, HarperCollins, New York, 2009, chapter 9.

CHAPTER 5: Economists and Their Models

1. This is the theme also of my book *Economics Rules: The Rights and Wrongs of the Dismal Science*, W. W. Norton, New York, 2015.

2. Dani Rodrik, *The Globalization Paradox: Democracy and the Future of the World Economy*, W. W. Norton, New York, 2011.

3. Peter A. Petri and Michael G. Plummer, "The Economic Effects of the Trans-Pacific Partnership: New Estimates," PIIE Working Paper 16-2, January 2016.

4. Jeronim Capaldo and Alex Izurieta, with Jomo Kwame Sundaram, "Trading Down: Unemployment, Inequality and Other Risks of the Trans-Pacific Partnership Agreement," Global Development and Environment Institute Working Paper no. 16-01, Tufts University, Medford, MA, January 2016.

5. *Market Access and Sectoral Issues*, in *Assessing the Trans-Pacific Partnership*, PIIE Briefing 16-1, vol. 1, February 2016: 3.

6. David H. Autor, David Dorn, and Gordon H. Hanson, "The China Shock: Learning from Labor-Market Adjustment to Large Changes in Trade," *Annual Review of Economics*, vol. 8, 2016: 205–240.

7. See the reaction to Steve Rattner's comments at the Peterson Institute, Steven Rattner "What's Our Duty to the People Globalization Leaves Behind?" *New York Times*, Opinion Pages, January 26, 2016, https://www.nytimes.com/2016/01/26/opinion/whats-our-duty-to-the-people-globalization-leaves-behind.html?_r=2.

8. Fabrice Defever and Alejandro Riaño, "China's Pure Exporter Subsidies," Centre for Economic Performance Discussion Paper No. 1182, London School of Economics and Political Science, December 2012.

9. The original paper is Carmen M. Reinhart and Kenneth S. Rogoff, "Growth in the Time of Debt," NBER Working Paper No. 15639, January 2010.

10. Thomas Herndon, Michael Ash, and Robert Pollin, "Does High Public Debt Consistently Stifle Economic Growth? A Critique of Reinhart and Rogoff," *Cambridge Journal of Economics*, vol. 38(2), 2014: 257–279.

11. Alberto F. Alesina and Silvia Ardagna, "Large Changes in Fiscal Policy: Taxes Versus Spending," NBER Working Paper No. 15438, October 2009.

12. Paul Krugman was a persistent critic of the austerity school. See his discussion of the Alesina-Ardagna paper at Paul Krugman, "Night of the Living Alesina," *New York Times*, Opinion Pages, March 13, 2013, https:// krugman.blogs.nytimes.com/2013/03/13/night-of-the-living-alesina/.

CHAPTER 6: The Perils of Economic Consensus

1. Justin Wolfers, "What Debate? Economists Agree the Stimulus Lifted the Economy," *New York Times*, July 29, 2014, https://www.nytimes .com/2014/07/30/upshot/what-debate-economists-agree-the-stimulus -lifted-the-economy.html?_r=0.

2. Greg Mankiw, "News Flash: Economists Agree," Greg Mankiw's Blog, February 14, 2009, http://gregmankiw.blogspot.com/2009/02/news-flash -economists-agree.html.

3. Dani Rodrik, *One Economics, Many Recipes: Globalization, Institutions, and Economic Growth*, Princeton University Press, Princeton, NJ, and New York, 2007.

4. Dani Rodrik, "Diagnostics Before Prescription," *Journal of Economic Perspectives*, vol. 24(3), Summer 2010: 33–44.

5. Kaushik Basu, "Two Policy Prescription for the Global Crisis," *Project Syndicate*, April 23, 2013, https://www.project-syndicate.org/commentary /lessons-from-the-world-bank-imf-spring-meetings-by-kaushik-basu.

6. Paul Krugman, "How Did Economists Get It So Wrong?" *New York Times*, September 2, 2009, http://www.nytimes.com/2009/09/06/maga zine/06Economic-t.html.

7. Paul Romer, "My Paper 'Mathiness in the Theory of Economic Growth,'" May 15, 2015, https://paulromer.net/mathiness/.

8. Carol Tavris, "How Homo Economicus Went Extinct," *Wall Street Journal*, May 15, 2015, https://www.wsj.com/articles/how-homo-economicus-went-extinct-1431721255.

9. Luigi Zingales, "Does Finance Benefit Society?" *Journal of Finance*, vol. 70(4), 2015: 1327–1363.

10. Jorge Luis Borges, "On Exactitude in Science, A Universal History of Infamy," 1946.

11. Rob Wile, "The Greatest Graduation Speech Ever Given Is This Bullet-Point List of 12 Economic Concepts," *Business Insider*, April 17, 2014, http://www.businessinsider.com/thomas-sargent-shortest-graduation-speech-2014-4.

12. Jonathan D. Ostry, Andrew Berg, and Charalambos G. Tsangarides, "Redistribution, Inequality, and Growth," International Monetary Fund Discussion Note, February 2014.

13. Nora Lustig, Luis F. Lopez-Calva, and Eduardo Ortiz-Juarez, "Deconstructing the Decline in Inequality in Latin America," Tulane Economics Working Paper Series, Working Paper 1314, April 2013.

14. James Manyika, et al., *Digital America: A Tale of the Haves and Have-Mores*, McKinsey Global Institute Report, December 2015.

15. Robert J. Gordon, *The Rise and Fall of American Growth: The U.S. Standard of Living since the Civil War*, Princeton University Press, Princeton, NJ, 2016.

16. Tyler Cowen, "Economic Development in an 'Average is Over' World," Working Paper, April 8, 2016.

17. Margaret McMillan, Dani Rodrik, and Íñigo Verduzco-Gallo, "Globalization, Structural Change, and Productivity Growth, with an Update on Africa," *World Development*, vol. 63, 2014: 11–32.

18. Dietrich Vollrath, "More on Decomposing US Productivity Growth," Blog, May 11, 2016, https://growthecon.com/blog/More-Decomp/.

19. Ricardo Hausmann, Dani Rodrik, and Andres Velasco, "Growth Diagnostics," in *The Washington Consensus Reconsidered: Towards a New Global Governance*, J. Stiglitz and N. Serra, eds., Oxford University Press, New York, 2008.

20. Isaiah Berlin, *The Hedgehog and the Fox: An Essay on Tolstoy's View of History*, Weidenfeld & Nicolson, London, 1953.

21. Daniel Drezner, *The Ideas Industry*, Oxford University Press, New York, 2017.

CHAPTER 7: Economists, Politics, and Ideas

1. George J. Stigler, "The Theory of Economic Regulation," *Bell Journal of Economics and Management Science*, vol. 2(1), Spring 1971: 3–21; Sam Peltzman, "Toward a More General Theory of Regulation," *Journal of Law and Economics*, vol. 19(2), 1976: 211–240; Jean-Jacques Laffont and Jean Tirole "The Politics of Government Decision Making: A Theory of Regulatory Capture," *Quarterly Journal of Economics*, vol. 106, 1991: 1089–1127.

2. Anne O. Krueger, "The Political Economy of the Rent-Seeking Society," *American Economic Review*, vol. 64(3), June 1974: 291–303; Gene Grossman and Elhanan Helpman, "Protection for Sale," *American Economic Review*, vol. 84(4), 1994: 833; Dani Rodrik, "The Political Economy of Trade Policy," in *Handbook of International Economics*, G. Grossman and K. Rogoff, eds., Amsterdam, North-Holland, 1995.

3. Robert H. Bates, *Markets and States in Tropical Africa*, University of California Press, Berkley, CA, 1981; Daron Acemoglu and James A. Robinson, "Economic Backwardness in Political Perspective," *American Political Science Review*, vol. 100(1), 2006: 115–131; Daron Acemoglu and James A. Robinson, *Why Nations Fail: The Origins of Power, Prosperity, and Poverty*, Crown, New York, 2012.

4. Charles W. Calomiris and Stephen H. Haber, *Fragile by Design: The Political Origins of Banking Crises and Scarce Credit*, Princeton University Press, Princeton, NJ, 2014; Simon Johnson and James Kwak, *13 Bankers: The Wall Street Takeover and the Next Financial Meltdown*, Pantheon Books, New York, 2012; Luigi Zingales, "Presidential Address: Does Finance Benefit Society?" *Journal of Finance*, vol. 70(4), August 2015: 1327–1363.

5. Grossman and Elhanan Helpman, "Protection for Sale," *American Economic Review*, vol. 84(4), 1994.

6. Mancur Olson, "Dictatorship, Democracy, and Development," *American Political Science Review*, vol. 87(3), September 1993: 567–576; Daron

Acemoglu and James A. Robinson, "Economic Backwardness in Political Perspective."

7. Jon Elster, "Rational Choice History: A Case of Excessive Ambition," *American Political Science Review*, vol. 94(3), 2000: 685–695.

8. Scott Atran and Jeremy Ginges, "Religious and Sacred Imperatives in Human Conflict," *Science*, vol. 336, 2012: 855.

9. Amartya Sen, *Identity and Violence: The Illusion of Destiny*, W. W. Norton, New York, 2007.

10. See Alexander Wendt, *Social Theory of International Politics*, Cambridge University Press, 1999; John Gerard Ruggie, "What Makes the World Hang Together? Neo-Utilitarianism and the Social Constructivist Challenge," *International Organization*, vol. 52(4), October 1, 1998: 855–885; Mark Blyth, *Great Transformations: Economic Ideas and Institutional Change in the Twentieth Century*, Cambridge University Press, 2002; Colin Hay, "Ideas and the Construction of Interests," in *Ideas and Politics in Social Science Research*, D. Béland and R. H. Cox, eds., Oxford University Press, 2011.

11. Daniel Béland and Robert Henry Cox, *Ideas and Politics in Social Science Research*, 10.

12. Robert Howse, "Thucydides and Just War: How to Begin to Read Walzer's Just and Unjust Wars," *European Journal of International Law*, vol. 24, 2013; Jack L. Goldsmith and Eric A. Posner, *The Limits of International Law*, Oxford University Press, Oxford and New York, 2005.

13. Alberto Alesina and Howard Rosenthal, *Partisan Politics, Divided Government, and the Economy*, Cambridge University Press, 1995.

14. See for example, Alberto Alesina, Guido Cozzi, and Noemi Mantovan, "The Evolution of Ideology, Fairness and Redistribution," *Economic Journal*, vol. 122(565), 2012: 1244–1261; Stefano Della Vigna and Ethan Kaplan, "The Fox News Effect: Media Bias and Voting," *Quarterly Journal of Economics*, vol. 122(3), 2007: 1187–1234; and David Yanagizawa-Drott, "Propaganda and Conflict: Theory and Evidence from the Rwandan Genocide," *Quarterly Journal of Economics*, vol. 129(4), November 2014.

15. George Akerlof and Rachel Kranton, "Economics and Identity," *Quarterly Journal of Economics*, vol. 115(3), 2000: 715–753; George Akerlof and

Rachel Kranton, "Identity and the Economics of Organizations," *Journal of Economic Perspectives*, vol. 19(1), 2005: 9–32.

16. Martin Gilens and Benjamin I. Page, "Testing Theories of American Politics: Elites, Interest Groups, and Average Citizens," *Perspective on Politics*, vol. 12(3), September 2014: 564–581.

17. Arlie Russell Hochschild's *Strangers in Their Own Land: Anger and Mourning on the American Right* (New Press, New York, 2016) masterfully describes the ideational world of poor, white conservatives in Louisiana.

18. Pratap Bhanu Mehta and Michael Walton, "India's Political Settlement and Development Path," unpublished paper, 2012: 17–18.

19. See Theodore W. Schultz, *Transforming Traditional Agriculture*, Yale University Press, New Haven, CT, 1964; Anne O. Krueger, "Trade Policy and Economic Development: How We Learn," *American Economic Review*, vol. 87(1), March 1997: 1–22.

20. This example is provided by Avinash Dixit and Jörgen Weibull, who show that even with rational Bayesian updating, a common signal may exacerbate posteriors—increase polarization—when priors differ. See Dixit and Weibull, "Political Polarization," *Proceedings of the National Academy of Sciences of the United States,* vol. 104(18), 2007: United States 7353.

21. Daron Acemoglu and coauthors show that differences in beliefs need not disappear even asymptotically when there is disagreement over the interpretation (that is, informativeness) of the signals received. See Daron Acemoglu, Victor Chernozhukov, and Muhamet Yildiz, "Fragility of Asymptotic Agreement under Bayesian Learning," unpublished paper, February 2009.

22. See, for example, Arthur T. Denzau and Douglass C. North, "Shared Mental Models: Ideologies and Institutions." *Kyklos*, vol. 47(1), 1994: 3–31; Mark Blyth, "Ideas, Uncertainty, and Evolution," in *Ideas and Politics in Social Science Research*, D. Béland and R. H. Cox, eds., Oxford University Press, New York, 2010.

23. Rohini Pande, "Can Informed Voters Enforce Better Governance? Experiments in Low-Income Democracies," *Annual Review of Economics*, vol. 3, September 2011: 215–237.

24. Johnson and Kwak, *13 Bankers.*

25. Calomiris and Haber, *Fragile by Design.*

26. Mark S. Mizruchi, *The Fracturing of the American Corporate Elite*, Harvard University Press, Cambridge, MA, 2013.

27. James Surowiecki, "Moaning Moguls," *The New Yorker*, July 7, 2014, http://www.newyorker.com/magazine/2014/07/07/moaning-moguls.

28. For a good discussion of how economic ideas can shape politics, see Edward López and Wayne Leighton, *Madmen, Intellectuals, and Academic Scribblers: The Economic Engine of Political Change*, Stanford University Press, Stanford, CA, 2012.

CHAPTER 8: Economics as Policy Innovation

1. Dani Rodrik, "The Political Economy of Trade Policy," in *Handbook of International Economics*, G. Grossman and K. Rogoff, eds., vol. 3, Amsterdam, North-Holland, 1995.

2. Daron Acemoglu and James A. Robinson, "Economic Backwardness in Political Perspective," *American Political Science Review*, vol. 100(1), 2006: 115–131. See also Daron Acemoglu, "Why Not a Political Coase Theorem? Social Conflict, Commitment, and Politics," *Journal of Comparative Economics*, vol. 31(4), 2003: 620–652.

3. Raquel Fernandez and Dani Rodrik, "Resistance to Reform: Status Quo Bias in the Presence of Individual-Specific Uncertainty," *American Economic Review*, vol. 81(5), December 1991.

4. Acemoglu and Robinson, "Economic Backwardness," 126–128.

5. Lawrence J. Lau, Yingyi Qian, and Gerard Roland, "Reform Without Losers: An Interpretation of China's Dual-Track Approach to Transition," *Journal of Political Economy*, vol. 108(1), 2000: 120–143.

6. Quoted in Robert P. Inman and Daniel L. Rubinfeld, "Federal Institutions and the Democratic Transition: Learning from South Africa," *Journal of Law, Economics, & Organization*, vol. 28(4), 2011: 784.

7. Inman and Rubinfeld.

8. Dani Rodrik, "The Rush to Free Trade in the Developing World: Why So Late? Why Now? Will It Last?" in *Voting for Reform: Democracy, Political*

Liberalization, and Economic Adjustment, S. Haggard and S. Webb, eds., Oxford University Press, New York, 1994.

9. I. M. Destler, American Trade Politics, 4th ed., Peterson Institute, Washington, DC, 2005.

10. Wayne Leighton and Edward López, *Madmen, Intellectuals, and Academic Scribblers: The Economic Engine of Political Change*, Stanford University Press, Stanford, CA, 2013, p. 147.

11. Michael Walzer, "The Problem of Dirty Hands," *Philosophy & Public Affairs*, vol. 2(2), Winter 1973: 174.

12. Paul S. Segerstrom, T. C. A. Anant, and Elias Dinopoulos, "A Schumpeterian Model of the Product Life," *American Economic Review*, vol. 80(5), December 1990: 1077–1091; Philippe Aghion and Peter Howitt, *Endogenous Growth Theory*, MIT Press, Cambridge, MA, 1998.

13. Daron Acemoglu and James A. Robinson, "Economics versus Politics: Pitfalls of Policy Advice," NBER Working Paper 18921, March 2013.

14. Leighton and López, *Madmen*.

15. Leighton and López, *Madmen*: 134.

16. Leighton and López, *Madmen*: 178.

17. Jesper B.Sørensen and Toby E. Stuart, "Aging, Obsolescence, and Organizational Innovation," *Administrative Science Quarterly*, vol. 45(1), March 2000: 81–112.

18. Richard R. Nelson and Sidney G. Winter, "Evolutionary Theorizing in Economics," *Journal of Economic Perspectives*, vol. 16(2), Spring 2002: 23–46.

19. Leighton and López, *Madmen*: 155–56.

20. James Leitzel, *The Political Economy of Rule Evasion and Policy Reform*, Routledge, London and New York, 2003.

21. Leitzel, *Political Economy of Rule Evasion*: 23.

22. Mark Blyth, "Powering, Puzzling, or Presuading? The Mechanisms of Building Institutional Orders," *International Studies Quarterly*, vol. 51, 2007: 762.

23. Franklin D. Roosevelt, "Address at Oglethorpe University," May 22, 1932.

24. Kurt Weyland, "Toward a New Theory of Institutional Change," *World Politics*, vol. 60(2), 2008: 281–314.

25. Paul J. DiMaggio and Walter W. Powell, "The Iron Cage Revisited: Institutional Isomorphism and Collective Rationality in Organizational Fields," *American Sociological Review*, vol. 48(2), 1983: 147–160.

26. Matt Andrews, *The Limits of Institutional Reform in Development,* Cambridge University Press, 2013.

27. Sharun Mukand and Dani Rodrik, "In Search of the Holy Grail: Policy Convergence, Experimentation, and Economic Performance," *American Economic Review*, vol. 95(1), March 2005: 374–383.

28. Acemoglu and Robinson, "Economics vs. Politics."

29. Acemoglu and Robinson, "Economics vs. Politics": 174.

CHAPTER 9: What Will Not Work

1. Nouriel Roubini, "Globalization's Political Fault Lines," *Project Syndicate*, July 4, 2016, https://www.project-syndicate.org/commentary/globaliza tion-political-fault-lines-by-nouriel-roubini-2016-07?barrier=accessreg.

2. Harold James, "Rethinking Labor Mobility," *Project Syndicate*, January 3, 2017, https://www.project-syndicate.org/commentary/displaced-workers -globalization-mobility-by-harold-james-2017-01?barrier=accessreg.

3. Dani Rodrik, "Why Do More Open Economies Have Bigger Governments?" *Journal of Political Economy*, vol. 106(5), October 1998: 997–1032.

4. Stefanie Walter, "Globalization and the Welfare State: Testing the Microfoundations of the Compensation Hypothesis," *International Studies Quarterly*, vol. 54(2), June 2010: 403–426.

5. Lawrence Mishel, "Tired of Economists' Misdirection on Trade," Economic Policy Institute, April 26, 2016, http://www.epi.org/blog/tired-of -economists-misdirection-on-globalization/.

6. Kenneth F. Scheve and Matthew J. Slaughter, "A New Deal for Globalization," *Foreign Affairs*, July/August 2007: 35.

7. The mechanism is the following: trade liberalization increases the global supply of that country's exports. This in turn reduces the world price of these commodities. Countries exporting similar goods then suffer an adverse terms-of-trade shock.

Chapter 10: New Rules for the Global Economy

1. Dani Rodrik, *The Globalization Paradox: Democracy and the Future of the World Economy*, W. W. Norton, New York, 2011.
2. The deadline ran out at the end of 2016. The United States and the EU have both declined to declare China a "market economy."
3. For a recent example, see Stanley Reed and Keith Bradsher, "China's Steel Makers Undercut Rivals as Trade Debate Intensifies," *New York Times*, May 3, 2016, https://mobile.nytimes.com/2016/05/04/business /international/chinas-steel-makers-undercut-rivals-as-economy-slows.html? referer=https://t.co/uUtRw9xuEt.

Chapter 11: Growth Policies for the Future

1. Gary Shteyngart, *Super Sad True Love Story: A Novel*, Random House, New York, 2011.
2. Gaaitzen de Vries, Marcel Timmer, and Klaas de Vries, "Structural Transformation in Africa: Static Gains, Dynamic Losses," University of Groningen Growth and Development Centre, GGDC Research Memorandum 136, http://www.ggdc.net/publications/memorandum/gd136 .pdf. See also Xinshen Diao, Margaret McMillan, and Dani Rodrik, "The Recent Growth Boom in Developing Economies: A Structural-Change Perspective," Harvard University, unpublished paper, January 2017.
3. Jim O'Neill, "The World Needs Better Economic BRICs," *Global Economic Paper Series*, November 30, 2001.
4. "Statement by BRICS Leaders on the Establishment of the BRICS-Led Development Bank," Durban, South Africa, March 27, 2013.
5. "Arvind Subramanian on what is holding back investments in India," *Rediff Business*, October 1, 2015, http://www.rediff.com/business/report /arvind-subramanian-on-what-is-holding-back-investments-in-india /20151001.htm.
6. Andrew M. Warner, "Public Investment as an Engine of Growth," International Monetary Fund Working Paper, August 2014, https://www.imf .org/external/pubs/ft/wp/2014/wp14148.pdf.
7. Girish Bahal, Mehdi Raissi, and Volodymyr Tulin, "Crowding-Out or Crowding-In? Public and Private Investment in India," International

Monetary Fund Working Paper, December 2015, https://www.imf.org /external/pubs/ft/wp/2015/wp15264.pdf.

8. See Stephen S. Cohen and J. Bradford DeLong, *Concrete Economics: The Hamilton Approach to Economic Growth and Policy*, Harvard Business Review Press, Boston, MA, 2016; and Michael Lind, *Land of Promise: An Economic History of the United States*, HarperCollins, New York, 2012.

9. Josh Lerner, *The Boulevard of Broken Dreams*, Princeton University Press, Princeton and Oxford, 2009.

10. National Research Council, *Energy Research at DOE: Was It Worth It? Energy Efficiency and Fossil Energy Research 1978 to 2000*, Committee on Benefits of DOE R&D on Energy Efficiency and Fossil Energy, Board on Energy and Environmental Systems, Division on Engineering and Physical Sciences, 2001, http://www.nap.edu/catalog/10165.html.

11. Fred Block and Matthew R. Keller, "Where Do Innovations Come From? Transformations in the U.S. Economy, 1970–2006," in *Knowledge Governance: Reasserting the Public Interest*, L. Burlamaqui, A. C. Castro, and R. Kattel, eds., Anthem Press, 2011.

12. Fred Block and Matthew R. Keller, *State of Innovation: The U.S. Government's Role in Technology Development*, Paradigm Publishers, New York, 2011.

13. National Research Council, *Energy Research at DOE*.

14. Mariana Mazzucato, *The Entrepreneurial State: Debunking Public vs. Private Sector Myths*, Public Affairs Press, New York, 2015.

15. See Fareed Zakaria, "The Rise of Illiberal Democracy," *Foreign Affairs*, November/December 1997; and Steven Levitsky and Lucan A. Way, *Competitive Authoritarianism: Hybrid Regimes After the Cold War*, Cambridge University Press, Cambridge and New York, 2010.

CHAPTER 12: It's the Politics, Stupid!

1. Dani Rodrik, *Has Globalization Gone Too Far?* Institute for International Economics, Washington, DC, 1997.

2. Rawi Abdelal, "Writing the Rules of Global Finance: France, Europe, and Capital Liberalization," *Review of International Political Economy*, vol. 13(1), February 2006: 1–27.

3. Anat Admati and Martin Hellwig, *The Bankers' New Clothes: What's Wrong with Banking and What to Do about It*, Princeton University Press, Princeton and Oxford, 2013; Simon Johnson and James Kwak, *White House Burning: The Founding Fathers, Our National Debt, and Why It Matters to You*, Vintage Books, New York, 2012; Thomas Piketty, *Capital in the Twenty-First Century*, Harvard University Press, Cambridge, MA, 2014; Anthony B. Atkinson, *Inequality: What Can be Done?* Harvard University Press, Cambridge, MA, 2015; Mariana Mazzucato, *The Entrepreneurial State: Debunking Public vs. Private Sector Myths*, Public Affairs Press, New York, 2015; Ha-Joon Chang, *Economics: The User's Guide,* Penguin, London, 2014; J. Bradford DeLong and Lawrence H. Summers, "Fiscal Policy in a Depressed Economy," *Brookings Papers on Economic Activity*, Spring 2012; Jeffrey D. Sachs, *Building the New American Economy: Smart, Fair, and Sustainable*, Columbia University Press, New York, 2017; José Antonio Ocampo, *Development Cooperation in Times of Crisis,* Columbia University Press, New York, 2012; Joseph E. Stiglitz, *The Stiglitz Report: Reforming the International Monetary and Financial Systems in the Wake of the Global Crisis*, New Press, New York, 2010.

4. Jeffry Frieden, "Will Global Capitalism Fail Again?" Bruegel Essay and Lecture Series, Brussels, n.d. http://scholar.harvard.edu/files/jfrieden/files/GlobalCapFallAgainWebversion.pdf?m=1360041998.

5. Anthony B. Atkinson, *Inequality*.

INDEX